When you choose a GGF Member, you can be assured that they:

1. Will comply with the new Building Regulations (relating to windows) and ensure you get the appropriate certificate via the Fenestration Self Assessment Scheme (FENSA).

2. Will have been in business for at least three years.

3. Have all been vetted to ensure they provide a quality service, the vetting procedure includes taking up references, looking at their accounts and site visits.

4. Work to the Federation's Code of Good Practice and technical guidelines.

In addition the GGF will provide you with:

1. A free conciliation service - should you and a Member company not see eye to eye over work carried out.

2. Protection for your deposit - the GGF Deposit Indemnity Scheme is backed by Norwich Union and safeguards deposits up to £3,000 or 25% of the contract price, whichever is lower.

3. A Customer Charter.

TRUST MARK
Government Endorsed Standards
Registered through:
Glass and Glazing
Federation

Contact us on: **020 7939 9101** for a list of members in your area or see **www.ggf.org.uk**

advertisement feature

The Complete Guide to
Investing
in Property

The Complete Guide to
Investing
in Property

5th edition

LIZ HODGKINSON

LONDON PHILADELPHIA NEW DELHI

Publisher's note
Every possible effort has been made to ensure that the information contained in this book is accurate at the time of going to press, and the publishers and author cannot accept responsibility for any errors or omissions, however caused. No responsibility for loss or damage occasioned to any person acting, or refraining from action, as a result of the material in this publication can be accepted by the editor, the publisher or the author.

First published in Great Britain and the United States in 2006 by Kogan Page Limited
Second edition 2007
Third edition 2008
Fourth edition 2009
Fifth edition 2010

120 Pentonville Road
London N1 9JN
United Kingdom
www.koganpage.com

© Liz Hodgkinson, 2006, 2007, 2008, 2000, 2010

ISBN   978 0 7494 5624 5
E-ISBN   978 0 7494 5922 2

British Library Cataloguing-in-Publication Data

A CIP record for this book is available from the British Library.

Typeset by Saxon Graphics Ltd, Derby
Printed and bound in Great Britain by MPG Books Ltd, Bodmin, Cornwall

Mixed Sources
Product group from well-managed
forests and other controlled sources
www.fsc.org Cert no. SA-COC-1565
© 1996 Forest Stewardship Council

Contents

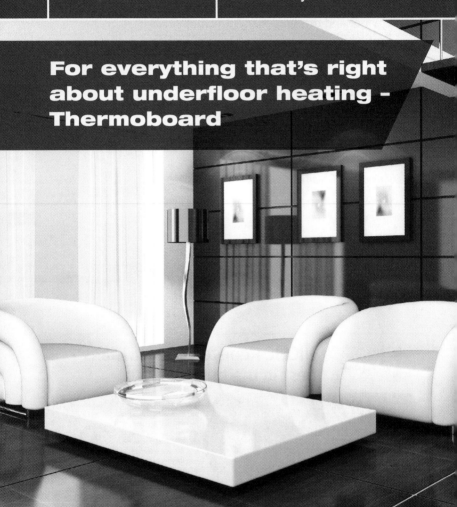

INVEST IN UFH TO INCREASE THE SALEABILITY OF YOUR PROPERTY

Underfloor Heating (UFH) is now immensely popular in the UK – some would say it is to homes now what central heating was thirty years ago. UFH is widely used now as more and more homeowners and developers recognise the value it adds to properties.

Chris Simmons, Commercial Manager for Thermoboard, the UFH division of Wavin comments:

"Property advisers have said that a shift in the market in respect of people's expectations when renting or buying a property has already occurred. Architects and developers are realising that if a home is equipped with sustainable features such as UFH, it can increase the value of the property. We're now seeing this change in perception filter down through the property market with increasing numbers of homeowners choosing underfloor heating or looking for it in housing adverts."

Importantly, a recent survey by YouGov showed that people ranked energy efficiency as the third most important attribute when choosing a new home. UFH outperforms more traditional forms of heating such as radiators when it comes to energy efficiency.

Chris continues, "We are all aware of spiralling fuel costs, so investors in property will be glad to learn that UFH only requires water heated to

45–55°C. This is significantly less than other forms of heating, making it more attractive to potential tenants in terms of using less energy and increasing money savings. Chris adds, "The radiant heating effect of UFH means that air temperatures can be set 1–2°C lower whilst still maintaining the same comfort level provided by radiators, reducing heat lost through essential air changes by 10–20% over a year."

"This radiant blanket of heat provided by UFH through conduction, convection and natural radiation, prevents cold spots and drafts that may occur when using radiators. With UFH the advantage is creating comfort by giving homeowners a cool head and warm feet. UFH also offers design flexibility, particularly with difficult room layouts that require maximum space for furniture placement"

The UFH systems of today are increasingly sophisticated and now offer homeowners complete control in terms of the flexibility to heat and control the temperature of individual zones easily and efficiently, independently or simultaneously.

Chris continues, "To meet the demand of modern consumer lifestyles we introduced a comprehensive range of UFH controls which allows for the customisation of each UFH system to a customer's chosen requirements. Homeowners can alter their own heat settings for individual circumstances; for example when having visitors over for dinner they may wish to increase the temperature for when guests arrive and cool the room slowly throughout the evening. Homeowners now also have the option to access their UFH settings from a PC which is useful when on holiday or at work.

The adaptability of UFH is also popular with developers as groundfloor UFH systems can be partnered with upstairs radiators, if desired. Complex projects, using more than one type of system, can be accommodated. Our own team can help developers and installers by creating full system designs via our Thermoboard FullSpec service, so that, however complex the project, the installer can be clear when completing the job.

"Moving into the next decade, UFH will no longer be seen as the luxury option, it's fast becoming an expectation for homeowners. Why risk the premature need for an upgrade when you can invest in UFH now as a method of future proofing a home's saleability?"

For more information please call the Thermoboard UFH helpline on 01392 444122 or visit www.thermoboard.co.uk

Introduction

Why invest in property?

This book is written in the belief that for the person who wants to attain financial security, and have some fun, excitement and flexibility in the process, property still makes one of the best kinds of modern investment, in spite of the credit crunch.

But what does it actually mean to 'invest' in property? What is the real difference between 'owning' property, which the vast majority of people do anyway nowadays, and 'investing' in it?

Don't we automatically 'invest' when we buy property, given that property generally goes up in value? Yes, in a sense, but the main difference is that when you consciously invest in property, as with any other type of investment, you are buying with the express and overriding intention of making a profit.

When you specifically invest in property, you are doing more than just depending on a rising market. Instead, you are hoping to make a gain whatever the market, as you are using money-wise skills rather than just wishful thinking.

At its most basic level, when you invest in something, you put a certain amount of money into that commodity in the hope that you will get vastly more money out, and that during your ownership, that commodity will have increased enormously in value.

Investing is a different matter from just saving, where you put your money into a totally safe, if unexciting and low-yielding bank or building society account. There is no risk but there is precious little gain, either.

BUT – when you invest, as opposed to just saving, this means you are taking an element of risk with your money. Unless there is some risk, it is not investing. And while you may make a lot of money from your investments, you will stand to lose as well. Investments are never guaranteed, but wise investors balance the risk so that the scales are heavily weighted in their favour.

When you invest, whether in property or any other commodity, you are basically backing a hunch, but you cannot know for an absolute certainty that you will gain.

But of course, the more you know what you are doing, the smaller the risk becomes. Although this may sound an obvious thing to say, all day and every day people are investing in products about which they know nothing at all. Nowhere is this more true than on the money markets, where amateur investors are losing fortunes all the time because they haven't a clue what they are doing, and have not bothered to understand the nature of their investment.

There are many products to invest in, from equities to fine art, antiques, wine and classic cars, and many investment 'opportunities' are being advertised all the time.

This book explains what is meant by investing in property, as opposed to merely buying property, and why the author believes that property is probably the best and safest choice for the amateur or part-time investor, so long as you know what you are doing, and why you are making certain choices.

Over the past few years, property has generally increased in value so much that there is a general belief that, over time, you just can't lose.

The truth is that you can lose, but even so, property does historically come good most of the time – eventually. Also, investors in property can now, quite literally, have the whole wide world in their hands – or in their portfolios. It is now possible to invest in property in most countries in the world, so that your property portfolio can look as international as you like. Nowadays, anybody can be an international investor and financier! Anybody can swagger around brandishing an impressive-looking international property portfolio!

So why do I believe that property, in general, makes a good type of investment?

In the first place, everybody understands property, simply because everybody has to have a roof over their heads. Everybody also understands that home occupiers have to pay rent or a mortgage in order to continue living there. It is also self-evident that even when fully owned and mortgage-free, there are continuing costs attached to living in a home.

Big-time property investor Dominic Farrell, a former Army officer, shares my view. He believes that property is an asset that will never go out of fashion, in contrast to certain other types of investment, such as vintage wines or antiques which, while they may be nice to have, are not absolutely necessary to everyday existence, and are also very subject to the vagaries of fashion and taste. And although the property market moves in cycles, statistics show that it has always risen in value over time, usually way beyond inflation.

Another point Dominic makes is that property, unlike other investments, can be leveraged, which means that it can be used to secure a lot of borrowing. Put simply, this means that you can buy a £100,000 property for £10,000 down, and borrow the other £90,000 which you pay back over a very long time. We are all familiar with buying property through long-term mortgages and in most cases the existence of the property is security enough for the lender.

Although a house price crash is often forecast, most experts believe this is unlikely to happen, at least in the UK, because current planning restrictions are such that in many areas it has become difficult, if not impossible, to build new housing. This means there is a constant excess of demand over supply. Also, according to David Miles, chief UK economist at Morgan Stanley, as the population becomes ever wealthier, housing will become an ever more valuable commodity.

Yet throughout 2008, the property world was sent reeling by two terms, 'sub-prime' and 'credit crunch', describing phenomena which have apparently mysteriously been responsible for house prices plunging all over the world. Investments which many people imagined were safe have proved anything but as mortgages and loans became more difficult to secure, fixed-rate deals came to an end and instead of a nice bank balance building up from a property portfolio, many investors faced bankruptcy from fast-falling prices, especially on newbuild properties.

And there was more bad news as many major developers and housebuilders either stopped building altogether or drastically cut back their expansion plans. Nor did it end there, as off-plan and newbuild flats were often being offered at auction for less than half their original purchase prices.

What caused all this panic and plunge? In very simple terms, much property expansion and investment since the mid-1990s was predicated on the assumption that property prices would only ever go up, that property investment was relatively risk-free, and that investors would always be able to borrow on extremely favourable terms, and then secure a high rental from these properties until such time as they came to sell.

It all looked like guaranteed win-win-win, and the acronym OPM – Other People's Money – was a term used to denote the clever investor, who was able to finance an ever-growing property portfolio by this means.

Using OPM in the form of mortgages and rents made sense when property prices were on an inexorable rise and when borrowers could secure cut-price mortgages in a highly competitive lending market.

But then it all went horribly wrong. Lenders, always looking for new markets, started to encourage the so-called sub-prime sector – people with bad or adverse credit histories – to borrow large sums of money for the dream of owning their own house, but at higher interest rates than normal. The cynical idea here was that if the high-risk sub-primers defaulted on their mortgages, the properties would be repossessed and the lenders would make a huge profit on the increased value of the foreclosed homes.

And lo and behold it came to pass, and they did default. The only problem was that many of these properties were found to be unsaleable, in America at least, where most of the sub-prime market existed.

At the same time, in the UK, large mortgage lenders such as Northern Rock and Bradford and Bingley fell on hard times as their own financial houses of cards came tumbling down. Huge debts they had racked up could not be repaid, owing to extremely complex financial vehicles known as Collateralized Debt Obligations (CDOs). These are credit derivatives made up of different loans and bonds, all sliced up and based mainly on sub-prime lending. Financial institutions around the world bought up around $3 trillion worth of American CDO debt.

The main American rating agencies, such as Standard & Poor's, Moody's and Fitch Ratings, rated CDOs with sub-prime debt as 'very good risks' – which, as it turned out, they were not. All would have been well, however, if the repossession companies had been able to sell the foreclosed houses at a profit. The problem was, nobody wanted these properties at any price, which meant that the collective debt outstanding on the homes remained.

For property investors the result was that lenders had no choice but to restrict their mortgage deals. Because these institutions had taken on great mounds of unpayable debt on the assumption that the music would never stop, they began to demand higher interest when competitive fixed-rate deals came to an end. The attractive deals dried up, particularly for first-time buyers and buy-to-let investors, the supposedly growing market aggressively targeted by lenders.

Many new blocks of flats, particularly in inner cities, were built on the assumption that their values would continue to rise, meaning that investors who bought off-plan would realise a tidy profit when they came to sell.

As it happened, there was such over-supply in some areas that investors could neither sell nor rent out, and many new or amateur investors became bankrupt, owing literally millions of pounds. This also happened abroad, where, again, many investors with very little money to spare were targeted by off-plan developers and high-pressure sales techniques.

The overall effect was that the supply of money worldwide, which had been sloshing around as if there was no end to it, dried up, leaving many investors stranded.

Falling property prices also meant that people would find it harder to be able to take equity out of their own homes to start building up a property portfolio. Equity is taken out on valuation; if that valuation shows you are already in negative equity, there will be no money available with which to start your investment process.

Fast and fabulous new floorings!

For investors in property, a new floor is an ideal way of giving an older property a fast face-lift or a new build the finishing touch.

Ready-to-install
Gerflor, one of the world's leading manufacturer's of self-adhesive floorings, specialises in cost effective, luxury vinyl tiles that come ready-to-install with a commercial quality, pre-applied adhesive backing for quick, easy and low cost fitting, making them perfect for when installation times really count.

Minimum maintenance
Featuring hardwearing, hygienic surfaces, only simple routine cleaning of these floorings is required without the costly maintenance regimes of waxing and polishing. Gerflor tiles and planks will therefore remain looking good for longer in the home.

Good looking
Looks being paramount, Gerflor's designers travel the world focusing on key trends in design and colour while drawing inspiration from natural wood and ceramics as well as new textures, finishes and effects.

For example, the Senso collection of beautifully realistic, vinyl planks captures the mood of real wood in six distinctive ranges, each with a style of its own, and including an extra slip resistant option, three widths and many inspirational colours.

Innovation
For those preferring the distinctive appeal of stone, Gerflor has introduced Caractère Distinctive, a revolutionary, self-adhesive, 100% recyclable, mineral composite floor tile that resembles real stone, yet it is up to four times lighter and far easier to handle. Available in three fashionable tile sizes, five attractive colours and featuring a built-in grout for added realism, Caractère Distinctive is warmer, more comfortable and far quieter than a traditional ceramic floor. Thanks to its impact, scratch and heel-proof surface, it is also virtually indestructible.

Easy fitting, self-adhesive floorings
Gerflor's self-adhesive flooring ranges include: Caractère Distinctive, Caractère Elegance, Senso Rustic, Senso Classic, Senso XXL, Senso GripX, Senso Origin, Aqua, Design and Prime.

Buy on-line!
For quick and simple flooring solutions with an easy sampling and ordering service visit **www.gerflorstore.co.uk**

So you may now be asking if all this property investment was a ridiculous bubble which was bound to make many people come a cropper. And how does it look for the future?

There is an old saying: when the going gets tough, the tough get going. In fact, the property fallout is going to mean that investors with money – and who do not rely on wishful thinking – are in for a better time than ever. The days of the 100 and 125 per cent mortgages are at an end, and lenders are demanding ever bigger deposits. In addition, interest rates are higher. This means that although the OPM idea of investing will not now be so attractive, for those with cash in the bank, property investment can be more lucrative than ever.

The two upsides to this property crash – well, not exactly crash, but 'correction' in estate-agent terms – are:

1. Many more people are going to have to rent in future; this is good news for those who buy cleverly and can make sure of a ready, steady rental market.
2. Property has, for the foreseeable future, become a buyer's market.

For those interested in buying abroad for investment, exactly the same thing applies. And as ever, the longer you can hang on to your property, the more likely it is to come good. The idea of flipping – selling on your off-plan property before completion so as not to sign up to a 20-year mortgage – was never really going to work out: nobody can ever say for sure whether a particular property will be worth more or less in two to three years' time. People can make predictions but all kinds of unforeseen events can alter the situation in the meantime.

So, the way it looks at the time of writing is that investors with money in the bank will be able to make a killing, but those who have to rely on 100 per cent mortgages or raise deposits via credit card borrowing – always a high-risk method but encouraged by property seminars and property clubs, many of which have now gone out of business – will find the going extremely tough.

Whatever the property market, the following considerations must be borne in mind:

▮ All property transactions, of whatever kind, are feeding a lot of mouths. Whether you pay cash or buy on a mortgage, you are paying, for example, lawyers, estate agents, removal firms, furniture companies, utility companies, surveyors, architects, developers, curtain and carpet companies. There will be taxes to pay when you buy and when you sell, as well as on an ongoing basis: local taxes such as council tax have to be paid all the time and income tax will have to be paid on any income received from renting or leasing a property.

▮ All mortgages and loans to buy property have to be paid back with interest, usually over many years. The longer the term, the less the interest appears to be, but the more money, in fact, will have to be repaid.

▮ The only certainties in property are what you buy the place for and what you sell it for. All projections of capital growth are exactly the same as betting on a horse. You can shorten the odds by studying form but you can never be sure your horse will romp home first. Anything can happen with property, as with any other investment, so wishful thinking should never play a part.

▮ The purchase price and the selling price of any property are only part of the story. You have to factor in how much it costs you to make the purchase and how much it costs you to sell it, as well as how much it costs you to maintain it while it is in your ownership.

▮ When it comes to renting, whether holiday lets or homes, certain inescapable factors apply. One is that, in most areas, people renting are on a certain salary and cannot pay more than a certain amount in rent. The people at the top of the pyramid who can pay more or less anything are in very short supply and will only ever go for the highest-end places. This also applies to holiday lets. Even if there is a dire shortage of properties to rent in a certain area, rentals will never go up to more than the average person can afford to pay. Often it's not even a matter of competition, simply a fact of what people can afford. In a recession, one of the first things people cut back on is holidays, which are not an essential expense. For ordinary rentals, if tenants think they are paying too much rent, they will simply hand in their notice and find somewhere cheaper, even if it is not as nice and is in a worse location.

A personal story: I do not understand high finance, which is why I have written this book. It is for people like myself, who find small print difficult to decipher. So I just go with what I can understand and what works for me. The thing is, I am always looking for properties to buy. I never stop looking but I rarely buy. Why? Because in most cases, the figures simply don't add up. In order for me to invest successfully in property, I have to be able to make more money – when all the figures are taken into account – than I could from just having the money in the bank. I know that money in the bank gives a safe, albeit low, return. I also know that investing in property can deliver spectacular rewards, but by the same token, this means you must never take your eye off the ball.

My property investments give me an income I can just about live on – now, not at some indefinable time in the future. This is the case whatever the market may do. My property investments are pretty much ring-fenced, whether prices rise or plummet, and mean I am not having to factor in some capital growth plucked out of the air to make sense of my investments. It means little to me that properties rose in a certain country by 10, 20 or whatever per cent, because until I come to sell, those figures mean nothing at all.

The least that any property investment has to be able to do is 'wash its face', in estate-agent parlance. That means that you do not have to feed it, but also that, even if it's not actually making money, it is at the very least covering its costs.

In spite of temporary doom and gloom all over the world, property is booming as never before. And while this does not, of course, mean that it is impossible to lose, it certainly means that property is becoming an ever more exciting commodity. Business journalist Chris Walker, of *The Independent on Sunday*, wrote on 1 April 2007:

The boom in global real estate reflects a market struggling to come to terms with the industrialization of many countries simultaneously. In this scramble to establish value, bubbles may well occur, but so favourable a backdrop is difficult to imagine. There's money still to be made in bricks and mortar.

We all understand the basics of property. By contrast, you have to be quite financially sophisticated to understand how equities and other aspects of the money markets work. You also have to be numerate and actually enjoy number-crunching. Successful city people are doing sums in their heads the whole time; it is second nature to them. But few ordinary people really understand how and why stock markets crash, or how the stock market performance in, say, Japan, can intimately affect other stock exchanges around the world.

And as a result of the near-collapse of Northern Rock and other apparently rock-solid financial institutions, most property investors have also now come to have at least a nodding acquaintance with technical financial terms like 'futures' and 'derivatives'. Many property investors – the present writer included – used to assume, in their innocence, that mortgage lending was a relatively simple operation whereby money was made from lending out at interest. We had simply no idea that big financial institutions were playing high-risk international money markets with OUR money.

So do property investors now have to come to terms with these complicated financial vehicles? Not really, but it does mean that every single aspect of borrowing, including mortgage-arrangement and exit fees, has to be carefully calculated and added up, and that although property investment is usually considered a medium-to-long-term proposition, the figures have to make sense now, not at some indefinable time in the future.

The main new aspect which investors have to consider is whether they have an exit strategy that will not leave them out of pocket, whatever markets may do in the future.

The good thing about the property market is that it is virtually certain to recover. Investors have to be sure they can ride out a downturn as well as an upturn and not look for a quick profit. The investors who have come to grief are those who were led to believe they could turn in a quick profit; sensible investors will always regard such a possibility with extreme caution.

Historically, at least, property is solid and substantial and far less liable than equities to stock market fluctuations, to crashes and recoveries. Obviously house prices fluctuate, but there has rarely, if ever, been a complete crash. One reason for this is that all real estate is built on land which will never go away. A further reason for the dependability of property is that everybody needs a home, whereas we can manage without a car, foreign travel, the latest electronic gadgetry, if we have to.

Then, there is almost always a shortage of housing.

And while house prices can go up and down, there is always going to be some value in land. By contrast, the entire value of an equity can be wiped out, in a severe downturn of the market, when major contracts are lost, when there is a takeover, or poor performance in the High Street. And there is little the individual shareholder can do about this, except to buy and sell at the right time.

Property is also a very versatile type of investment. Not only can you see it, feel it, touch it, there are many things you can do with it. You can buy it and go and live in it yourself, you can buy a wreck to do up and sell on, you can rent your property out or you can buy land and build your own home. In other words, you can enjoy property in a hands-on way which would be difficult to do with purely financial investments.

You can stamp your personality on a piece of real estate, which you cannot do with equities. You can make your home look lovely, you can renovate, decorate or extend it.

You can use a property as your main residence, or for holidays. You can enjoy your home for part of the year and rent it out for the rest of the year. Or you can have lodgers or paying guests, run holiday cottages or use part of your home as an office. You can create a separate flat in the basement or in the garden. As opposed to equities, you can use and enjoy your property as a full- or part-time home all the while it is (with any luck) making you money.

Then for many people, property has an emotional pull which merely playing the money markets does not possess. There is only one kind of beauty in a share – when it goes up in value. But you can take an aesthetic interest in a beautiful home which you cannot do with a beautiful share. A home can be an architectural gem or 'full of charm and character' in estate-agent speak. You can fall in love with a property in a way that would be difficult when just moving money around.

It is this aspect, I think, which gives property its special appeal. You are not merely hoarding for the future, you are getting pleasure and excitement from it in the present.

In my adult life, I have owned or lived in more than 20 different homes and each one has been exciting, challenging or highly profitable. Not all the homes have provided every ingredient on the wish list, but each has been important in its way, and each has had something special about it, at least to me. And while I lived in or owned them, I put something of myself in them. Then, when they were sold or I moved away, the next owner changed their personality again.

These are the considerable upsides of investing in property. What are the downsides?

Here are the main ones:

1. Property is much less easy to liquidize than stocks and shares. Although you can sell a share at any time, or instruct your broker to sell, you may have to wait a year or more to sell a house or a flat. Because any property represents a considerable sum of money, you have to wait for a buyer to come along. With a share, you can sell at any time, even though you may not make a profit.
2. It is more difficult and expensive to sell a property than other types of investment. This is mainly because property is subject to the laws of tenure, some of which go back to Roman times. In selling, title has to be established, plus any costs or debts attaching to the property, and searches have to be carried out. All these not only take time but cost money. Then mortgages have to be arranged, stamp duty paid, utilities sorted out. Buying and selling property is a complex

and time-consuming business, even when you have a ready and willing buyer.

3. Property is not always 'owned' in the way other commodities are owned. Although most houses are sold on a freehold basis, the majority of apartments, at least in the UK, are leasehold. This means you have bought the right to occupy the property for a certain length of time, and not the property itself. When the lease ends, the property reverts to the freeholder for nothing. Not everybody realizes that the shorter the lease, the more value the property loses. The fact of 'leasehold' is peculiar to property ownership, and is yet another complication. Short leases are the main reason why some properties go down in value.

4. Property is expensive to purchase. You can buy a share for just a few pounds, but any piece of real estate is going to cost five figures minimum, and usually six figures, these days. And the purchase price is not the only cost involved. There will be stamp duty to pay, lawyers and agents to pay, surveyors to pay, removal costs, insurance costs and, possibly, renovation costs.

5. Although most people buy property through mortgages, in most cases you still need to have a considerable deposit available. This is particularly the case when buying property purely for investment. You will also have to have spare cash for incidental costs. Then when you sell, there will be Capital Gains Tax to pay, unless the property is your principal private residence.

6. Property is a high-maintenance investment. You can't just buy it and forget it, as you can with stocks and shares or when putting money into a bank account. All property needs constant updating and modernizing.

7. And as I've mentioned, there are also ongoing costs when owning property, such as council tax, utilities, mortgage payments, service charges and repair bills. All these can add up, so you have to be sure that your property constitutes an asset and not a liability.

So – do the upsides outweigh the downsides?

In my view yes, very much so. The main upside is that property is much less liable to intense market fluctuations than other types of investment.

Even when property 'crashes' it still retains considerable value. For instance, upmarket estate agents Knight Frank reported in July 2008 that country cottages had experienced the worst fall in prices, at around 5 per cent. This means that a country cottage which would have sold for £500,000 in 2007 would probably go for around £475,000 in 2008 – still a lot of money. It's hardly wiping out an entire investment, and somebody selling such a cottage would probably have made a considerable profit on it anyway, unless they had bought it less than a year previously.

And the cheaply erected inner-city flats, many of which experienced dramatic price drops during 2008, were still selling at auction for between £120,000 and £150,000 each. Although this may have left the original buyer way out of pocket, by no means all the value had disappeared, especially as such properties had each cost around £45,000 maximum to build.

The investors who lost out were mainly buy-to-let investors who had been promised a high rent they simply could not achieve, and had bought on that basis. They had to sell because the achievable rents would not service the mortgage; a cash investor would have been able to survive until prices and rents picked up.

By comparison, if you invest in, say, fine art or antiques, the artist or furniture-maker you have confidently backed may well go out of fashion. Property is vastly less subject to the vagaries of fashion and style than most other commodities.

A further point is that it is relatively cheap to borrow money to buy property. Mortgages on your own home constitute very low-interest loans, and even mortgages on buy-to-let or investment properties, while higher, are still lower than loans for other types of goods. This is because property is generally seen as good security for the lender, and mortgage providers will not usually advance more money on any property than they believe it to be worth – and what they could get for it on repossession, come to that.

Something I am always being asked is: is it better to pay cash or borrow on a mortgage when property developing – always assuming of course that paying cash is a choice? Here I probably differ from most others writing on property investment who always advise their readers to use other people's money, or OPM, as it's called.

My own view, which may be old-fashioned or not financially sound, to some people's way of thinking, is that it is extremely stressful to live with large amounts of debt and that where property is concerned, there are many costs apart from simply servicing the debt. This means you have to be very, very careful when borrowing large sums to buy property because, apart from the cost of borrowing – paying back with interest, in other words – property attracts many other costs, both one-off and ongoing. When working out the figures, you have to be sure that you can not only service the debt, but can afford all the other costs associated with owning property. Whatever is promised, never forget that once you have bought your property, the developer or property club operator goes away. From the moment the property is yours, the responsibility is yours as well.

Another very specific risk for the property investor is currency risk: all currencies move daily in relation to each other. So if you are putting your money into investments in another country – and investing in property abroad is becoming increasingly popular – you have to be aware that values may move up and down, making it difficult to know whether you are in profit or not. Inflation and interest rate changes can dramatically affect the value of your investment property.

The Financial Services Authority, the UK's financial watchdog, also points out that before investing you should have sorted out your debts and made sure you have built up some savings. This will be the case whatever kind of financing you decide on, as bricks and mortar, unlike stocks and shares, need regular maintenance, and repair and renovation bills can be high. Also, mortgage interest rates are notoriously subject to change, and most advertised fixed deals only last for a certain length of time.

The book *Maxed Out: Hard times, Easy credit*, by James D Scurlock, takes a wry look at the way we are getting ourselves ever deeper into debt. One reason cited for the huge increase in property prices over the past 50 years has been shortage of housing, but according to Scurlock this is by no means the only factor involved. The ever-growing mortgage industry and the increasing ability to borrow many times your salary, have also been responsible for the huge hike in property prices. If we all had to pay cash, property prices would stay relatively stable and would not be so vastly in excess of earnings. Very few people these days can afford to buy a home outright, and now this has spread to investing as well.

It is considered clever to use OPM but hikes in interest rates, a sudden fall in property prices or a sudden dramatic downturn in personal circumstances, such as losing your job, can all wipe out your so-called investment. Mortgage companies have very little mercy when you cannot meet your payments, and repossessions can easily happen.

What happens during a repossession?

We hear a lot about repossessions these days and often the hardest hit are investors who can no longer meet their mortgage require-ments. Since 2008, this has often been exacerbated by tenants defaulting on rent or by landlords experiencing long void periods between tenants. Mortgage lenders are likely to show much less mercy to a buy-to-let investor than to turn somebody out of their own home although, of course, it may involve turning a tenant out of their home.

The first thing that happens is that the mortgage company con-tacts you about late payments. This is a standard, round-robin type of letter and not usually personal. If this is ignored and no arrangement made to meet at least some of these payments, the next stage is a letter from a solicitor or appointed debt collection company. This will usually kick in when you are three months in arrears.

After this, comes a possession order, and the final stage is a possession warrant or bailiff's eviction notice.

As well as repossessing your property, the mortgage lenders will also come to you for the costs involved in bringing this action;

any shortfall between the amount outstanding on the mortgage; and any costs involved in selling on the property.

You, as the defaulter, will discover that you cannot get any credit and may not be able to get back on your feet for many years. It is a nasty business all round and it is becoming more common as investors who may have bought up, say 10 properties off-plan on the promise that they would rent out easily and profitably, find they simply have no funds at all to meet their mortgage requirements. In addition, the property will likely have lost value in the time between being bought and under threat of repossession.

Most bank repossessions are sold at auction and, very often, the bank will be glad to offload them at any price.

But even so, lending money for property purchases has come to be seen as relatively safe for the lenders. This is in itself an indication of the relatively low level of risk in property investment; lenders are actually falling over themselves to lend you money to buy ever more property.

Even when many mortgage deals are drying up, long-term mortgages still constitute low-level borrowing: 7 per cent sounds high for a mortgage, compared to what we have got used to during the 1990s and early 2000s, but it is still a cheap loan compared to any other type of borrowing available.

These are the main advantages of investing in property but overwhelmingly, the greatest appeal is that with property, you remain in control. You do not abdicate the care of your valuable investment to fund managers who may not have your best interests at heart. It is up to you to buy, sell, rent, upgrade or whatever.

But in general and historically, you the owner are responsible for your property. Yes, you have to look after it and yes, owning property can certainly cause anxious moments and sleepless nights. And you cannot control every aspect of your property investments, such as freak weather conditions or neighbours from hell. But while you are the owner, a property remains your concern and yours only.

It is fun, creative, challenging and exciting to invest in property. I have been doing it for many years and still get a thrill from it.

My personal story

I am not clever with money or figures and indeed, I am almost innumerate. My number-blindness has been a severe handicap throughout my adult life and is rather like dyslexia in the world of words. But even so, I have made a lot of money and am heading towards an extremely financially comfortable old age by investing over many years in property.

By contrast, not one of the purely financial investments I have entered into over the years has been even remotely worthwhile, from the Savings Certificates given to me at birth, to the Save and Prosper scheme, where I Saved but never Prospered, to pension funds (Robert Maxwell took mine) or any kind of bank account.

Mind, for a long time I didn't even realize I was 'investing' in property. So far as I knew, I was just doing my best to buy nice homes in attractive locations that I would enjoy inhabiting. The fact that in the main they turned out to be highly profitable investments was an added bonus.

Also, I have enjoyed the buying, selling, renovating, developing and buy-to-let processes that I have got into over the years. Dabbling in property has been an exciting addition and sideline to my life as it has never been my 'day' job.

But don't just listen to me. Marion Mathews and Renske Mann have amassed three very nice homes, two in London and one in Devon, simply through property trading over the years. Renske says: 'In reality, most people cannot save from their salary. Most of us never earn enough to save for a decent pension and in any case, it is virtually impossible to discipline yourself to save out of your net salary.

'Marion and myself could never have saved enough or contributed enough to any kind of pension scheme to give a decent retirement. But through investing in property we not only have more than enough assets to see us out, we have choices about where to live as well as being able to earn income on our properties. Even our main home is producing income, as it is partly commercial premises.'

TIUTA

Bridging loans are the ideal funding solution to help property aspirations stay on track – as they provide quick, short-term finance. During recent times their true value has come to the fore, as the flow of long-term credit facilities slowed substantially.

A bridging loan is a loan to an individual or a company that is taken out on a short-term basis and secured against; land, a residential or commercial property. As their name suggests, they bridge the gap in finance shortfalls typically until the security is sold or refinanced with a long-term lender.

Tiuta, is a specialist bridging finance provider, offering a vast array of market-led products especially created to specifically help buyers grasp opportunities and complete valuable transactions. Rather than focusing on purchase price, they lend on open market value, which makes them an easy choice when purchasing at auction or buying under valued properties. Tiuta employ traditional commercial underwriting both in terms of the borrower and the property. This enables us to consider propositions that often fall outside of the more "tick box" approach employed by some High Street lenders.

As the ability to move quickly is key in the property sector, Tiuta gives Decisions in Principle within an hour and funds could be available in a little as 24 hours – if not before. This means our clients can achieve the same advantages and successes that cash buyers do. Flexibility is also a vital ingredient of Tiuta's bridging loans: each loan can be tailored to match individual circumstances, and have no early redemption penalties or exit fees.

Bridging loans are no substitute for mainstream, long-term mortgages but, with an exit strategy in place from the outset and when taken out with a reputable lender, they can play a crucial role in seeing property transactions succeed.

To find out more about what Tiuta can do to support your property ambitions call 0870 777 7205 or visit WWW.TIUTAPLC.COM, now.

What does Renske believe is the secret of successful property dealing? 'You have to be prepared to hang onto it until the market is right for selling. I would say you cannot be in it for the quick buck but have to wait 10 years for it to come good. Also, any property you buy, whatever its condition, has to be a little bit special. The bog-standard properties will never really gain that much in value. The old adage, location, works best every time.

'If the property is not very special in itself, it has to be in an exceptionally attractive location to increase significantly in value.'

Writer Val Hennessy decided to sell her big house in Totnes, Devon and move to a two-up, two-down cottage in Whitstable, Kent, which cost less than half the selling price of the Totnes house. Val says: 'Thanks to selling my main house, which had no mortgage on it anyway, I now have enough money in the bank to see me out and if ever I can't earn any money by writing, I will never have to worry financially.'

Totnes, near Torquay, is in any case a highly desirable part of Devon, and Val's beautiful house, with its stupendous views, sold for the full asking price in only two days. The secret is always to buy highly desirable properties.

So far as I am concerned, at this stage of my life I have several hundred thousand pounds in the bank, five fully-owned properties, no debts, no dependants and no absolute need to work for a living.

And that is without being remotely clever, or dishonest, with money. I am so naïve about money that I would not even know how to be dishonest. And most of my money-wise friends inform me that I have a peasant mentality when it comes to money. This is in common with many writers and artists who like to live 'like a poor person with money', as Picasso once put it. We have other things on our mind, so that if we do end up with money in the bank, we have been extremely fortunate.

Many writers and artists earn large sums in their lifetime, only to end up with nothing in the bank. Examples include Scott Fitzgerald, Simon Raven and Roy Boulting. Why? It never occurred to them to invest in property during their high-earning years; instead, they just spent.

As I am a property investor, there are always new things happening with my properties. When the last edition of this book was published, I was living at two addresses, one in London and the other in Worthing on the south coast. Then I lived solely at the Worthing address and rented out my London flat. Why the change?

I was teaching journalism part-time in a London college and this meant I had to be in London for the part of the week I was teaching. But in July 2006 I decided to leave this job, which meant that I no longer needed the London flat. As it had been comprehensively renovated the previous year, it was in perfect condition and I had two choices: to rent it out or to sell it. At the time, the property was worth maybe £230,000 and I would get a maximum of £13,500 a year on rent, making a gross yield of just under 6 per cent – not a great yield but probably the best that could be hoped for at the time. Percentage yields on rental flats have been steadily declining since 1995, when it was quite easy to get a 10 per cent gross yield. However, since there was no mortgage on the place and its value was likely to rise because of its excellent location, I decided to rent it out. I managed to find a suitable tenant right away and so gave up my London home.

If I had sold the property, I would have had to pay capital gains tax on it and this, added to legal and estate agent's costs, would have reduced my take to well under £200,000. Coming out with, say £190,000, I would struggle to get 5 per cent interest at the bank and would get gross around £9,500, as well as losing a valuable property asset in a popular London location. For me, the figures favoured renting the property out and, for the time being, hanging on to it.

But I had another problem, which was that I no longer had an office, as the London flat doubled up as my office. The lack of office space meant that I would either have to sell my existing south coast flat and buy a bigger one, or buy another flat to use as an office. I chose the latter course and bought a small flat within the same building at £69,000. Just a year later, that same little flat was valued at £90,000, making it another good buy. Again, putting that £69,000 into a bank account would yield at most £3,450 pa. Instead, I have already made a paper profit of £21,000 – before costs, of course. But I am not intending to sell this little flat yet. Another thing: if I fall on hard times, I can always rent out the flat for around £410 a month or £5,000 a year and still get more than I would at the bank, at the same time, with any luck, as the asset is increasing in value.

This is the thing about property development: things keep changing and you have to keep your eye on the ball. I have now added another property to my portfolio and I have put the London flat temporarily out of my use, which means I don't have such an easy way of staying in London overnight. With property, there are always choices to be made, and any situation needs constant review. Although property may not be so easy to sell as stocks and shares, your portfolio still needs constant reviewing and number-crunching. You can never afford to be complacent: you have to act according to small shifts in the market, in interest rates, rental yields and also maybe major changes in your own life.

In spite of the 2008 downturn in property prices, my London flat has increased considerably in value since the last edition of this book. This is because it is about two minutes' walk from the huge new Westfield London Shopping Centre, the biggest in Europe. The proximity to this shopper's paradise has also had the effect of increasing achievable rents in the area, as more upmarket people are becoming attracted to the location.

Yes, this is a lucky strike, but it is an example of the many complex considerations the canny investor has to take on board. Another London area I am looking at is Peckham, SE15. Property values here, long depressed because of lack of transport links, will shoot up once the projected Underground is up – or rather down – and running.

The whole point, I believe, of successful property investment is to give yourself lifestyle options as well as money in the bank.

My present happy financial state of affairs is purely the culmination of buying and investing in property since my early twenties. And I have, like many people these days, had a divorce along the way, thus halving my monetary assets at a stroke.

This is how it all began. After renting a series of extremely grotty flats, I bought my first house in 1967 with a small legacy of

£1,000 from an aunt. The six-bedroom house in Newcastle on Tyne, where I was then working, cost just under £3,000. Even in those days, it was cheap for such a large house and it was cheap because at the time Victorian properties were not highly desirable. Most people wanted to live on modern estates, plus, you could not get a full mortgage for an old property. Because I was able to put down a one-third deposit, it was easy to secure a mortgage for the rest.

The top floor had already been converted into a flat, which my then husband and myself rented out to university students. Later, another student rented our spare bedroom, and the rent from these three students more than paid our mortgage.

Thus we lived rent-free. When we sold the house three years later to come to work in London, we hardly made any money on resale, just a few hundred pounds. But because the rental income had more than covered the mortgage, it was still a good buy.

We found we could hardly afford anything in London, and eventually struggled to buy a tiny two-up, two-down cottage in Richmond, Surrey, for £7,800. We had two small children by now and were ridiculously overcrowded. We were also poverty-stricken and had no spare rooms to rent out. It was altogether hellish and we stuck it for just one year before putting the immaculate cottage on the market for £11,500. It sold for the full asking price, thus making us a terrific gain in that time. This tiny house, therefore, proved to be a good investment although it was far from being an ideal place to live.

We bought the tiny cottage because we could not get a mortgage on a rundown property, which we would have preferred. However, our next house was more like it: a four-bedroom terraced house on the slopes of Richmond Hill, which we bought for £14,000. Because of the great gain made on the tiny cottage, we could secure a mortgage on this very dilapidated house. We stayed there for seven years, in that time renovating it completely. Then the lack of a garden meant we had to move again to accommodate our growing family.

We sold this house easily and quickly for £34,000 – a good gain in that time, although it was back on the market in 2004 for £1 million!

The next purchase was a large, five-bedroom Edwardian house with a huge garden, again in Richmond, which we bought for £33,000. This too was in dreadful condition and we set about extensive renovation. Seven years after this, my then husband and myself were out on an evening walk by the river when we saw a For Sale sign up at a beautiful but totally dilapidated Queen Anne house on the river.

We had to have it! The house contained squatters, had trees growing through the living room floor and there was no parking. It was a pig in a poke and a ridiculous buy, really, but anyway we went ahead and bought it for just under £200,000; selling the Queen's Road house for £170,000. A legacy of £24,000 from an aunt of my husband's came in useful here as well.

We then set about trying to get planning permission to turn the space in front of the house into two parking spaces. This resulted in an almighty, two-year-long fight with the local council, but eventually the decision went in our favour, meaning that the value of the Grade Two listed property doubled overnight.

Not long after we won our epic fight with the council, some-body rang up out of the blue and offered us £550,000 for the house, about a hundred grand more than it was really worth at the time.

We took the money and ran – in opposite directions. This bonanza enabled us to afford to get divorced, and we moved into separate establishments, this time in Prime Central London, as it is now called. I went to live in Notting Hill and my now ex-husband bought a place in South Kensington, after taking a 50 per cent share each of the proceeds of the Richmond sale.

My large maisonette in W11 was again very rundown. I bought it for £300,000 and sold it in perfect condition six years later for £415,000 – not such a great gain in that time, but it was a wonderfully trendy and vibrant place to live in those years.

With the family now grown up and gone, it was time to down-size and I bought a three-bedroom terraced house in Hammersmith, London W14, outright for £200,000, thus not only zapping the mortgage but giving myself some useful capital as well. I now started investing in buy-to-let properties, buying and selling as markets changed. I also began buying properties on the south coast with my new partner, who died in 2004, leaving me our joint purchases.

The Hammersmith house was sold in 2004 for the full asking price of £650,000, within a day of going on the market. This time I did not even have to pay removal costs, as I walked out leaving my buyer everything, even down to cutlery and crockery. He was extremely grateful, as he had been thrown out of his house by his ex-wife, and had nothing to call his own.

Four years later, that Hammersmith house was worth £750,000. This meant that its value had risen by £25,000 a year – far less than the interest I was getting on the money at the bank over that same period. So it was a good decision to sell it at that time.

Meanwhile, the remaining properties on the south coast had increased in value, which meant I still had a fully-owned property portfolio worth in excess of £600,000.

Everything changed again in January 2009. The year-long bonds I had invested in since selling my London house were no longer available, and the 6.7 per cent interest payable at the time had gone down to 0.75 per cent. Clearly, I then had to think of doing something else with my money other than leaving it in the bank paying tiddley-squat. It seemed there were no funds of any kind worth investing in and no point in having large sums of money at the bank. At the same time, pension funds had gone down, rents from buy-to-let were also plummeting as the 'reluctant landlords' unable to sell were flooding the market, and property prices were decreasing because nobody could get a mortgage or raise the high deposit now demanded.

There seemed no way to turn, whether you had money or not. So I started thinking about buying property again and after looking at a number of possible locations, hit on Oxford. Why Oxford? Well, it was one of the few areas where property prices were pretty much holding up, and properties were selling fast, often for the asking price and within a week or so of coming onto the market. Oxford University is world-famous and thriving, mainly because of the numbers of foreign postgraduate students flocking to its prestigious colleges. The actual city is quite small and so heavily built up that there is no room for the kind of inner-city developments that have lost so much value in Northern cities, although a few gated modern developments have been squeezed into central locations.

Then, Oxford is in the middle of the country, with easy access to London, the West Country, the South and Midlands. There are several motorways going into Oxford and it is a city of beautiful (and ugly!) buildings, with huge historical and tourist interest. But – in early 2009, mortgages were as hard to get in Oxford as anywhere else, so cash buyers were able to cash in. Although properties were going fast, they were much cheaper than two years previously, and because I had the cash doing nothing at the bank, I decided to pounce, and bought a beautiful three-bedroom apartment in Central North Oxford, at the top of the Banbury Road, in possibly the best residential location in the whole of the city.

At the same time I had to think about what to do with my Worthing properties. I put the two small studio flats on the market but although there were several viewings, nobody made an offer. I did not put the main flat on the market as I knew I would only get a very low price for it through estate agents but, lo and behold, a buyer for whom this flat ticked a lot of boxes, made me an offer for it. Then, blow me, another cash buyer made an offer of the full asking price.

So – although estate agents came round and shook their heads at the price I was hoping to achieve for the property – two people came out of the blue and offered it. The price was, in any case, around £30,000 lower than it would have been two years before.

My situation at the time of writing is that I will probably have to rent out the small studios, when I would have preferred to sell, but I have a beautiful Oxford apartment with a couple of spare rooms I could rent out to a couple of postgraduate students if I fell on hard times, and this to me seems the best thing I could have done under the circumstances.

The credit crunch has affected just about everybody, but property remains a good buy so long as you choose a location that – as far as one can ascertain – will always be desirable, and not adversely affected price-wise by lots of new buildings and developments. My two other buy-to-lets, one in West Kensington and one in Worthing, are still performing reasonably well, with good tenants in each.

One reason why properties have lost so much value in America is because there is plenty of land, which means that land does not have the same intrinsic value as it will always have in a small, overcrowded country like England. So, although the property market was said to have 'crashed' in 2009, in fact, all this meant was that the property values were lower. For most people, the price of property in the UK remains high and one reason for this is that during 2009 foreign investors flooded in owing to the weak pound. Although property prices will always fluctuate, meaning that investors must constantly be on their guard, they are unlikely to fall as dramatically as in some other countries with space for many new buildings, resorts and developments.

I tell this story, not to boast about how clever I have been, because I am not that clever. Also, when I was buying and selling, there were no property investment seminars, no investor shows, no makeover programmes on television and certainly no books about the best ways to invest in property; in fact, there was no expert advice available at all. I had to learn as I went along and I made plenty of mistakes along the way.

When investing in property, you have to be prepared to suffer short-term discomfort for long-term gain and also, keep updating as tastes and ideas change. I have spent Christmas Day up a ladder painting a ceiling, gone to DIY warehouses on Bank Holidays, and got up at five in the morning to do painting and decorating. Why? I have to say that in some masochistic way, I enjoy it.

If you seriously want to invest in property, it is also important to have at least some competence with DIY as otherwise you are constantly getting stuck because of having to rely on a workman being available. It is not always practical, and it is always expensive, to call workmen out for tiny jobs.

The secret, I think, lies in knowing where to spend and where to save, but unless you are prepared to put in quite a lot of work yourself, the cost of property renovation and development will probably be prohibitive. My friend Ivan Twigden, who became a multi-millionaire through building and construction, is always prepared to mend a drain or get up onto a roof himself. If it's cheaper to do it himself, he will always have a go, rather than pay over the odds for an emergency call-out service. Even as a rich man – particularly as a rich man – he doesn't like to waste money.

Most people who have been successful property developers and investors have been prepared to get their hands dirty and pile in themselves.

But it is not a good idea to try to do highly technical or skilled jobs yourself, such as electrics or plumbing. These must be done by a qualified professional.

Then, nothing beats doing your own research, slogging round streets and looking at properties, whether or not you intend to buy. I am always poking my nose into new developments, show homes and houses for sale. That way, I keep getting ideas of both what to do and what not to do. Otherwise, your tastes can get stuck and you can become old-fashioned in your thinking.

Everything in property is a learning experience, whether you always make money or not. As Robert Kiyosaki, author of the best-selling book *Rich Dad, Poor Dad*, puts it: 'Sometimes I make money – and sometimes I learn.'

But by putting in the right kind of effort, you can greatly minimize the chance of losing, and maximize the possibility of gaining.

Nowadays, there are many more opportunities to invest in property than when I first set out, and the whole game has been made much easier by the availability of buy-to-let mortgages, property clubs, self-build magazines and advice from every quarter. Buy-to-let has become a mature industry and there are many ways to invest in property that were not easy or possible in the past. Overseas mortgages are becoming ever easier to obtain and self-build mortgages are also available.

Also, when I bought my early properties, most people did not regard their homes as 'investments'. You bought in order to have somewhere decent to live, as there was very little acceptable rental property available. In those days, property development was only for the rich and the few. Now, at least in theory, everybody has the opportunity to invest in property. The whole business has become democratized, much as the business of buying stocks and shares was democratized in the 1980s.

But even without the advantages that today's property investors possess, buying property has eventually provided me with the type of pension and retirement income that no other product could possibly have done. In most cases, you have to have earned a lot of money to stack up a decent pension; as a writer I have had good years and bad years, good decades and bad decades. But property has been much more reliable.

So, is property the new pension? Many people in recent years have been disappointed with the way their pensions have been performing. The days when you could retire after 40 years in the same job with a nice inflation-proof pension (which my father-in-law, and later his widow, enjoyed during their retirement) seem to be over.

My in-laws did not need to invest in property: my father-in-law's pension, from his job as a senior local government officer, was assured from the word go. Nowadays, things are very different. If I had relied on a company or private pension I would now be very poor indeed.

Again during 2009, very many people – and the present author is one – discovered that owing to the financial meltdown, the value of their pensions seriously plummeted. One couple who retired with a pension of £800 a month, found to their horror that in 2009, its value had gone down to £150 a month; nowhere near enough to live on with even the most stringent economies. The answer to financial security is becoming ever more clear: never rely on others to invest your money for you. Journalist Hadley Freeman, writing in *The Guardian* on 15 July 2009, makes this point:

> The recent crash has surely proved that these (financial) experts often know, at the best, nothing... There was an acronym on 80s Wall Street that investment banks used to put next to the names of certain investors – WDIS, standing for the only question these clients would ask: 'Where do I sign?'.

In the past, all too many of us have taken the attitude that worrying about savings, pensions and investments is boring and have cheerfully left it to others.

Was it Groucho Marx who said that a stockbroker is somebody who invests your money for you until it's all gone? The Bernie Madoff scandal has shown the world how careless even very rich people can be with their money and this is where, time and again, investing in property can be a relatively simple – financially speaking – method of providing for yourself.

However, property is not a risk-free, fail-safe method of providing for your retirement. Most financial experts warn that there are dangers from investing in a single, undiversified asset as you could retire and need to cash in at a time when house prices are falling.

And then you have to be able to sell a very valuable house indeed for it to provide enough for a decent pension. Also, it is never sensible to rely on upward-only property prices. As became evident during 2008, property prices are almost entirely dependent on available mortgage deals. When world money supplies are drying up and mortgages become more difficult or expensive to obtain, house prices inevitably fall. When mortgages are cheap and easy to obtain, house prices rise.

It's almost as simple as that. Other factors can certainly affect property prices, but mortgage availability is by far the biggest determining factor. Lenders advance sums based on what they believe they could get for the property on repossession, if the worst came to the worst. So property investment is always a moving target, with no certainties.

There are, I believe, two overriding aspects to successful property investment: always be prepared to sell, and never sell out of desperation.

Always be prepared to sell

That is, provided the right buyer at the right price comes along. This has happened to me three times in my lifetime and I have not passed up the opportunities which may not have come my way again.

Such luck cannot, of course, be guaranteed, but sometimes you have to make your luck by agreeing to sell when and if the right buyer shows up. That is what investment means – there is no room for lingering sentiment, even with your own home.

My philosophy with investing in property is that I will always be prepared to sell to the right buyer, even if it means turning myself out of my home. Very often, buyers come out of the blue, rather than walking into estate agents' offices and going away with a fistful of hyped-up brochures, none of which describe exactly what they want. In fact, the best deals I have ever done on my properties have been with buyers of this type; the ones who really, really want it as opposed to buyers who negotiate and haggle and are prepared to walk away.

By the same token, some of my best purchases have been of properties that just caught my eye when I wasn't even looking for somewhere. In order to invest successfully in property, you very often first have to go with a hunch – then number-crunch.

If living in an apartment building, always let the caretaker know if you are interested in selling or buying a particular property. Passers-by, casual visitors and renters often ask the caretaker if they know of any properties for sale in the building, and this personal approach can often work better than going through an estate agent. In 2009, three properties were sold in this way in my block of flats in Worthing. Sometimes caretakers will live on the premises, and they almost always know more than anybody else what's going on in the building.

Never be desperate to sell

I always remember the words of a millionaire art dealer who said the secret of his success was that he held on to his artworks until the market was right to sell. Never be so desperate that you have to sell at any price – as this way you will never get a good price.

House markets fluctuate all the time, but eventually the right buyer will come along. If you sell for a knockdown price, though, you will never be able to recover that money and may curse yourself for years to come when, if you had waited another few months, your ideal buyer would have happened along.

Of course, the property must be correctly priced. Estate agents are fond of saying that if you put your house on the market at a price that is too high, you will end up selling it for a price that is too low.

An example: in 2004 I sold my London house for £650,000 as soon as it went on the market. My neighbours, with a virtually identical house, believed it sold so quickly because it was underpriced, and put their house on the market for £680,000. A year later, they were forced to accept an offer of £560,000. Yet if they had put it on at £640,000, say, it would have sold instantly for the asking price. Moral: never be too greedy!

Finally, if you want to invest in property, I do believe you have to have a definite 'feel' for the product, which is a mixture of interest, knowledge and insight. Robert Kiyosaki believes that unless you love real estate, you shouldn't invest in it because 'if you don't love it, you won't take care of it', and, as we have seen, property takes a lot of care. There also has to be some chemistry between you and the property. However much the deal works on paper, if you feel unhappy with the property, or uncomfortable with it, you should always walk away. I always work out the figures very carefully before buying, but I definitely go on instinct and gut feeling as well.

So, if you are a beginner to property investment, or are keen to expand your portfolio, where do you start? There are so many options to choose from that it can seem difficult to hit on the 'best buy'.

We will now take a look at the extent of today's ever-expanding property investment opportunities.

1 Determining the market

There is so much choice when it comes to investing in property that it can be hard to know where to start, or what to do for the best, as there are many more options than most people imagine. Of course, none of these is mutually exclusive! Many investors have a go at several types of property investment, in order to have a varied portfolio.

At one time, house prices may rise, and your own home becomes ridiculously valuable. At other times, prices may stick or plummet, and buy-to-let becomes a more attractive option. Buying overseas may sometimes make more sense than investing in the home country, and so on. Commercial property can also be a good bet for some people. It is as well to note that the smart money always moves to where the best investments are at any one time, and when one type of investment has outlived its usefulness, moves on without sentiment or regret to the next up and coming opportunity. Smart money, for instance, would not have continued to invest in horses and carts once the motor car had been invented, but put money instead into the new horseless carriages.

Although that may sound obvious with the beauty of hindsight, it has to be remembered that, at the time, many 'experts' were predicting that the motor car would never catch on. As with all investments, the smart operator has to know when it is time to forget about one type of product and move on to the next.

In this chapter, we shall take a look at the main modern types of property investment, and briefly mention the pros and cons of each one.

Here they are:

1. Investing in your own home
2. Investing in buy-to-let
3. Buying a second home or holiday cottage
4. Buying abroad
5. Buying off-plan, either home or abroad
6. Buying a wreck and doing it up (developing)
7. Buying commercial property
8. Buying a business such as a hotel or B&B
9. Buying property to put into a SIPP or a REIT
10. Selling your main home and pocketing the proceeds
11. Buying ground rents and freeholds
12. Buying at auction.

1. Investing in your own home

What it is: You buy somewhere to live in yourself and it will be your main home, or principal private residence. However, you fully intend to use it as an investment or financial asset in that you will sit tight there until the market is at its peak, at which time you will sell and move on somewhere else. In other words, the primary consideration is always the investment potential, rather than a cosy home.

Here, you obviously have to be fairly sure that the place you have chosen to live is a present or future 'hot spot' and that it is likely to increase greatly in value during your residence there.

Pros: Because you are choosing a place as your main home, you are likely to take more care over it than when buying purely for investment, as with a buy-to-let or off-plan purchase, where you may be beguiled by sales talk and smart show homes. Also, because the place is your own home, you will not be liable for capital gains tax when you sell.

If you are building a new home from scratch, you will also be able to claim VAT relief on the new build. But beware: this can be a high-risk strategy as you must not be seen by the taxman to be buying or self-building purely for profit.

Cons: You may be in danger of entering into a nomadic life-style, where you are constantly buying with an eye to future profit rather than looking for a nice place for you and your family to live. This attitude can set in motion a rootless, temporary type of existence.

Also, although you are avoiding capital gains tax, it is expensive to keep moving. Every time you move, you will encounter legal fees, estate agents' fees, stamp duty, removal costs and renovation costs, for instance. The furniture and fittings which suited your last place may not fit into the new home. A further point is that you will not be able to claim any tax relief on renovations or improvements, which you can do with investment properties and second homes.

There is also the temptation to renovate your own home to a far higher standard than you could hope to recoup on the open market. The trick is to renovate to just the right standard, and this is not always easy to determine.

2. Investing in buy-to-let

What it is: You buy a place that is not your main home in order to make money by renting it out or, alternatively, you bank on the property making a huge capital gain in a few years and rent it out to make it pay for itself in the meantime. These days, most investors look at the total yield, that is, rental return plus potential capital gain, when deciding whether to buy.

Pros: Buy-to-let, in all its various guises, has become by far the most popular method of investing in property in recent years, and is the main way used of making money – or turning you into a 'property millionaire' – at property clubs and investment seminars. The idea is that you get regular income through rental yield which offsets the many costs involved in buying and maintaining a property, and in the process you become a landlord.

Although you incur capital gains tax on resale, there are very many costs you can set against this tax, such as refurbishment and improvement, utility bills, council tax, service charges, accountancy fees, purchase costs and legal fees.

A further benefit is that buy-to-let mortgages are easily available and constitute cheap borrowing. The idea is that you make a killing by selling at a profit when you have bought with cheaply borrowed money. Mortgages are still the cheapest kind of long-term loan available, and a prime reason for so many people investing in buy-to-let.

Cons: There can never be any guarantee that your place will successfully rent out. Although many property developers are now offering a 'guaranteed rental' for a period of time, you as the owner do not know whether this is a genuine rent, or whether the property will rent out at that amount when the guarantee period ends. Or, indeed, that it will rent out at all.

In many areas, landlords struggle to find tenants as the buy-to-let phenomenon has caused serious oversupply of properties, with many developers now building apartment blocks specifically aimed at this sector, and canny tenants negotiating rents ever downwards. Rents also do not always cover mortgages, as Tony and Cherie Blair found to their cost when they had to keep lowering the rent on their West London house.

Being a landlord is hard work and requires input from you. Renting out a property is emphatically not the same as hiring out a car, for instance, as the complicated rules of tenure always apply. Tenants are human beings, and being a landlord involves very human transactions – it is emphatically not simply a matter of moving money around.

There are very many regulations governing renting out properties and also many ongoing costs associated with buy-to-let. Figures have to be worked out very carefully indeed, to make sure the expected rental will adequately cover your costs – and not merely the mortgage.

Tenants nowadays expect smart, modern, clean properties, and this means constant work maintaining and renovating your property to a high standard. The unexpected – such as no tenants, the boiler breaking down, the roof coming off in a high wind – can always happen.

The other major factor here is that if buying mainly for capital gain, you are taking a big gamble as you can never know for sure that the capital gain on resale will be worth it. You are looking into the future, a place where nobody has a reliable crystal ball.

Although many property professionals are in the business of prediction, as with all financial predictions, they can actually only go on past performance. Anybody who could genuinely and accurately predict future trends would indeed soon be a billionaire, but that person has never yet come forward.

3. Buying a second home or holiday cottage

What it is: You buy a second home that is not your main home, either because you believe the area or the property will rise in value, or because you want to make the place pay for itself by renting it out as a holiday cottage when you are not there yourself.

Pros: You enjoy a second home which, if you rent it out, helps to pay for itself, and with any luck, you will be both getting rental income and enjoying capital growth. Also, the rents from holiday cottages and short lets are higher than with the assured shorthold tenancies you will be entering into with buy-to-let.

Another plus is that renting out a holiday cottage is considered a business, which means there are many more things you can offset against tax than with buy-to-let, which continues to be assessed as unearned income.

Cons: It is almost always the case that the times of highest rental interest will be the times you will want to use the property yourself. Also, you will have to keep the place meticulously tidy to satisfy the rental agency, and have plenty of changes of linen, towels and so on. Holiday cottages and flats have to come completely equipped with everything.

As occupants usually stay only a week or so – and stays are becoming ever shorter, with many holiday homes being rented only for weekends – the quick turnover means a lot of cleaning, clearing and preparing – and wear and tear. As one holiday cottage owner said: 'It's three times the money and six times the work of ordinary rentals.'

The other thing is that the holiday home must be in an area of high rental potential, where you may well be competing with other holiday cottages. As with buy-to-let, holiday lets have become a competitive business, both fuelled by the easy availability of mortgages.

4. Buying abroad

What it is: You buy a place abroad in the belief that by doing so you will make more money than by investing in the home country. You may also, into the bargain, hope to get some enjoyment from the place yourself, although increasingly investors are buying abroad purely for investment and do not ever expect to visit their foreign properties.

Pros: Buying abroad is exciting, challenging and exotic. It is often much cheaper to buy abroad than in the UK and there are dramatic opportunities for capital growth, as many foreign markets are emerging, are nowhere near their peak, and have plenty of growth potential. It is possible to make a far greater capital gain by buying abroad than in the home country.

It is now also possible to buy on a mortgage in most currencies, and is becoming easier all the time. The other huge advantage of much of 'abroad' is the vastly better weather. There is also the aspect that you are buying a dream, and that people will pay a lot of money to realize a dream. Your investment could rise hugely in value, if you have bought into a highly desirable area or country.

Cons: There are many unknowns about buying abroad, so while it can be an extremely profitable exercise, it can also be very risky. Changes of government, currency differences, developers going bust, labyrinthine legal procedures, poor infrastructure, language problems, high-pressure sales talk, fragile economies, can all mean you have been sold a pup in the belief you were buying a reliable investment.

Also, the actual process of buying abroad can be more expensive than buying in the UK. Then there is the cost of flights, getting to and from your investment, as well as paying ongoing costs such as local taxes, service charges and land taxes. Each country has its own financial and legal rules, and you may well find that you are bound by the rules of the country when it comes to inheritance, buying and selling, renting and advertising.

5. Buying off-plan, either home or abroad

What it is: You buy a property long before it is finished in the belief that by so doing, you will make a significant profit on resale, maybe renting it out for a time before you come to sell. Here, you are buying a place you will never inhabit yourself as you are purchasing purely for investment purposes.

Pros: You buy at an early stage in the development, at a discount, because you have to use your imagination to visualize what the property or development will look like on completion. Because the property is unfinished, you pay in stages, often over several years, so do not tie up all your money at once. You buy cheaply because you are buying something which does not yet exist. The idea is that you gain a cash incentive by helping the developer to defray some of his costs, and enable the project to continue and be completed.

With any luck, as an off-plan buyer, you will be getting the pick of the prime units. But the major advantage of buying off-plan is that you can buy to flip, which means that you can sell your property after exchange of contracts but before completion. This allows you to take advantage of capital growth without completing the purchase or applying for a mortgage. You also avoid paying stamp duty land tax as the eventual lease will be in the final purchaser's name.

Obviously the earlier in the proceedings that you buy your as yet non-existent unit, the greater the potential profits. Off-plan properties are now available all over the world. If you decide not to flip and complete the purchase, you will probably need a mortgage, which will lock you into long-term borrowing, with severe penalty payments for early redemption.

Cons: Buying off-plan is the most heavily marketed of all property investments. You are taking a risk that (a) the finished property will be as attractive in reality as on the computer-generated pictures and (b) that the completed development will rise in value as much as the hype. Marketing people point to previous growth figures but with future developments, nobody really knows. Not all off-plan properties are sold at a discount, either. The more the developer reckons he can obtain full price, the less likely he is to offer discounts to early buyers. When buying discounted properties through a property club, the club will also extract its fee. You have to be sure that the purchase price plus the property club's fee plus the buying and running costs plus interest on the loan add up to a genuine cut-price deal.

In any case, your money will be tied up for a long time, maybe several years, before the development is even ready. Very many developments go seriously over time. There may be service charges, council tax and other ongoing costs to pay as well as the stage payments.

Property clubs – those which promise to make you an instant millionaire – are heavily into off-plan buying, and there are many unscrupulous operators in this game.

Other risks are that developers can go bust, the apartments may not be finished to the high standard expected, and the hoped-for capital growth may not happen, especially if there is a serious downturn in the market. These are all potential risks that the off-plan investor has to take on board.

There are two main ways to make money from off-plan developments: one is to rent the completed property out until such time as its value has increased enough to secure a substantial profit, and the other is to 'flip' – sell on at completion without either yourself or anybody else ever having lived in it.

At times of quickly rising house prices, flipping can be a sensible option. When house prices are levelling off or plummeting, you stand to lose a lot of money, bearing in mind that you have to pay interest on borrowed money all the time, whether or not you make a profit yourself.

6. Buying a wreck and doing it up (developing)

What it is: You buy something in bad condition, renovate it and immediately sell it on for a high profit. This type of amateur property developing is beloved of countless property shows on television, where we are almost always shown the things that can go horribly wrong.

Pros: Developing property is exciting and challenging, not least because you are turning something horrible into something wonderful. Property developing appeals to some deep instinct in us, which is to make something beautiful and usable out of unpromising material. In fact, all kinds of makeovers have this appeal, which is why they make such popular television, from *DIY SOS* to *How to Look Good Naked* to *Extreme Makeover* and *10 Years Younger.* We all love this kind of transformation, of turning the ugly duckling into a swan.

Cons: It can be difficult to make money unless you are extremely strict with yourself and work to the tightest budget and the shortest timescale. You have to know where to spend and where to save, where to cut corners and where to be lavish; also, you must be very exact with the market you are aiming at, and what that particular market requires. This is again where research comes in.

In order to make this kind of developing work, you have to be able to coordinate builders and building trades; work out your realistic expenses at every stage, not forgetting interest charges, council tax, stamp duty, VAT, capital gains tax, estate agents' fees, for instance. There are very many costs involved in developing, including 'dead' costs such as stamp duty. These all have to be recovered on resale, otherwise you have not made a profit. You cannot just look at the purchase price and the selling price, and assume you have thereby made a killing.

When developing an existing property, as opposed to building from scratch, you cannot reclaim VAT. This means you have to add on 17.5 per cent (in the UK – VAT levels may differ in other countries) to all your building and renovation costs, including kitchen and bathroom appliances.

It is also difficult to make a good profit from a quick turna-round on property. Usually, a house or flat takes several years to reach its peak value and recoup buying and selling costs.

It is very, very easy to overspend on renovation. A friend's old-fashioned terraced house was valued at £600,000 in its 'raw' state. He then embarked on a major renovation that eventually cost in excess of £350,000. When the renovation was complete two years later, he had the house revalued. The estate agents were very excited at the impeccable renovation and believed they would have no trouble at all selling at the recommended guide price of £850,000. But – while the modernization had added a good £250,000 onto the price of the property, the works had cost far more. In addition, my friend had to rent a flat for six months while the bulk of the work was being done, and this added another £8,000 or so to the cost.

It is true that in those two years, property prices had gone down and it is probably also true that in years to come, the full price of the renovation will most likely be recouped on resale. But whenever contemplating any renovation, first discover from the local agents how the prices compare for an unmodernized house and a fully renovated state of the art property, especially if you need to sell the property instantly on completion of the works. You might find it is less than you imagine.

7. Buying commercial property

What it is: You are buying property for commercial or business purposes rather than for residential use. As with residential buy-to-let, you can buy this type of property to rent out, except that this time you are renting to a business, rather than a person. Commercial property can include offices, shops, sheds, ware-houses and factories, and as with buy-to-let you have two bites of the profit cherry: rental yield and capital growth when you come to sell.

Historically, it has also been possible to put commercial prop-erty only into a SIPP (Self-Invested Personal Pension), and this remains the case, thanks to a dramatic U-turn by the Government in December 2005.

Pros: In the recent past, yields from commercial property have vastly outstripped not only shares and bonds but also residential property.

Commercial tenants tend to be far less hassle than residential tenants as they are usually responsible for all the repairs and renovation to the property. They also tend to stay longer – 15 years is not uncommon – and as well as being responsible for all maintenance and repairs, they agree to regular, upward-only rent reviews. Residential tenants, by contrast, can negotiate rents down for agreeing to stay.

Commercial tenants must also hand the property back in perfect condition, agree to insure the place, handle any planning permission and pay for any improvements.

Cons: There is more to go wrong when investing in commercial property, and much more to understand than with residential property. Many investors go for residential property simply because they understand it, and are frightened off by commercial property. You would definitely need a qualified expert to guide you through the maze and this, of course, will cost you. Every commercial lease is different and each has to be separately analysed. Then there is such a bewildering choice of commercial property that it can be hard for the beginner to know which might be best to choose.

Some swanky new office blocks, for instance, fail to attract the expected tenants and lose thousands daily. It can also be difficult and expensive for the individual investor to break into commercial property as the entry level is high.

8. Buying a business such as a hotel or B&B

What it is: You are buying a property which gives you both a home and an income.

Pros: Going for this option may well mean that you are living in a much nicer, bigger and grander place than you could otherwise afford. And whatever the hotel or guest house may produce in income, the chances are that the real estate will keep increasing in value.

Cons: It is difficult to make a living from a small hotel or bed and breakfast, and very hard work. Also, you constantly have strangers in your house. You have to enjoy the actual process of running a hotel and also be the kind of person who can cope easily with strangers. Definitely not for everybody!

It is also essential that the hotel is situated in a location which will attract a high number of visitors, but where there is not already oversupply. Many, many hotels in seaside towns in the UK, for instance, have had to close as there are simply not enough summer visitors to enable the business to keep going.

You will also have to keep meticulous records of incomings and outgoings. Also, you will have to conform to current health and safety regulations, and may need licences for running a restaurant or selling liquor, for instance.

9. Buying property to put into a SIPP or a REIT

What it is: You buy property which is then transferred to a trust and 'wrapped up' in a pension scheme which will yield you, with any luck, an excellent return when you retire.

Pros: Such investments are protected from the taxman and thus, as tax-free vehicles, yield far more money than they would if you had to pay tax on them. Investments put into SIPPs can be bought and sold in the same way as other properties, and rents can be received from buy-to-let investments – all tax free. You can bequeath these investments to your heirs, thus creating the famous, or notorious, 'trustafarians'. You can also avoid paying inheritance tax, or your executors can, when you die.

Cons: By 'wrapping up' your investments, you are not only protecting them from the taxman, but also from yourself and your heirs! The point about putting property – or indeed, any other type of investment – into a SIPP is that you can never yourself get at the bulk of the capital.

The reason for this is that the investment does not belong to you any more, but to a trust you have created. You can administer the trust, but you remain a trustee, not the owner. As such, you only benefit from the interest or yield received.

Also, these vehicles need professional management and you will have to pay a fee to fund managers. Another aspect is that, really, you need to be quite rich to invest in a SIPP. There are also upper limits to the amount and type of property you can put into a SIPP. Because there are many rules, it is imperative to take professional advice, and you need to know that your adviser is completely trustworthy.

REITs – Real Estate Investment Trusts – introduced into the UK in January 2007, are companies which own and manage income-producing property. This can be commercial or residential and the idea is that the bulk of the income is distributed to investors.

Instead of investing directly in property, you put your money into a REIT which buys, manages and lets out property on behalf of the investors. REITs were first established in the United States, then migrated to Australia and finally to the Netherlands as a means of investing in a property portfolio. REITs are closely linked to buy-to-let, and – so property experts maintain – are set to change the face of property investment in the UK. As you invest in the company rather than the property itself, REITs are an indirect means of property investment, rather like stocks and shares, although there are several important differences.

As REITs get going, they will probably appeal most to those who feel they understand bricks and mortar, but don't want all the hassle of dealing with it directly.

10. Selling your main home and pocketing the proceeds

What it is: This is the famous 'downsizing' that older people are increasingly choosing to do when the family has grown up and gone, and the big house and garden are no longer needed.

Pros: By downsizing, you get your hands on a large lump sum you can use how you like. By choosing this option, you avoid all costs, fees and complications. There is also nobody to take your money off you, such as fund managers or other financial advisers, and nobody is making any money out of you either. You become a totally free, financially independent individual, living like the camel, off your hump. The huge hike in property values in recent years has enabled ever more people to take advantage of this simple option.

Cons: Can there possibly be any cons to this option? Yes, just a few. In the first place, the fabulous lump sum you have in the bank is extremely vulnerable to the taxman. You will not only pay tax on the interest received, but in effect, your capital will lose value just sitting in the bank.

Then, with 'unwrapped' money, you will also have to pay your full whack of inheritance tax on your estate – or your executors will – when you die. As you never know how long you have to live, or what care you may require in later years, it is hard to budget for having just enough to last you out – a financial planning difficulty that has not escaped the taxman.

11. Buying ground rents and freeholds

What it is: Now that there are many more flats and apartments being built than houses, leaseholds, once rare, are becoming ever more common. All apartments in blocks are sold leasehold as to have a freehold property means that you own the land on which the property is built; clearly this cannot happen with a third-floor apartment, for instance.

All leasehold properties are owned by a freeholder; that is, somebody who owns the whole building, and who leases out the separate apartments to the leaseholders. But freeholds frequently change hands, for a variety of reasons. The initial freeholder or developer may have gone bust, they may have died, or they may have tired of the business of collecting ground rents, service charges and so on. It is possible to buy the ground rents off the freeholder and so own the building. This business is only going to grow as ever more apartment blocks are created.

Pros: Ground rents and freeholds are often sold extremely cheaply. You see ground rent investments being advertised for as little as £4,500. But the collectable ground rents may only come to £300 a year. People who buy ground rents and freeholds usually view them as a very long-term investment, and as their business. It's no use just buying one; you have to own a lot to make it work.

The main reason why people buy ground rents is that when all the leasehold interests of a property run down, the buyer of these ground rents now owns the freehold. In practice these days, lease-holders are likely to get together to collectively enfranchise – buy the freehold between them – and in order to do this, they have to negotiate with the person who owns the ground rent interest.

The shorter the leases, the more the ground rent owner stands to gain from selling the freehold. The whole business is subject to extremely complex calculations and legal processes and either way, whoever owns the ground rents stands to gain – eventually.

For instance, if the leaseholders get together to buy the free-hold, they must make the freeholder – or ground rent owner – an offer which includes the sum of all the ground rents for the total length of time that all the leases have left on them – as well as a sum to compensate him for the loss of the freehold.

If ground rents come to a total of £300 a year and there are 100 years left on each lease, this means the ground rent owner stands to lose £30,000 – without any adjustment for inflation. When you buy a ground rent, you are buying this element only and not any other covenants that may affect the building. You are simply buying the covenant to pay this rent.

First of all, you have to obtain an application pack from Land Registry containing forms GR1 and GR2, or they can be down-loaded from the internet. Then you have by law to give the tenants in the building the right of first refusal before going ahead with the purchase. To make it worthwhile, you would need to buy ground rents of properties with leases of 80 years or less; the shorter the lease has to run, the more it becomes worthwhile to consider buying the ground rent element of the building.

There are now many companies that buy up ground rents; this is a specialist area and one, really, which is not highly recommended for the amateur. The business of buying ground rents is best left to the seasoned property investor who has, maybe, started off by buying and selling their own home, graduated to buy-to-let, buying at auction, and gradually become more confident and experienced in the kind of property investments that ordinary people do not readily understand.

Very often, companies or individuals buy up ground rents with the intention of increasing them once bought, as some ground rents are nominal and are charged on a never-increasing basis. Some ground rents can be as little as £25 or £50 a year. Also, nowadays people are buying up ground rents to make money from enfranchisers – that is, the ever-increasing number of leaseholders who collectively buy their freehold. When enfranchising, leaseholders must compensate the ground rent holder for the total income stream he or she will lose and the present value of the ownership he or she would have secured when the leases expired.

As you can see, buying ground rents can be a very complicated business and those interested should take advice from a lawyer, or a company such as Rosetta Consulting, which specializes in ground rent and enfranchisement law.

When you look at it like this, it becomes easy to see why ground rent investments can be a canny buy. But you have to know what you are doing, and also, these days, know your way around the extremely complicated collective enfranchisement laws.

Cons: You have now got yourself a huge responsibility! One reason freeholders offload their freeholds is because collecting charges from leaseholders can be a thankless task. In some cases, people may not have paid service charges for years. In addition, the property may be in very bad condition and need six figures spending on it. That money has to be raised from the leaseholders, a group of people who notoriously hate paying out, especially when they believe they are putting money into the hated freeholder's pocket. In general, the business of buying ground rents and freeholds is a specialist business not really suitable for the amateur investor. Another aspect is that leaseholders are now allowed to enfranchise, which means they can buy the freehold for themselves and so wrest control from an outside freeholder. As against this, investors can make a lot of money from selling the freehold to the residents.

When buying abroad, it can be difficult to establish title, which can make buying the freehold extremely risky, as you think you own the building, then discover that you do not.

12. Buying at auction

What it is: Instead of going through an estate agent, you buy property at a property auction. These are becoming increasingly frequent and many investors nowadays only buy at auction.

Pros: You can often get bargains at auction in a way that might be difficult otherwise. In general terms, properties sell at auction for 10–15 per cent less than through ordinary estate agents.

Cons: If there are many people bidding for the same property, it may end up being the opposite of a bargain. At one recent property auction, a garage valued at around £7,000 went for £14,500. You must have all the finance, surveys, mortgage and so on in place before going to the auction, as when the hammer comes down, the property will be yours. Buying at auction has become sophisticated and most auctions are now full of professional auction-buyers. You are competing with these.

There is usually a very good reason why something is sold at auction, which is that it cannot, for some reason, be sold in the ordinary way. Properties sold at auction may have a sitting tenant paying £6 a week rent; they may be in truly terrible, uninhabitable, condition; they may be in out of the way places; not have a high value; or there may be legal problems attached. You would need to find out exactly why a particular property is being sold at auction.

You would also need to act fast as there is usually a gap of only a few weeks before the catalogue is sent out and the auction itself. The kind of places that often go at auction are unmodernized houses which need total renovation and houses with sitting tenants, which often come at about 30 per cent cheaper than those sold with vacant possession. Then when the tenant leaves, the property gains its full value. But if the tenancy is regulated, and the tenant is paying hardly any rent, you may have a very long wait indeed, as they can never be evicted.

Brief guide to buying at auction

Catalogues are published around two weeks before the sale, and guide prices are included, usually on a separate sheet. Note: the guide price is expected to be exceeded at the sale. Lots are identified by description, such as Vacant House, Ground Rent Investment, Commercial Property and so on.

Dates and times of viewings are also published on a separate sheet in the catalogue. These are almost always block viewings and there is no need to book in advance. The property will be open for about 15 minutes only. Tenanted properties are not usually viewed in advance.

If you are interested in a particular property, you can obtain a legal pack from the agents, and this should be sent to your solicitor. You can also contact the vendor's solicitor; the agent can put you in touch.

Finance must be arranged before the auction sale. There are financial companies which specialize in auction sales, and your agent should have a list. They will also usually advertise in auction catalogues.

Pre-auction offers can be made by phone, fax, e-mail or in writing. If you make an offer you must be in a position to exchange contracts immediately. A lot will not be withdrawn from the auction until a legally binding contract is exchanged.

It is possible to bid by proxy, via the internet or telephone if you are unable to attend the sale personally. We have all seen footage of such bidding on television.

If you plan to attend the sale, you should first check as to whether there have been any last-minute alterations, as lots are sold subject to these alterations. The auctioneer will announce the lot by number and invite bids at a suggested level. You bid in the usual manner, by raising either your hand or the catalogue. If you are the highest bidder, the auctioneer will strike the gavel and the property is yours – there and then. A legal and binding contract happens at the time of the sale.

Then you will be asked to complete a purchase slip and attend the contract desk where the legal formalities will be concluded. You then have to pay the 10 per cent deposit plus a purchaser's administration fee of, typically, £150 including VAT for each lot purchased.

The balance of the purchase money must be paid within 28 days of the auction. If you are interested in seeing the progress of a property auction before taking the plunge, you can obtain a Result Sheet the day after the auction.

Auctions are becoming ever more popular and it seems the days of amazing bargains, at least for properties, are now more or less over. Ever more vendors put their properties up for auction because they expect to get more for them, rather than less. Most lots have a guide price on them which is usually the very lowest price at which the lot will be sold. Unless it comes up to the guide price on the brochure, it will be withdrawn from the sale.

So although the auctioneer will usually start the bidding low to get the room warmed up, don't imagine that you will secure the property at this low price, even if there are no other bidders. For instance, if a property is up for auction at £140,000 and the highest offer made is £95,000, don't expect the hammer to come down. Instead, the property will be put up on the 'lots withdrawn' website the next day.

The main reason vendors sell at auction these days is for a quick sale; a property sold at auction will typically take five to six weeks to sell, rather than the three months or so by the ordinary high street estate agent route. By law, the auction house must mention any problems pertaining to the property, such as lack of planning permission, unpaid rents, unpaid service charges or disputed title. Then it is a case of *caveat emptor* – let the buyer beware.

In the old days, most properties sold at auction had something drastically wrong with them, and there was some very good reason why they could not be sold by the normal route. Although it is still true that many property lots at auction will have a problem attached, ever more put up for auction will be perfectly ordinary properties where the vendor wants a quick fight to the death rather than the often long drawn-out agony of estate agent-generated sales.

(Information courtesy of Andrews and Robertson: 020 7703 2662; auctions@a-r.co.uk)

There is a lot to take on board in the complicated business of buying property for profit!

The important questions to ask yourself

When considering investing in property, you have to ask yourself why you are investing and what you hope to get out of the investment, whether in the short, medium or long term. Property investment is currently extremely fashionable and 'everybody' seems to be doing it, but that doesn't mean everybody is automatically on their way to vast wealth.

All forms of property investment are highly complex, and every aspect of the transaction needs to be completely understood before you proceed. This is what is known in the trade as 'due diligence' and you would be extremely unwise to proceed without it, as there are very many sharks out there, waiting to take your money off you.

Never forget that there are very many ways of making money out of you, the investor. There are mortgage lenders, who make vast sums from borrowers, there are surveyors, project managers, builders, insurers, developers, property seminar providers, furnishers, decorators, paint manufacturers, financial advisers, letting and estate agents, pension providers, managing agents, freeholders, solicitors, investment advisers – just to name a few. And let us also not forget that the government too makes huge sums out of you, the investor, as well, through income tax, stamp duty, capital gains tax, VAT, inheritance tax, council tax. Every time a property changes hands, the government takes its whack, one way or another. VAT is just as much a tax as income tax, stamp duty and capital gains tax.

As such you have to be sure that you know exactly what you are doing, and that you are very clear about WHY you are investing in property – and what you hope to get out of it in the long run.

If you need usable income now, you would probably consider some form of renting or letting. If you have a spare room or rooms, you can rent those out to lodgers or paying guests. This is the time-honoured way of making money from your property, and still the most popular.

There is, of course, a big difference between making a usable, useful extra bit of cash and earning an income you can live on. You would need to have a very big property portfolio indeed in order for it to yield a full-time income, and the bigger the property portfolio, the more work and effort it takes. There will always be repair jobs, difficulties with tenants, plus ongoing administration.

If you are looking for financial independence in the future, then you will be thinking about pensions, or pension alternatives, or maybe buying bigger and better homes to live in with a view to eventually downsizing and living off the capital.

You may also consider buying off-plan in order to sell in 10 or 15 years' time at a sizeable profit.

It may be that you are looking to afford the otherwise unafford-able, such as a second home overseas or in the country. In which case, you will buy a place that can be rented out when you are not using it yourself.

Whatever your eventual aim, you have to ask yourself some searching questions about property investment, such as:

▮ Am I prepared to put in the necessary work of maintenance, repairs and renovation? Building costs can easily run away with you and make no mistake – all property will need maintenance and regular updating. The property that looks after itself has not yet been invented.

▮ Am I prepared to put in the kind of research that sensible property purchases demand? This means never buying anything on impulse, but only after careful consideration and evaluation of the costs involved in buying and owning the property.

▮ What kind of risk am I prepared to take which will allow me to sleep at night? Everybody has their own 'risk profile' and this needs to be carefully assessed before making any investment purchase. The more risk-averse you are by nature, the more you need to proceed with caution. The kinds of risks you are taking on include: interest rates rising, house prices plummeting, no tenants appearing for your lovely property, tenants trashing your apartment, an unexpected huge repair bill such as for a new roof or new boiler, and your investment turning out to be worth much less than you were led to believe.

▮ Am I good at working to a very tight budget? When investing in property, every last penny has to count and costs can include petrol or air fares to get to your investment, phone calls (more than you would ever believe possible), accountants' fees, legal fees and continuous overheads. However big your budget, you can always expect fees to run away with you and there will always, always be unforeseen costs.

▮ Over how long a period do I want to invest? Obviously, for anybody who invests, there comes a time when they want to see a return on their investments. With buy-to-let or holiday lets, there can be an instant return in the form of rents, but when developing property, you will only realize a return when you successfully sell. In general, the advice is to regard property as a medium- or long-term investment, as it can take time to realize its full potential.

As well as all these, there is another important consideration – what kind of property interests me most? Am I more interested in smart newbuild properties which (with any luck) are absolutely perfect at the time of completion, or romantic hideaway cottages? Am I an urbanite or a country person? Can I stand living cheek by jowl with other people, as in an apartment building, or must I have a big house standing in its own grounds? Everybody has strong preferences when it comes to property, and with which they feel most comfortable. I always feel most at ease with property where I can add my own touches and add some value, rather than somewhere highly designed by somebody else.

Then, different places appeal as your lifestyle changes. When I was bringing up a family, I would not have wanted to live in a flat; now, flats make more sense as they offer more security and, in general, take less maintenance than a house. Your work may require you to live in a big town or city; then, when you retire, you may prefer to move to the country, to another country, or to the seaside. All these considerations will affect your attitude towards the kind of property investment that will most suit you.

Regard it as a business

When considering investing in property, it is essential to regard it as a business, as the sums of money involved are too high and the competition is now too great for it to be treated as a hobby. Bear in mind that when investing in property you will have many mouths to feed, such as (for instance) developers, currency brokers, estate agents, lawyers, surveyors, architects, builders, mortgage lenders and also governments, which these days are dedicated to extracting every little bit of tax from anywhere they possibly can. You have to be sure that your investment will feed your mouth as well as all these other people's. And, most importantly, feed your mouth best.

If you are serious about investing in property, you need to do constant research. This involves going round to see show homes, looking at properties on the market, pretending to be a tenant to keep up to date on how the buy-to-let market is operating, closely studying the property pages in local and national newspapers, and keeping up to speed with all the property websites and price guides on the internet.

The 'fatal flaw'

It is also important to keep in mind that there is no such thing as the perfect property. Every single piece of property, without exception, will have a fatal flaw – or several flaws, much like human beings.

Any piece of property will be too big, too small, too near the road, too far away from the road, too far away from transport links or shops, not near a good school, too near a school for comfort, not near enough to the sea, in a location which is either too crowded or too isolated.

The *Guardian Weekend* magazine has for several years run a feature detailing pros and cons of properties currently on the market. Without fail, every single one has a major drawback. It may be that the bathroom is downstairs, or there is no garden, or that the front door opens directly onto the high street, or the third bedroom is too small to take an actual bed.

There is no point in trying to find the property that is perfect from every angle because such a place simply does not exist. You just have to make sure the property you are interested in ticks more boxes than not, but first of all, you have to have a very clear idea of what you want and what you are prepared to compromise on.

Most property investors go to many auctions, view many properties, keep their eye in all the time – but only rarely do they buy.

2 Using your own home

There are a number of ways you can use your own home as a property investment, thus killing two birds with one stone – enjoying your property as it makes you money, the ideal scenario! You cannot do this with a bond or a share.

For the purposes of this chapter, 'your own home' is defined as your principal private residence as opposed to a second home, a buy-to-let, holiday cottage, home abroad or any type of property other than what is designated your main abode.

There are many tax advantages to using your own home as an investment, but the government only allows each person ONE principal private residence (PPR). If you are an unmarried couple, you are each allowed a PPR but if you are married, then it's one between you. The new Civil Partnership Bill, which came into force in December 2005, allows same-sex couples in genuine relationships to leave property to each other free of inheritance tax. This right does not extend to cohabiting heterosexual couples, on the grounds that they could marry if they wished.

A civil partnership has to be registered, and cannot be an informal arrangement, at least if property and other assets are to be inherited, as with spouses. There is a legal document which each partner must sign and this is legally binding. Civil partnerships have to be dissolved in much the same way as a marriage. Once the formalities are over, civil partners are treated in exactly the same way as married couples as regards tax, pension and inheritance rights. And as with married partners, each civil partner has to make a new will when registering the partnership, as previous wills will be invalid.

Of course, as with married people, inheritance tax will be payable in the normal way when the survivor dies.

Cohabiting, but not married, heterosexual partners, are not allowed to enter into a civil partnership, on the grounds that they could marry if they wanted to. This is the case however long the heterosexual partnership has endured – time does not add to the legality.

Civil partnerships, marriages and cohabitation all have serious consequences for the property investor, and national laws will always override any private arrangements. Wherever property is involved, it is essential to discover your inheritance or partnership rights and to make arrangements accordingly.

Buying a house together – advice for couples

If you are a married couple buying a house together, you will usually be joint tenants. This means that you both own the whole of the property and if one dies the survivor automatically inherits. But if you are a cohabiting couple, you would be wise to choose the tenants in common option, whereby you each own half the property. Where this happens, it is vital for each partner to make a will stating that, on death, the deceased's half of the property goes to the remaining partner. Otherwise, it just goes into the estate. Inheritance tax does apply, however, as the only exemption is for married couples leaving property to each other, or same-sex couples who have declared a civil partnership.

I bought three properties jointly with my partner, who died suddenly in 2004. Because we had each drawn up a will specifically stating that the survivor would own the properties, I automatically inherited them on his death. Otherwise I would have had to sell them to administer the estate. The question of joint or common ownership is very important indeed when investing in property and cannot be left to chance.

There are other vital considerations when you are investing in property with another person, such as: Does one person have ownership and if so, what rights does the other person possess? Who pays the mortgage and how will this affect the equity on resale? What happens when one party wishes to sell and the other does not? What happens in the event of death? How are outgoings to be apportioned? What about life insurance? What if there is negative equity? Who pays for repairs?

Before you ever start investing with another person, whether this is your spouse, partner or friend, it is essential to draw up a legally binding document. If you are a close friend or intimate partner, it can seem harsh and calculating to do this, but it is essential.

Anybody possessing property assets and who is about to get married or enter into a civil partnership should seriously consider a formal pre-nuptial arrangement, drawn up by a solicitor. This makes provision for division of assets in the event of a divorce or break-up.

Ever more solicitors are offering these pre-nups, which although not necessarily legally binding, are becoming more recognized by UK courts, and the existence of a pre-nup will certainly have an influence on what a court decides.

It is very likely that the law regarding pre-nups and post-nups will soon change. Initial consultations instituted by the Law Commission began in September 2009 and a report and draft bill is likely to be published in September 2012, which will harden and clarify the laws on pre- and post-nuptial arrangements.

In the meantime, anybody with any property or financial assets or investments who is about to get married or enter into a civil partnership should see a solicitor before the big day and enter into a 'full and frank disclosure of assets' as solicitors put it.

The situation at present is that if and when a relationship breaks down, the terms of any pre-nup will be considered, and one stipulation is that they must have been inherently fair at the time they were drawn up.

Couples can also enter into post-nuptial agreements whenever circumstances change, and these will also be taken into account when the relationship ends. Wherever property and other valuable assets exist, it is always better to enter into a legally drawn-up agreement while still friends and lovers, rather than try to slug it out when you are no longer on speaking terms and have come to hate each other. Both the pre- and post-nuptial 'piece of paper' are rapidly becoming as important as the change of legal status that marriages or civil partnerships bring about.

Many couples are reluctant to draw up pre-nups, as they are seen as 'unromantic'; but there is nothing more unromantic than seeing all your hard-earned financial assets disappear into the gaping maws of divorce lawyers.

If you have decided that the best and safest way to invest in property is to use your own home, you must be very careful that you are not seen to be running any kind of property development business for profit, as HM Revenue and Customs will take a very dim view if you are, and tax you accordingly.

The main methods of using your own home as an investment are:

▌ buying a place in an up-and-coming area, living in it for a few years, then selling it on at, you hope, a vast profit;

▌ buying a wreck, doing it up and then selling it on, while living in the place in the meantime;

▌ building your own home from scratch, living in it and then selling it on when finished;

▌ having lodgers or paying guests;

▌ renting out your home to overseas visitors as a holiday let when you are not there yourself;

▌ buying a place that has a self-contained flat in the basement or in the loft, or converting part of your home into a self-contained flat;

▌ letting out your home to TV and film crews;

▌ running a small hotel or B&B at the same time as living in the place yourself.

Finance

The first, and most important, aspect to any investment is getting the finance right. First of all, you must do all you can to save costs on the actual buying process, as these are 'dead' costs which cannot always be recouped on resale. And when you are using your own home for investment, you cannot claim anything back on tax, as you can with properties acquired purely for investment. So far as the government is concerned, your own home is supposed to be a tax-free zone, apart from paying stamp duty on purchase and VAT on just about everything else, of course.

So far as estate agents and lawyers are concerned, it is important to remember that, contrary to what most people believe, it is always possible to negotiate on costs and fees – these are not as fixed as you might imagine. Most professionals charge what they believe they can get away with, and it is up to you to obtain the best price possible.

At a time of falling property prices, it can be tempting to 'gazunder'; this means offering a vastly lower price than mutually agreed, literally hours or minutes before exchange of contracts. Gazundering is not illegal, as there is no binding contract until exchange, but it is dishonourable, sharp practice and not to be encouraged. Another wheeze is to put in a counter-offer after survey; this is less despicable but its possibility should be made clear at the outset, ie any offer made is subject to a full structural survey.

When choosing a conveyancing solicitor, get three quotes, as with builders. You can simply call them and ask what they charge for conveyancing, or for their scale of charges. Firms of solicitors like to believe they are above 'quoting' but they are only people touting for business, after all. I would always recommend using a specialist conveyancing solicitor, rather than a general solicitor who does a divorce one hour, a county court judgment another, and a motoring offence another, for instance.

A conveyancing solicitor deals exclusively with property transactions and is an expert in this field. UK Conveyancing Solicitors is a nationwide organization of lawyers dealing only with property matters and members are accredited as specialists in the law of land and real estate. These solicitors will also carry out all legal work connected with property. They will quote you an all-in price for your property transaction, but make it clear that they can only act on behalf of either the purchaser or the seller, not both.

In my view, solicitors are absolutely crucial to the success or failure of a property investment.

The same goes for surveyors, estate agents and removals firms. If you can be bothered, always get three quotes.

When making an offer on a property, always ask what will be included in the sale, as this can make a huge difference to the eventual costs of purchase. Most agents' particulars quote 'space' for washing machine, fridge and so on. I always ask vendors to throw in the white goods as there is little resale value, they are a lot of effort to move, and always look dingy and second-hand in the new property, apart from which it saves me from having to buy appliances right away. Carpets and curtains should always be included in the sale as well; again, they have little or no resale value. And even if they are not to your taste, they will serve for a while.

In the olden days, I used to try to charge for curtains and buyers never wanted to pay anything for them. So I ended up taking them down, storing them for a few years then throwing them away as they never fitted my next windows. Now I can't be bothered, and I just leave the curtains and blinds without ever entering into negotiations. Curtains and blinds also go out of fashion after a few years, as with other furnishings.

Whatever deal you are able to secure from your lawyer or agent, remember that there are always many costs involved in moving house. These have to be calculated and set against any profit you may make when selling one place and buying another.

As well as the price of the house, these costs also have to be taken into account: land registry fee; stamp duty, now called stamp duty land tax; local searches; Mortgage Indemnity Guarantee; valuation fee; homebuyer or full survey fee; fees for specialist tests where applicable, such as damp or drains; lender's arrangement fee; mortgage broker's fee; insurance premiums; removal firm; storage costs; van hire; disconnection and reconnection of services and utilities; carpet laying or other flooring; animal care; mail redirection; change of address notices; purchase of appliances; immediate redecoration or renovation.

Although some of these costs, such as redirection of mail, may be small, they all add up and eat into your wonderful profit.

Getting a mortgage

(Note – this section applies only to mortgages or loans taken out on your principal private residence. Mortgages for the specific purpose of buying investment properties are discussed in Chapters 6 and 8.)

There are very many different types of mortgage and also fierce competition for custom from mortgage providers. Even so, whatever the incentives from particular companies, a mortgage amounts to borrowed money on which you pay interest.

Many people imagine the word 'mortgage' refers to the loan itself. In fact, the term denotes the document which puts up the property as security for the loan. This ensures that the property cannot be sold without the loan being paid off. In the UK, this is unlikely to happen, but when buying property abroad, care has to be taken that there is not a loan outstanding on the property, which frequently happens.

A mortgage has two main elements – the capital plus the interest. All mortgages are repaid with the interest calculated at variable, fixed or discounted rates. The usual length of time for a mortgage to be paid off is 25 years, although some mortgages can stretch to 40 years. The longer the period, the lower the monthly repayments, but the overall cost of the loan will be greater as you are paying interest for longer.

There are usually penalties for paying off your mortgage early, as the mortgage provider considers that by so doing you have reneged on the deal by doing them out of their full whack of interest.

The mortgage business, regulated in the UK by the Financial Services Authority, is complicated and becoming ever more so. Here is a handy guide through the maze to enable you to decide which sort of mortgage would most suit your needs.

Although there are hundreds of different mortgages on offer, they fall broadly into about half a dozen types.

Variable

The basic mortgage rate which most lenders offer is a standard 'variable' rate (SVR). Here, the interest paid varies according to Bank of England base rate charges. Where there is a special rate, this reverts to the SVR at the end of the deal period.

Fixed

This type of mortgage sets the interest rate payable for a given period of time – not the entire length of the mortgage. This type of mortgage enables you to budget for a certain length of time as you know for certain what the outgoings will be. But when the fixed period expires, the mortgage reverts to the SVR.

Fixed-rate mortgages can be both good and bad news. If interest rates rise above the level you are paying during the deal period you will save money, but if they go down, you will lose out.

Fixed-rate mortgages usually last for between one and five years, although some lenders offer fixed-rate mortgages for up to 10 years. In a few cases, you can get a fixed rate for the entire mortgage term, although these rates will be higher than usual. Fixed-rate mortgages have been extremely popular, but they are not such a good idea when interest rates keep falling. At the moment, the government (in fact all governments) are doing their utmost to keep inflation low, so fixed-rate mortgages may not be such a good deal in future as they have been in the past.

Capped

These mortgages guarantee that your monthly payments will never go above a certain figure. Below that set figure, the rate can move up and down in line with the SVR. The advantage of a capped-rate mortgage is that you can be certain of the maximum amount you will have to pay and may benefit from lower rates if interest rates fluctuate downwards.

Discount

This type of mortgage gives a discount on the lender's standard rate for a specified period of time.

Tracker

These mortgages track the Bank of England base rate so that every time this changes, your payments will change as well. Tracker mortgages are good news when rates are going down, but if interest rates go up, your monthly payments rise accordingly and you could be paying above the odds.

Note: after interest rates were cut by 1.5% in November 2008, most lenders pulled tracker mortgages for new lenders, although existing trackers will continue.

Flexible

These mortgages calculate interest rates daily and also allow overpayments, so that your mortgage can be paid off early. Most flexible mortgages allow you to make underpayments and go on mortgage 'holidays' as well.

Portable

If you move home, you can keep the same mortgage product without incurring an early repayment charge.

Although the mortgage business is hugely competitive, never forget that mortgage providers are only in it to make money out of you – lots of it! So the sensible advice is never to be tempted by wonderful-sounding offers but work out the full cost of the deal, including the lending fee, valuation fee, legal fees and any redemption penalties. The mortgage does not start and end with the repayments.

Every time you move home, you will have to go through all the mortgage business all over again, with another set of unavoidable fees, unless you go for a portable product.

Warning: many mortgages which purport to discount interest rates come with extra charges for arranging the loan. Application fees for discounted and fixed-rate mortgages come in at around £400. Only a small proportion of mortgages do not charge this application fee.

Then there is often an exit fee, of typically £300, when you change mortgage providers. The advice here is to shop around, as many apparent deals come with high entry and exit costs.

Also, many of the mortgage options are, in reality, so much window-dressing and their differences are more apparent than real.

New types of mortgage

Mortgage lenders are always trying to find ingenious new ways of lending people money and, as such, new mortgage products are coming onto the market all the time. Of these, the most controversial is the so-called 'sub-prime mortgage'.

These mortgages, also known as 'non-conforming' or 'bad credit' mortgages, originated in the United States and are fast catching on in the UK. They are aimed at people with impaired credit rating, those who have been declared bankrupt, or who have county court judgments against them. In other words, they are specifically aimed at those who have not managed their finances well in the past.

Since the credit crunch of 2008, it has become more difficult to secure a sub-prime or adverse-credit mortgage, and many mainstream lenders are no longer offering them. They are not, however, impossible to obtain, and many lenders are advertising on the internet. The Council of Mortgage Lenders advises that anybody in search of a sub-prime mortgage must ensure that the lender or broker is registered by the Financial Services Authority; this can be checked by logging on to the FSA website.

In general terms, anybody who has been made bankrupt or is subject to a County Court Judgment or an Individual Voluntary Arrangement (IVA) will not be able to secure a mainstream mortgage, and will have to resort to a sub-prime version. Since 2008, such mortgages are no longer so competitive and may include extremely high fees. However, once you have proven that your finances are back on track, a sub-prime mortgage can often be converted to a prime, or near-prime, version.

Self-certification mortgages, which are also becoming more common as self-employment increases, may or may not be sub-prime, depending on your credit history and income. To obtain a standard mortgage, you would have to show pay slips or, if self-employed, three years' worth of audited accounts. If you have been self-employed for less than two years, you may not be able to provide documentary evidence of your income. Self-cert mortgages were originally designed for these people, and they depend on your own assessment of your income without any accompanying official documentation.

To secure a self-cert mortgage, you would typically have to put down a deposit of between 10 and 25 per cent more than with an ordinary mortgage and also pay a slightly higher interest rate. This may not be significantly higher – perhaps 0.25 per cent more than ordinary high-street mortgages – but when investing, it is these apparently small margins that can make all the difference. If you cannot provide documentary evidence of your income, you will be assessed on your debt and credit history.

Generally, it is better to secure a mainstream mortgage than a self-certification deal, but if the self-cert appears to be your only option, take advice from a specialist broker first and never lie about your circumstances in order to secure higher borrowing.

Interest-only mortgages are popular with investors of all types because they mean lower monthly repayments. This is because you are only paying interest and are not paying off any capital at all. In particular, investors often switch to an interest-only mortgage when cheap fixed-rate deals come to an end or interest rates increase. Investors usually justify interest-only mortgages as they expect the value of their house to keep on increasing, and see the interest-only option as a short-term solution to keeping their finances afloat. The danger is that these interest-only repayments can come to seem normal and the time to start paying off capital is never right.

Interest-only mortgages can be high risk: if prices are falling rather than rising, you may have no way of paying off the difference between what you owe and the original amount borrowed. In such cases, lenders may be perfectly entitled to repossess your property. In addition, investors often take out interest-only mortgages and then completely forget that they are not paying off any capital. Such mortgages can be a good bet at a time of fast-rising house prices, but you may come a cropper if you need to sell quickly and prices have fallen in the meantime.

So think very hard before deciding on any of these less than mainstream mortgages. They are aimed at those with tight finances and accordingly, as ever in the financial world, you pay a high price for the privilege.

Jesus saves, Moses invests – but what about Mohammed?

Many Muslims are interested in investing in property, yet the Koran emphatically states that they must not lend or borrow at interest.

The idea, in Sharia law, is that there should be no interest on money for no effort. Yet few Muslims, in common with others, probably have the entire cash sum sitting in their accounts ready to buy property. The solution has been to set up special 'Muslim mortgages' which operate differently from the usual ones.

Lloyds TSB, for instance, have both a current account and mortgage on offer which comply with Sharia law. The current account pays no interest and charges no interest because there is no overdraft facility. With the mortgage, the bank buys the home for the customer who pays for it with a fixed monthly sum plus rent.

Bristol and West, now part of Britannia, have a Muslim-type mortgage on offer, and the Islamic Bank of London also offers a current and savings account which makes an arrangement charge rather than interest charges.

Because only about half a dozen lenders offer Islamic mortgages, there is less competition than with mainstream lenders, and as the arrangements are more complex, arrangement fees may be even higher than with ordinary mortgages. All lenders offering Islamic mortgages are required to have a Sharia Advisory Board consisting of recognized experts before they can offer such mortgages. Anybody interested in obtaining an Islamic mortgage should check that the lender complies with this. Such mortgages can be equally suitable for freehold and leasehold properties.

The Murabaha mortgage is an arrangement whereby you pay around 20 per cent of your home's value on the day of purchase. From that day the property will be registered in your name, and then you may pay off any debt outstanding on your home at any point. There is a fixed repayment period that is agreed between you the mortgagee, and the lender.

This type of mortgage works by you the purchaser agreeing the sale price with the vendor as usual, but the bank then pays the purchase price, after which the property is immediately sold to you at a higher price. This higher price is determined by the original price of the property plus the repayment period you have agreed with the lender, minus the quite large deposit you have to put down.

Another type of Muslim mortgage, the Ijara mortgage, is becoming slightly more popular as you do not need such a large amount of capital in the first place. Here, as with the Murabaha, the lender purchases the property and gains ownership. You then enter into a lease agreement with the lender in that each month you will pay rent, plus a contribution to the eventual purchase price of the property.

Islamic mortgages are available to anybody, not just Muslims, and they are now regulated by the Financial Services Authority. Getting round the no-interest element, though, usually means you pay more each month for the privilege of this special type of mortgage.

Under Muslim (Sharia) law, wives can only inherit one-eighth of their husband's estate, while men can inherit only a quarter of their wife's estate; the rest must be split between any children and surviving parents. These stipulations are set out clearly in the Koran, and all practising Muslims are supposed to abide by them.

This ancient, but still current, law has serious implications for inheritance tax, as this is payable on any estate worth £300,000 or more (in 2007/08; £312,000 in 2008/09), unless the entire amount is left to the surviving spouse, and applies to Muslims in just the same way as followers of any other, or no religion, as it is the law of the country by which all must abide.

This means that a married Muslim man with an estate of £800,000, following Sharia law, at least, could only protect £100,000 of this by leaving it to his wife free of tax. Of the rest, £285,000 would be exempt under the nil-rate band and the remaining £415,000 would be subject to inheritance tax at 40 per cent. Wealthy Muslims have been getting round this tax in the past by writing an 'interest in possession' trust which names their spouse as a lifetime beneficiary. But such trusts have now been targeted by the government's raid on these tax-planning (or tax-evading) measures.

Anybody of the Muslim faith who has significant property assets should take advice on tax, will and inheritance planning, in the light of both the ancient and the modern laws.

Before you ever buy a property for investment purposes, take careful note of:

Freehold or leasehold?

When buying property with a view to its future investment potential, you need to know, not just whether the property is being sold leasehold or freehold, but the length of the lease, and whether the property is being sold with a share of the freehold. Also, what the service charges are and whether there is a sinking fund, as all intimately affect the future value of the property.

In the old days, leasehold properties were relatively rare, but now that more flats are being built than houses, leaseholds are increasingly becoming the more common type of tenure. And anybody buying with investment potential in mind needs to look very carefully at all aspects of the lease before making an offer.

The main difference between leasehold and freehold is that with the latter, you own not just the home, but the land on which it is built; the 'real estate'. With a leasehold property, by contrast, you don't own anything at all! All you have bought is a length of time. You have bought, in effect, an extremely long rental, whether this is 99 years or 999 years. You can sell this lease on, but you are not buying or selling the actual property, which continues to belong to the freeholder, or landlord.

All types of property where there is more than one self-contained dwelling sharing common parts, a roof and foundation, are likely to be sold leasehold. Examples include: newbuild apartments, mansion blocks, conversions from large houses, conversions from former commercial buildings, such as 'The Old Fire Station', 'The Old Vicarage', 'The Old Post Office', and residential premises over shops or offices.

Many buyers, when looking at the length of lease, imagine that the longer it is, the safer they are. But this is an illusion. Whenever there is an outside freeholder, you, the leaseholder, can be charged thousands of pounds for repairs and renovation. When this happens, the value of your investment goes out of the (new) windows that have been forced on you by the freeholder, as subsequent buyers look at service charges very carefully before deciding to buy. Any leasehold property that has high service charges attached will put off potential purchasers and reduce the value of your unit.

Nowadays, very many people are buying newbuild flats – always leasehold in the UK – as investments, whether or not they intend to inhabit these properties themselves. But unless the property comes with a share of the freehold, your investment could actually lose value in time. And certainly, by the time the lease ends, your property will be worth nothing, and you will have nothing to sell.

Because newbuild apartments are heavily marketed, they can seem extremely attractive. In addition, service charges – always an aspect of living in an apartment building – tend to be very low, at first. This is because the building is considered unlikely to need repairs and maintenance for many years – although this is by no means always the case.

It is common for the service and maintenance charges to rise heavily after a few years of being kept artificially low. Also, the freeholder can sell the freehold on at any time he or she likes, above the heads of the residents, although residents must by law be offered the 'right of first refusal'. This very often happens, as selling freeholds is yet another way property investors can make serious money.

'Layer cake' developments

Increasingly, new apartment blocks will be 'layer cake' developments, which means there will be a layer of luxury apartments at the top, commercial premises on the ground floor and, sandwiched between the two, affordable or 'key worker' housing.

It is becoming increasingly difficult for developers to obtain planning permission and often the only way they can do this is to agree to provide some key worker housing within an apartment building or other development. The key worker or shared equity units are kept very separate from the full-price, luxury apartments or houses, and the key worker apartments are not usually finished to the same specification as the full-price units. They are in the same location, though.

In the past, buyers worried that the key worker element would reduce the future value of the full-price units and certainly at one time this was the case. But now that a sandwich of key worker apartments has become the norm in most new apartment buildings, the full-price units rise in value along with the general housing market.

The key worker units are run either by the local council or a housing association, and are organized separately from the full-price units. For instance, such units are never advertised and if you go to view a show home you will never be shown the affordable units. It's almost as if they were not there, and so far as most purchasers are concerned, they can be disregarded as they are never going to be bought and sold on the open market.

It is very difficult indeed to satisfy the requirements for being a key worker, and there is huge competition, as one can imagine, to acquire these units as they are usually in ideal locations and form part of a very nice new block or development. However, the key workers would not normally form part of any residents' association and the service and maintenance charges are calculated differently.

The presence of shared equity housing should no longer put off the purchaser of the full-price apartments.

Is there any way round the problem of not knowing whether, and how often, the freehold may be sold on? Yes – whenever contemplating buying leasehold properties, always ask whether they come with a share of the freehold. If they do, this means that you, and the other residents, are in charge and there is no outside freeholder. But beware if the property does not come with a share of the freehold, as you are then buying into something over which you have no control. Whenever there is an outside freeholder, you can find yourself, as a leaseholder, paying very high sums for renovation, painting, new windows or a new roof. In some cases, these bills can come to £90,000 or more per leaseholder.

There is especial danger here in buying a flat in a local authority block, where leases can be very short, mortgages difficult to obtain and leaseholders mugged with huge bills for repairs. The council tenants in the block, meanwhile, pay nothing except their own very low rent.

Ever since Mrs Thatcher announced the Right to Buy scheme in 1980, buyers have snapped up local authority flats as they are cheaper to buy than others. In addition, the flats are often in extremely desirable locations, and come with very low annual service charges. Again, the annual service charges on a local authority block are about half of what is charged by a private freeholder.

But if the council decided to update the building, you as the leaseholder would have to pay your share of this updating. And with a short lease and unknown service charges, you could discover that your apparent bargain buy is extremely difficult to sell.

Mortgage providers also are not keen to lend money on high-rise blocks; in any case, it is difficult to get a mortgage for a property with a lease of 80 years or less.

The reason for this is that mortgage lenders consider this length of lease a wasting asset, as the value of the property declines as the lease gets ever shorter. It is possible, legally, to extend your lease by 90 years or alternatively to collectively enfranchise – that is, buy the freehold together with the other leaseholders in the building – and it is possible to get a loan from a mortgage company specifically to do this.

But in general terms, if you buy a property on a short lease, you will have to buy it for cash, or get a very expensive shorter-term loan. Financing is now available on short and very short leases, at a price which takes into account the fact the property is likely to decrease in value as the years go by.

Many investors nowadays buy a short-lease property in two stages; one when they buy the lease initially, and the second stage when they either buy a 90-year extension, or collectively enfranchise with the rest of the block.

Properties with very short leases often seem like amazing bargains but investors must consider the resale value, which will get ever less as the lease runs down. The other aspect is that the shorter the lease, the more it costs to buy an extension or to enfranchise. But a property with a long lease or a lease which has enfranchised will have a greatly enhanced value, so these cheap-seeming properties can be a good investment.

These days, a landlord or freeholder must by law sell a lease extension or allow the leaseholders to enfranchise, although working out the price can be difficult and needs a specialist valuer.

So, always ask whether it comes with a share of the freehold. If it does, this means that you, and the other residents, are in charge and no outsider can impose heavy repair and maintenance bills. Having a share of the freehold means, in effect, that the lunatics are running the asylum.

If the property you own or are considering buying does not come with a share of the freehold, you should seriously consider enfranchising, which means clubbing together to buy the freehold from the existing freeholder. Current laws mean that leaseholders in a block are allowed to enfranchise if enough of them want to do it – but there has to be a majority decision.

Enfranchising can be expensive, as the freeholder naturally will want to get as much money as possible from relinquishing control of the building, and also lawyers specializing in enfranchisement law are extremely expensive. The legal fees alone for enfranchising can come to around £4,000 per leaseholder. There may also be people living in the building who complain that they cannot afford to enfranchise; alternatively, that the lease will 'see me out'. It can sometimes be very hard work persuading the majority of residents that enfranchisement is worth it.

The real problem with apartment blocks is that, although everybody wants them to be smart, clean and in good repair, nobody wants to spend any money on them. And although property generally goes up in value, an apartment block in bad repair will lose value, and you will be left with a liability rather than an asset.

If you are buying property abroad, particularly an off-plan apartment, it is vital to check the exact nature of the tenure, and to determine whether you have automatically bought a share of the freehold or merely a length of time in the property. Most countries do not have the complex leasehold laws which apply in the UK, but it is always essential to know exactly what you have bought. Whether the property is a new villa or apartment, or a resale property, make sure you understand exactly what kind of information is contained in the title deeds. This is particularly important if you are buying in a country where you do not speak or understand the language and where the laws of tenure may be very different from those you are used to.

Now we will take a look at the various ways of making money from your own home.

Buying a wreck in an up and coming area, doing it up and then selling on at a massive profit

I have taken advantage of this option on many occasions, and it has worked wonderfully. Here, you need to be very sure that an area is up and coming – and that it will not take forever to come up. Also, you have to be very sure that you can add value.

Be very careful when watching television property shows, as they never include all the many costs of renovation, development and time taken. They virtually never factor in costs such as stamp duty, interest paid on mortgages or other loans, loss of income if you have given up your job to renovate the property, estate agents' fees, or moving costs. Nor do they give the true cost of renovation, which is much, much more than the one or two grand stated on the shows.

The impression given on many television shows is that you can buy cheap and sell dear, while spending hardly anything on renovation in the process.

In general terms, you must allow at least £4,000 for a new bathroom; £5,000 for a new kitchen; £1,000 for redecoration of one room; £30,000 for a side extension or loft conversion and around £2,000 for garden landscaping. And these are minimum, not maximum amounts.

Then, all the time it stays on the market, the property will be costing you – in mortgage fees, parking fees, utilities, council tax, and service charges for a leasehold property. All these costs have to be added up before you can safely say you have made a profit.

But apart from the cost of renovation and selling, there has to be something special about your property which will make it stand out from the rest, and give it a certain cachet.

At times when property prices are falling, it makes even more sense to keep an eagle eye on estate agents' windows and websites, to see which properties go quickly, which ones hang around, and why. There is no sense in trying to be too greedy or bucking the trend with any market, especially at times when mortgages are difficult to obtain and ever larger deposits are being demanded.

It is also fair to say that at times when property prices are fluctuating wildly, estate agents' estimates of the value of your property may also vary considerably. It is not uncommon at times of falling prices, for there to be as much as £50,000 to £100,000 difference in valuations from different agents.

Also, beware of the 'my house' syndrome! Estate agents all complain that people selling their own homes frequently fall into this mindset, which means that however terrible it may appear to viewers, the 'my house' syndrome means that the owners refuse to see its faults and tend to overvalue it as a consequence. This psychological stumbling block means that people's own homes very often stay on the market for a very long time, because their owners remain emotionally attached to them. You can see this syndrome very clearly on television shows, where it reigns supreme.

The other tendency is to overvalue your own home, ignoring the market.

A friend put her immaculate, beautifully designed studio flat on the market for £120,000. At the time, such flats were selling for a maximum of £90,000. After lingering on the market for a year, my friend had to accept an offer of £75,000. Here, the 'my house' syndrome prevailed to such an extent that my friend tried to bypass estate agents' fees by selling it privately, expecting that people would fall over themselves to pay over the odds for the flat.

In the end, not only did my friend have to accept a low offer – incurring service charges and council tax all that time – but had to pay estate agents' fees of 1.5 per cent plus VAT – another £1,321.87 to add to the selling costs.

Many people, when selling their homes, pin their hopes on cash buyers. But you can never do this. Most people buy on a mortgage, which means the property will be valued according to what the mortgage provider is prepared to lend.

Yet the financial meltdown of 2008/09 was not such bad news for everybody. Although properties in some locations lost up to 40 per cent of their value, in others, prices held up or even increased. One such place was Oxford, where I bought a property in 2009.

During 2009, most people with money in the bank wanted it to do better than earn half a per cent interest and so they naturally looked to invest in property. Oxford – and Cambridge as well, come to that – in common with a number of other university cities, have ridden out the credit crunch far better than many other places and there are good reasons for this.

University cities with an international reputation plus enormous historical and tourist interest are likely to be good places to invest as they are less vulnerable to city bonuses and the availability of mortgages than many other areas. There are very few new developments in these cities, almost no high-rise blocks and none of the cheap buildings aimed mainly at buy-to-let investors. There is also no 'inner city' blight although of course Oxford does have its sink estates.

Wandering around both Oxford and Cambridge in 2009, two things struck me: one was the enormous amount of visitors and tourists and the other – possibly even more relevant to the property investor – was the sheer number of expensive shops and retail outlets.

Again during 2009, very many towns became ghost towns with retail outlets closing down and high streets full of To Let signs. This was not the case in Oxford and Cambridge, in fact quite the reverse. Another factor is that the universities in both cities are rapidly buying up properties and land in order to expand; another reason why such cities are good places to consider investing.

In my time, I have made wonderful profits on my main home, and the secret has always, always been that old cliché of location, location, location. That, plus always buying character properties.

Some research carried out by London agents Ludlow Thompson showed that most buyers prefer older, character homes over new-build. I have never in my life bought a new property, and would say, looking back, that many homes built from the 1950s onwards never do acquire a 'period' feel. Property developer Ivan Twigden, who started building houses in the 1960s, said that although some of his homes were now more than 40 years old, they still looked modern.

Wherever there is character, or period features, your home will attract a premium. So never destroy all the original character by ferocious updating.

Also, never forget that buyers are emotional people, too, and buy homes for many strange reasons. One buyer fell in love with a house of mine simply because it had a lovely expensive green curtain right across the back wall of the living room. 'I just had to buy it because of that curtain!' she enthused.

Successful and profitable selling of your own home – which contains, of course, much of your character, aspirations and lifestyle – depends not just on working out figures as exactly as possible, but on appealing to people's emotions. Even the right book on a coffee table can help to sell your house to the perfect purchaser. Never dismiss the amount of sheer emotion tied up in buying and selling homes.

Advice from Home Stagers

Tina Jesson runs a franchise company, Home Stagers, which will come into your home and suggest quick updating tips that will, she maintains, instantly add at least 10 per cent to the value of your property.

Among the quick tips she suggests are: updating the light fittings, adding a bit of colour to a very bland interior and updating the curtains or blinds. Tina recommends putting in leather sofas as these add a bit of colour and depth, and they can always be taken away to your new home. Cream and brown or black are the looks to aim at, in Tina's view, as touches of brown or black add some depth to an interior that can otherwise seem featureless.

But new light fittings, she maintains, are the quickest, cheapest and easiest way to upgrade a tired or old-fashioned looking home. As all properties vary, and different artefacts appeal to different markets, it may be worth contacting a Home Stagers adviser to come to the home you are considering selling, to obtain expert advice.

Home staging is an idea from America which has rapidly caught on in other countries; but even nowadays it's amazing how many sellers never think to 'stage' their homes before putting them on the market. Yet with the success of television shows such as *How Clean Is Your House?*, ever more buyers are looking for homes as clean as a five-star hotel.

Further quick tips include making sure that all appliances sparkle, windows are clean, there is no clutter, wardrobes are not full to bursting, and that the whole property has been deep-cleaned.

Staging a property becomes ever more important when there is a buyer's market, and it applies equally to sales and rentals. There is no doubt that rental properties which are immaculately clean and sparkling rent far more quickly than those looking tired and jaded. As an example, two identical properties in the apartment building where I live were being let at the same rental. One was smart and clean and the other was tired and old-looking. The smart one rented out within a few days but the tired one was on the market for two months with every agent in town, and even then the rent had to be reduced before anybody could be persuaded to take it.

At times when the market is tough, the better-presented your property, the more quickly it will find a buyer or renter. The garden, if any, should always look very neat, with the lawn kept mown. An untidy or unkempt garden, more than any other single factor, puts buyers and renters off.

Building your own home and selling it on

It is estimated that you can make 35 per cent more profit by building your own home than by buying a wreck and then renovating it. You also are allowed to do this work free of VAT. When you renovate an old house, you pay 17.5 per cent VAT, but no VAT on building your own house. The current situation, therefore, encourages people to knock down existing buildings and start again rather than renovate a wreck.

But you have to be very careful indeed, when doing this, that you are not seen to be property developing, or building purely for profit. If you want to avoid capital gains tax on selling, your property must not have been purchased for the sole purpose of making a profit, and you may have to prove this to HM Revenue and Customs; in addition, the property must be your only or main residence throughout the period of ownership. This means that you cannot build one house while living in another – at least, you can, but only one can count as your PPR, even if it is not yet built.

If you keep moving, HM Revenue and Customs may start asking awkward questions, as they are looking very carefully at the 'serial self-builders' who eventually may be taxed or deemed to be professional developers. In order to avoid capital gains tax, the property or land must emphatically NOT have been purchased for the sole purpose of making money, but rather, to provide a home for yourself and your family.

Obviously HMRC have to accept that you must live somewhere before your self-build home becomes habitable. This is how it works at present: if the building work is completed within 12 months of purchase, the self-builder is not liable to CGT while inhabiting two homes. In order to avoid this, most self-builders live in a caravan on the site while building is in progress. You can hire caravans for the specific purpose of temporary accommodation during the build.

You must show a degree of permanence, so the best advice is to try to live in your completed self-build house for more than just a few months before putting it on the market. As HMRC are very likely to swoop down, it is imperative that you keep all council tax bills, and all bills must be sent to the self-build address. If the self-build is seen to be driven by commercial considerations, then the exemption from VAT does not apply.

The biggest advantage of starting from scratch, as opposed to improving an existing building, is that you are exempt from VAT. But – what is starting from scratch, and if you live in a caravan on a site while your house is being built, does the caravan count as your main home? What about if you continue to live in your existing home while the new one is being built?

One way round this, of course, might be to rent, but even a rented home can count as your principal private residence. It is the occupation rather than the tenure that counts.

Self-build is becoming ever more popular, as by this means homeowners get exactly what they want. There is a big and growing business nowadays in selling plots for self-builders, who all have to be very careful that they are not seen to be commercial developers.

Mortgages

The problem with getting a self-build mortgage is that the lender has no collateral – that is, the house itself – to act as security for the loan. So with self-build, a different type of mortgage is required.

Here, you borrow in the short term to pay for materials and labour, then once the house is completed, you borrow in the long term just as with any other type of mortgage.

During the build, the funding is provided in four or five stages, each being linked to a phase in completion. Funds are released retrospectively after each stage is completed and approved by a Building Control inspector. There are a number of companies now offering self-build mortgages, and this is likely to increase as self-build becomes ever more popular.

Most self-builders believe you can save up to 30 per cent on building your own home as opposed to renovating a wreck or buying at the top of the market, and at the end of the build you have something unique to put on the market. (But not suspiciously soon after completion.)

Renting out a room (or rooms)

This option will not exactly make you rich, but is a time-honoured way of helping to pay the costs. Although I have been a buy-to-let landlord for many years, I have also rented out rooms in my own home over the years, and this has often enabled me to live in a better or more expensive home than I could afford otherwise, plus the rental income has enabled me to carry out renovations and improvements, thus greatly adding to the value of the property.

Under the government's rent-a-room scheme, you are allowed to charge up to £4,250 a year for rent without paying tax. Above this sum, you will be liable for income tax. But even without tax, the rental money will not be all profit. There will be greater wear and tear, your utility bills will increase with each new tenant, and you will have to pay more council tax if you are on the single person's 75 per cent rate. For this reason, many ad hoc landlords prefer bona fide students, as they are exempt from paying council tax.

The usual thing with renting out rooms in your own home, as opposed to letting self-contained properties, is that the rent is an all-in amount. With an Assured Shorthold Tenancy, the utilities are paid by the tenant on top of the rent.

The practicalities you have to consider are these: Do your tenants eat with you or get their own meals? If the latter, do they have use of the kitchen at certain times? What about baths and washing? Internet connections and telephone lines, including broadband? What if they want, or expect, satellite television?

Here are the experiences of Mike, somebody who has been renting out rooms for many years to mature students – mainly people aged 25 to 30 doing MBAs or other higher qualifications and who are simply there to work.

Mike says: 'It does not make me a fortune but is enabling me to stay in a home I would otherwise have to sell, as I am no longer employed. This means I can stay in the house until it reaches its maximum value on the market; otherwise I would have had to sell simply because I could not afford to continue to live here.'

BUT – be careful here, as HM Revenue and Customs are looking hard at people who rent out their homes for big events, such as Wimbledon tennis. At the moment, such people are banking a large amount of tax-free money, but HMRC are considering ways to tax this form of income.

Don't forget also that if you are a sole occupant paying 75 per cent council tax on your main home, this will go up to 100 per cent if you have a lodger. There are no exceptions to this apart from bona fide students. The council tax will definitely eat into both your rent and the £4,250 a year tax exemption, if you rent out to non-students.

You can expect a visit or letter from the council if letters are going to your home addressed to somebody else, and you have not informed the council tax people, as the Post Office are very likely to inform the authorities of a new person living at the address.

Renting out your home to holidaymakers and overseas visitors

Ever more people are now doing this and, as a result, many companies have sprung up which do all the arrangements for you. In most cases, your overseas visitors will be staying for a couple of weeks, and they are people who prefer to be in a real house rather than staying in a hotel. All the money is taken upfront, and it is advisable to rent out your house through a reputable agency. They will advise what you have to do to prepare your house for visitors and how much money you are likely to make. Again, you have to be careful that you are not seen to be using your house for profit, thus incurring the dreaded CGT when you sell.

You do not have to clear your house out but just make sure that the visitors have somewhere to hang their clothes and live free of your personal clutter. But those who take on other people's houses for holidays and visits are people who vastly prefer a family home to a hotel.

In general terms, you are not liable for tax if your home is just let out for a few weeks a year. In order to count as a holiday letting on a commercial basis, the home must be available for letting for at least 140 days a year, and actually let for 70 of those days. Also, the property must not be occupied by the same person or family for more than 31 days at a stretch. But this could soon change.

Using part of your home as a hotel or B&B

If your home is used partly for business purposes, or for income, you could lose the capital gains tax exemption which applies on your principal private residence. It is obviously wise here to take advice from a tax expert on whether some or all of your home will become liable for CGT when you sell.

Renting out a self-contained flat within your home

Here again you have to be careful, as the self-contained flat no longer counts as part of your home and will be liable for CGT when you sell, as you have been using your home partly for profit. If the house is divided into two, or more than two parts, each with its own separate utility supply, council tax bands will be affected.

You will also have to decide, if going for this option, whether you would sell the entire property as a going concern, or market the self-contained flat as a separate entity. If the latter, you would have to draw up a lease, as the property then becomes leasehold, and for this you would need the services of an expert property lawyer. In order to sell as separate entities, the flats have to be genuinely self-contained, in that you do not have to go through one flat to get to another.

Problems can arise if you have outbuildings on your property which you would like to turn into self-contained apartments. Here, before going ahead, it is essential to contact the council and ask how this will affect council tax. You would have to get planning permission, as well.

Some councils discourage homeowners from turning their houses into separate flats, while other councils actively encourage the provision of smaller units.

Three of my homes have had separate self-contained flats, and in every case, the flat was sold as an integral part of the main house, meaning that no capital gains tax was incurred, or necessity for drawing up leases.

Inheritance tax

This is one of the biggest concerns of everybody who invests in property; indeed, anybody who invests at all, in any assets, liquid or illiquid, above the current (2009) threshold of £325,000 is liable for inheritance tax of 40 per cent, and there is no quarter given, no relief, no way out.

Briefly, the situation is that for married couples or those in recognized civil partnerships, the joint home can pass free of tax to the surviving spouse. But that is all. Properties passed to your children are liable for this tax, as are properties owned by cohabiting partners. In October 2007, Chancellor Alistair Darling doubled the IHT threshold for married couples only.

Make no mistake, IHT is a terrible business and you may have to sell your investment properties to pay it. Also, all assets belonging to the deceased are frozen until probate is granted. Then you have to have all properties independently assessed by an estate agent (valuing properties for probate has become a lucrative sideline for selling agents); also, if HM Revenue and Customs are not satisfied, they may poke their noses in as well, quite legally.

Of course, there are ways round inheritance tax, but tax-avoidance schemes are in themselves very expensive to set up and you may be sure that the government has worked very diligently to plug as many loopholes as possible.

Also, the government is now cracking down on those who have put their properties into trust to avoid or minimize inheritance tax.

The new rules are complicated – as were the old rules – but the basic position is that trust funds and discretionary trusts set up to avoid IHT are now subject to inheritance tax, especially when capital is transferred to a beneficiary. It is very important when making a new will (and for anybody who owns property, a new will should be made every three to five years, or whenever circumstances change) to make sure the position on trusts and their relationship to inheritance tax is completely understood. Otherwise, you will be paying twice; once to set up the trust and again when you – or your beneficiaries – pay far more inheritance tax than they had expected.

Letting out your home to film and TV crews

If you have an interesting or unusual home, you may consider making money from it by letting it out for films and TV shows. There is a huge demand for all kinds of homes, with the following provisos: they must have rooms which are big enough to take film equipment and crews, and there must be easy parking. In particular, there must be enough room somewhere nearby to park the canteen van – most important!

In the old days, finding suitable locations was a hit and miss affair, with freelance location managers having to source suitable venues for filming. But now, all is made easy with the Space Men website, whereby any property owner can post their home on the site and add to the database which is constantly being scoured by film and television companies. Advertising agencies are also always looking for unusual homes as backgrounds or foregrounds for ads. Even the naff and the kitsch can have their uses!

In order to be suitable, your home must have some special quality, but this doesn't mean it has to be grand. An intact 1950s kitchen, even an unusual cupboard, can fit the bill, and there is constant demand for suburban semis of all ages, from Georgian and Victorian, to thirties, fifties and modern.

You can post your property on the website for nothing, and should somebody want to film there, you will be paid anything from £500 to £5,000 a day. Filming lasts between one day and several weeks, and in order to allow filming to proceed uninterrupted, obviously all occupants have to make themselves scarce during proceedings.

The film company hiring your home may want to paint your walls a different colour or move in different furniture, but they will undertake to return your home in the condition they found it, even if this means complete redecoration.

Obviously it is very disruptive to have a film crew hanging around your house for days, maybe weeks, on end but if your home suits the purpose, then it is good money for nothing, really, and an excellent way of turning your home into yet another money spinner.

David Rudland, founder of the leading website for this work, says: 'We get numerous requests from people wanting to have their homes used for locations, and have found some spectacular properties in this way. We have council houses, grand mansions, old and new. We even have apartments used solely for film and

TV work on our database. We take 15 per cent commission and try to get all the money upfront for our clients.

'Modern apartments are very popular for ads, but they must be very minimal, and large enough to fit in a film crew of, typically, 10 people.

'It can be a good way of making money from your property, so long as you have the right kind of property.'

Some investors are now going even further and buying properties specifically and solely to rent out to film and production companies. Television director Chris Short, for instance, has a property which is used purely by television chefs, and he has bought and prepared it for this specific purpose. Obviously, if you did this it would not count as using your own home to make money, but it is yet another way in which money can be made from canny property investment. Some people believe that buying a property for the sole purpose of renting it out to television and film companies is an easier and more effective way of making money than renting your property out as somebody's permanent home.

If you think your home might be suitable and you are not averse to undergoing the extremely disruptive experience of having an entire film crew in your house for maybe weeks on end, the best thing is to take pictures of your house with a digital camera and upload them to one of the many location libraries on the web. There is no charge for this, but the libraries take a commission, typically 15 per cent, on the daily rate you obtain when your house is hired out.

Tax matters

If you hire out your home to film companies on a regular basis, or otherwise rent it out for a short time, say for Wimbledon fortnight, you may be liable to tax on the rental income.

Homeowners who receive income from short-term lettings, from letting their home while they are away on holiday, or hire out their house for profit, must make sure they declare this income on their tax return forms. Any undeclared income could come back to haunt homeowners and may result in substantial penalties.

All profit received on your own home is fully taxable, although you may be able to set some expenses against tax, such as the cost of advertising your home, repairs, letting agent's fees, painting and decorating, gardening and window cleaning. Make sure you keep all bills.

If you are considering hiring or renting out your home for short periods, first take advice from your accountant as to whether generating income from your own main home will incur any capital gains tax liability. In general terms, HM Revenue and Customs will take a view on this, as tax and capital gains tax liability will depend on how much your home is used for purposes other than simply living.

3 Buy-to-let

Buying residential property to let remains overwhelmingly the most popular type of property investment and it is easy to see why. You have two potential bites of the profit cherry: income from rentals and capital growth on the property itself.

Added to that, there is the big plus that you can buy properties with cheaply borrowed money on a buy-to-let mortgage. It would be difficult to obtain such cheap borrowing for any other type of investment. Also, on paper at least, it seems that you cannot lose, given that there will always be a rental market and that property generally goes up in value over time.

But is it true that you simply cannot lose when buying to let? Well, not quite. Success in this endeavour depends on being able to work out your figures very carefully indeed so that you come out on top. There is also the little matter of being able to buy properties that will (a) rent out easily and profitably and (b) sell for a considerable profit in years to come. And with buy-to-let there are very many figures and percentages indeed to take into account, also many hidden costs not immediately apparent. Even buying paint and cleaning materials to smarten up your property adds up.

The big attraction of buy-to-let for many investors is that the projected rental income, rather than salary levels, is used to assess the level of borrowing. This makes it possible for investors to build up an impressive property portfolio very quickly indeed by the process known as 'gearing'.

To start the ball rolling, you have to have some level of cash deposit to put down on your buy-to-let. This will typically be 25 per cent of the purchase price. This initial cash is most often raised by releasing equity in the investor's main home and remortgaging.

When properties are rising fast in value, it can work to borrow the deposit in these ways; but in a market where house prices are falling, the more cash you have, the more able you are to ride out a property downturn. Despite talk of rents rising, the reality is that they will not rise significantly unless earnings increase as well. In most areas, tenants can afford only a certain amount of rent. And when utility bills are rising fast, it may be that they can afford even less.

Throughout 2009, rents continued to fall, not simply because earnings failed to rise but because in so many areas there was considerable oversupply of properties to rent. This was mainly owing to the existence of ever more 'reluctant landlords', a phenomenon last seen in the late 1980s, where owners put their properties onto the letting market because they were completely unable to sell them.

At the same time, many estate agents moved into lettings as they were unable to close any sales deals, and so there was the situation in many areas where whole streets were awash with To Let boards.

The Association of Residential Letting Agents (ARLA) always factor in capital appreciation in their figures, as well as the rent, but one cannot rely on property prices going up, especially when mortgages are becoming ever harder to obtain, and the criteria for lending becoming ever stricter.

When calculating the investment value of a buy-to-let investment, it is most sensible to go on what you can get now, not what you might be able to get in 10 years' time. Judith and Fergus Wilson relied on capital appreciation rather than rental income, and in common with most other investors, did not see the financial meltdown coming. In fact, nobody saw it – which just shows how very careful one has to be when projecting the value of investments into the unknown future.

Ever since the buy-to-let industry began in the early 1990s, the advice has been to think of property investments in the medium to long term, rather than as cash cows for instant gain. At the time it sounded like excellent advice, as properties kept going up in value, many different types of mortgages were being shovelled at investors, apartment buildings aimed more or less solely at investors were being constructed and it seemed that investing in property was more or less a licence to print money.

And this would have continued to be the case but for the financial crash that nobody saw coming. Nobody saw it coming because nobody – or at least very few people indeed – was in any way aware of the huge risks that financial institutions were taking with mortgage loans. When it all came crashing down, the carefully calculated gains were seen to be completely pie in the sky, castles in the air.

The only sensible way to regard buy-to-let – and the only sensible way *ever* of looking at it, is to work out what the yields mean now, not at some indefinable time in the future.

In the past, I have been advised by serious financial experts to invest in a number of properties rather than to keep buying for cash, which was seen as backward-looking, but now I'm glad that I have only a few buy-to-lets, all of which are producing useful income over and above their running costs.

Nor are the mortgage payments the only ongoing cost. If you arrange a mortgage through the Association of Residential Letting Agents (ARLA), you will have to use an ARLA agent to rent out your property, and these agents charge on average 10 per cent, plus VAT, of the yearly rental income achieved.

Buy-to-let multiple investors build up their portfolios by buying one property, then releasing equity in it by remortgaging, then buying more properties and repeating the process. In this way, quite ordinary people with no particular financial acumen have built up portfolios of dozens, maybe even hundreds, of properties, all of which pay their way through the rental income they generate.

Case study

Former maths teachers Fergus and Judith Wilson are among the most successful property investors in the UK. According to a story in the *Daily Mail* in January 2007, the Wilsons own over 700 houses in Kent, which are collectively worth around £240 million.

The secret of their success, they say, is supply and demand – plus, essentially, being able to do the meticulous number-crunching recommended throughout this book. The Wilsons believe that there is a chronic housing shortage which will most probably never be addressed, so property will always be a seller's market. 'The only way you can stop house prices rising is to build too many houses,' says Fergus, 'and for environmental reasons, that won't happen.'

The Wilsons have a few golden rules for success, among which are: never buy in an unfamiliar area, or any area that is too remote for you to keep an eye on. They will buy property in job lots, off-plan, at auctions, and their ideal buy-to-let property is a smart two-up, two-down new build mid-terraced house which, in 2007, costs them about £180,000. But they always buy in locations they already know well. And they always go for new, or newish, houses rather than character properties that may need extensive and expensive renovation.

The Wilsons' view is that bigger properties, such as three- or four-bedroom houses, are not only more difficult to let, but don't appreciate in value so quickly as the smaller houses. The Wilsons also prefer freehold houses to flats as there are no service or maintenance charges involved, or any problem about the unit losing value as the lease runs down.

Every single one of their houses is decorated, they say, in magnolia and white, with no variation, and they pick as tenants young professionals who are temporarily located in the M20 corridor.

Dedicated and clever investors such as the Wilsons have often been accused of pricing first-time buyers out of the market, but they maintain that developers and sellers would rather deal with a sensible, sound, middle-aged couple such as themselves, than a young first-time buyer who may have problems getting a mortgage or deposit together, and as such is likely to pull out at the last minute.

Obviously the Wilsons are both shrewd and sensible, but I believe the secret of their great success is that they are highly numerate, dealing in numbers all day and every day, and so leaving as little as possible to chance. They are also emphatically not victims of that arch-enemy of the successful investor: wishful thinking.

Judith Wilson, who was a deputy headmistress before deciding to concentrate on property investment, has become, so her husband proudly says, Britain's first buy-to-let lecturer.

However, at the end of 2008, the Wilsons announced that 'the party's over' and they would begin to sell their houses. Eighteen went on sale in March 2009 and a further 50 were to follow. They plan to sell all their buy-to-let houses over several years, the main reason being that the fixed-rate deals negotiated with Bradford and Bingley came to an end when the lender was nationalized. These mortgage deals, which had been set at 4.5 per cent, were due to rise to 7 per cent, an amount that would not be covered by the achievable rents.

In addition, several of their 900-plus tenants had fallen into arrears as they had lost their jobs, although the Wilsons maintained they were protected by rent guarantee insurance. But then, this kind of insurance costs a yearly premium and necessarily reduces the take from the rents. The Wilsons said they were not in arrears with their mortgages, which totalled a massive £150 million, but that for them, buy-to-let was no longer working. Another aspect was that some lenders wanted 5 per cent of the mortgage loan in arrangement fees, and all lenders were demanding ever higher deposits, with 25 per cent being about the lowest possible.

The Wilsons had originally banked on making their money from the capital appreciation of their properties rather than the rents, and believe that, in spite of estate agents saying that properties in their area had fallen by 20 per cent throughout 2009, in most cases they will gain on resale as they bought several years ago. They say they are not putting a glut of properties suddenly on the market, but selling them gradually, mainly to first-time buyers.

But buying up properties at great speed is a little like walking a tightrope in that you have to balance everything out very carefully indeed – and then have a safety net of cash to fall back on if interest rates rise, the boiler breaks down or you cannot rent the place out for love nor money.

Jackie Taylor, a former local government officer who is now a full-time landlord, has amassed a portfolio of 16 properties in eight years, all by mortgaging, remortgaging and gearing. She says: 'I am constantly juggling sums and figures to make it all work and it's very hard indeed. There is such fierce competition out there that your places have to be very smart and very central to attract tenants. Then they may negotiate you down as they have so much choice.

'I have had many sleepless nights, especially as I have had to replace boilers, redecorate and replace kitchens and bathrooms. Some of my properties have not rented out after a few years and I have had to sell them. There is no one perfect formula for success but my advice is that unless you buy a real dog of a property, eventually you are not going to lose.'

So what is a 'dog' of a property? There is no exact definition, but one rule of thumb is: can you imagine living in it yourself? If not, you have to ask yourself why anybody else should want to?

If properties are in bad condition when let, tenants will trash them even further. Homes get much harder wear with tenants than with owner-occupiers as the tenants don't really care and they will tend to make a tired, dated, dingy property even worse.

Yet not all 'dogs' are properties in bad condition. Some new-build flats can look wonderful when new, and they let out easily because they have this 'wow' factor. But very often, 10 years later they are flaking round the edges and have lost any wow they once possessed.

But a real 'dog' is one you cannot sell at any price. Many properties that may work quite well as rental propositions, are simply not popular on the sales market because they are too small, because they don't represent value for money and because many are single-occupancy only. In addition, some very small studios in large apartment blocks come with very high service charges that tend to negate the cheap purchase price. Other apartments that can be hard to sell are those with communal heating and hot-water systems as, again, while this may work for a rental investment when included in the rent, these central systems also considerably hike up service charges.

Always consider the exit strategy when buying an investment property, unless you intend to keep the property purely as a buy-to-let and are never likely to sell. But, again, nobody has a crystal ball to look into the future and unexpected events can force quick decisions.

Jackie Taylor continues: 'You do have to be prepared to hang on to them though, for about 10 years, to see a good return and you may not get a good yield in rent. You always have to think about repairs and maintenance and how you might pay for them.'

To make the enterprise work, you have to number crunch very carefully indeed, taking into account service charges, ground rent, fees to letting agents, cost of renovation, decoration, appliances, furniture and fittings, mortgage repayment, legal fees and stamp duty for buying and all other purchase costs and then set all these against the amount of rent you believe you can realistically achieve.

When all the numbers are computed, the rental yield should give you at least a clear 6 per cent gross yield. Any less than this and you will lose money, at least if buying on a mortgage. It sounds obvious, but if your mortgage repayments are set at 5.5 per cent and the best rental yield you can hope for is 4 per cent, this means you will pay to borrow! The rental yield has to be better than a bank account will produce, otherwise it will be costing you to rent out the property, rather than making anything on it.

The reason you have to work out the figures very carefully is that there are always unexpected costs when letting property, such as rental voids, a sudden hike in service charges (in lease-hold properties), an increase in interest rates or a major repair or renovation. The mortgage repayments are far from being the only ongoing cost of a buy-to-let property.

Here are the figures for rental yields from Knight Frank, the London estate agents, posted in July 2009:

■ The average gross yield in prime central London has fallen below 4 per cent for the first time since September 2007 – hitting 3.79 per cent in June 2009.

■ Gross yields hit a recent peak of 4.17 per cent in September 2008 – but have suffered from falling rents and, more recently, rising property values.

■ Residential rents in central London fell 1.9 per cent in the three months to June 2009, but prices actually rose by 3.7 per cent – putting downward pressure on yields.

■ A reduction in the volume of new lets suggests a further significant decline in rental values is unlikely.

■ Investors looking to add to their London residential rental portfolios in the current market need to pick their stock far more carefully and plan further ahead.

Obviously these figures only reflect prime London properties, in which Knight Frank specializes, but these percentage yields are an indication of what is happening in other parts of the country and show that rental income, in most cases, would not even begin to cover mortgage repayments and other running costs such as service charges.

Figures from the Association of Residential Letting Agents (ARLA) for the second quarter of 2009 give an average of 5.07 per cent gross rental return all over the UK, including Scotland, and 4.66 per cent net return. Again, although the figures are higher than for prime central London, they are still probably not enough to cover the average mortgage.

In their five-year projection of returns from rental investments, ARLA factor in annual capital appreciation of 6.66 per cent. But this depends on whether property prices start to rise again or continue to decrease still further, and of course nobody knows what may happen.

At the same time as having no income from rentals, investors would have faced ongoing costs, such as repayments on their loan, service charges (always a fact of life in apartment blocks), council tax and utility bills, thereby adding considerable insult to the injury of nil rent and negative capital growth.

Then the costs of entry and exit from this sector are relatively high. If you sell too soon you can lose an enormous amount of money, rather than gaining, which is the object of the exercise. And as we have seen, there are always considerable costs to buying and selling, whatever your eventual gain. Also, the sums of money involved in buying any property are very large; usually into six figures.

Most investment experts warn that buy-to-let is no longer a get-rich-quick scheme, if ever it was, and that it is unrealistic to expect a quick turnaround on profit. Because of the high entry and maintenance costs of this type of investment, it has to be viewed as a medium- to long-term venture, say 10 to 15 years, before genuine growth and profit can be realized.

In recent years, the emphasis has been mainly on buying new or off-plan properties for buy-to-let investment, on the assumption that they will not need immediate maintenance and as they are smart, new and clean, they will appeal to the increasingly sophisticated and choosy rental market. Mostly as well, these new developments of apartment blocks are in city centres or regeneration areas where workforces tend to be concentrated.

However, in 2008, the off-plan and newbuild buy-to-let market came crashing down, with investors buying up to 50 per cent of new properties and then finding themselves unable to rent them out, or at least unable to rent them at the high amounts promised by the developers.

Because so many newbuild properties came onto the market during 2008 and could not be sold for anything like the purchase price, the Council of Mortgage Lenders introduced new standards of practice in September 2008, whereby lenders can no longer offer a mortgage based on too high a valuation. Now builders and developers have to declare any incentives or discounts offered to buyers, to ensure that the valuation is always reliable and presents the true value of the property.

It has to be said that very many investors bought these properties after being fired up at expensive property seminars. They bought there and then, expecting that the vaunted 'due diligence' had been carried out by the companies offering the properties and that the rents were actually achievable. During the property downturn of 2008, several of these seminar companies went into administration, blaming the fall in property prices. But from an investor point of view, it was always a high-risk strategy to buy literally millions of pounds' worth of property without even seeing it, and without conducting very close research into whether the rental market was as buoyant as promised.

While buyers may be caught out, it might be thought that the lenders should take a share of the blame as well. In fact, there is no comeback in these situations, and lenders can just walk away once they have obtained their commission and arrangement fees. You, the investor, are left to pick up whatever pieces can be salvaged from such folly.

But although they may walk away from responsibility, mortgage lenders do not walk away from the debt. Monthly mortgage payments are relentless and the debt builds up until eventually the investor loses everything, even any initial deposits put down.

But as with everything in property matters, there is a wide choice of properties which may be suitable for renting out, and also a wide variety of tenants. You do not have to go for newbuild where, when all is said and done, the resale value has not been established on the open market.

Houses or flats?

As we have seen, Judith and Fergus Wilson believe it makes sense for buy-to-let investors to go for freehold houses rather than leasehold flats. It is certainly true that individual houses do not come with the same amount of 'baggage' you take on when buying a flat.

With flats, you have a complicated lease that tells you what you can and cannot do, and serious breaches of the lease could lead to forfeiture and repossession by the freeholder. Some apartment buildings do not allow subtenants and in any case, you as the leaseholder will be responsible for service charges plus any levies or extra costs for major repairs. These can be high: in my apartment block, the cost to some leaseholders of their share of a new roof was £20,000.

As with everything else in life, there are pros and cons. Flats tend to be cheaper than houses and you can get smaller units that may be easier to rent out. As opposed to the Wilsons, another successful property investor I know believes in going for studio flats, as there is always a demand for very small, self-contained units. Single people, particularly young women, would usually prefer to live in a flat than a house, as apartment blocks feel more secure than houses, which are easy to break into. Also, studio flats constitute the cheapest type of self-contained accommodation available, and increasingly, renters would prefer a fully self-contained unit, however tiny, than having to share a kitchen and bathroom.

The main thing, I believe, is to go for self-contained units rather than a houseful of bedsitters which constitute a House in Multiple Occupation or HMO. HMOs are complicated to administer and bedsits, or non-self-contained units, come right at the bottom of the rental market, where there may not be such good tenants available.

From the investor's point of view, it always comes down to adding up the numbers to see where you can get the best operating profit overall. My investor top tip is always to have a calculator handy. I have them all over the house so that wherever I am I can work out whether a particular property adds up to a good investment or not. Mostly, I have to say, they don't.

In my own case, I have always bought flats rather than houses as buy-to-let investments as they usually give a better yield than houses. The other problem with houses is that they are rarely suitable for single tenants, and the more tenants you have in each property, the more potential problems increase.

Also, the small terraced houses favoured by the Wilsons are not available in every location. Nor are many being built; for developers, the executive-type luxury five-bedroom detached house is far more profitable than a row of cheap one- or two-bedroom houses.

But there are very many property types to choose from. You can invest in upmarket properties in prime areas which appeal to corporate tenants; houses for families or for student occupation; one-bedroom flats for singles or couples; two- or three-bedroom flats for sharers; and properties suitable for social housing. Not all tenant markets operate in all areas, so the thing to do first is thoroughly research an area by talking to letting and selling agents, to

see what the market consists of, how much property costs to purchase, and the kind of rents that can be achieved.

Before ever buying a property, it is a good idea to pretend to be
a tenant looking for somewhere, rather than going on what developers or agents might say. When actress Annie Hulley decided to
start investing in property, she discovered that the rents promised to landlords were very different indeed to the rents actually
achieved. She said: 'As a landlord, I was told by agents that I
could get £425 a week for a type of flat I was considering buying.
But when I pretended to be a tenant looking for a similar flat, I
was told £350 a week. It's no good just going on what agents say
– you have to work on what you can realistically achieve in any
given market.' The other advantage of pretending to be a tenant is
that you get to see the competition. You learn what is on offer at
specific rents, and how smart or otherwise the properties are. You
also hear the spiel given by letting agents, which may be very different from what you would be told as a landlord.

ARLA's report for June 2009 says that there is not now very
much difference in yields between houses and flats, and it all
depends on the area. In inner-city areas investors are unlikely to
find houses but in country areas where there is more space, there
would be more houses available.

Local Housing Allowance (Housing Benefit)

In some areas, most of the available tenants will be on housing
benefit (HB); these will typically be families and often single
parents with two or more dependent children.

When deciding whether to start or expand your portfolio to
include this type of tenant, even more careful calculation is
required. The rent amounts and the accommodation allowed for
each type of claimant are both carefully calculated and not subject
to any variation. For instance, a single man will be entitled to a
one-bedroom flat at a pre-designated rent considered typical for
the area; a family consisting of two parents with a boy aged 12
and a girl aged 14 will be eligible for a three-bedroom house with

a separate living room and kitchen. Again, the rent will be fixed by the local authority and is not subject to any negotiation up or down.

Rents are paid four weeks in arrears directly to the tenant, who must then pay the landlord. Only if the rent is more than eight weeks in arrears can the landlord elect to have the rent paid directly by the local authority. It will be difficult, if not impossible, to recover any arrears, and a deposit to safeguard against this may not be payable in situations where the tenant has no financial resources.

Also, when circumstances change and, say, the children grow up and leave home, a couple might have to move from their three-bedroom house into somewhere smaller, as they will no longer have the same bedroom requirements as before.

Some landlords find this sector profitable. But before buying a cheap property with this market in mind, it is essential that you do thorough research at your local council offices to see whether you feel you can handle this sector. Find out the types of accommodation most in demand, the rents allowed, and any other conditions pertaining to HB tenants.

Working out the yield

Before ever deciding on a buy-to-let property, it is essential to work out the achievable rental yield, to see whether it is worth it. A sum of £1,800 a month, or £21,600 a year, sounds a lot of money, but if your property is worth £700,000, that is a yield of less than 3 per cent, probably less than you could get with even an ordinary interest account on that amount at the bank.

Assuming for the moment you buy a two-bed flat for £200,000, stamp duty at 1 per cent comes to £2,000; legal costs, say £940; renovation and decoration, another £5,000.

Service charges come in at £1,000 per annum. Your expected rental is £250 a week, or £13,000 per annum. Your gross return therefore is just under 6.5 per cent – about the minimum workable return. Allowing a 10 per cent plus 17.5 per cent VAT letting fee

(£1,527.50) and taking into account the service charges, your actual yield now reduces to £10,472.50.

Then you will have to pay income tax on the gain, plus insurance, gas certificate, repairs and renewals.

However, if you are a cash buyer, you will still gain a usable income. If you are buying on a mortgage, you will have to depend on capital growth to come out on top, which is always an unknown.

To qualify for a mortgage, your expected rental return has to be 130 per cent of the mortgage repayment costs. To give a simple example, if the loan costs you £1,000 a month, the expected rent must be at least £1,300 a month. This will give you a rental income of £300 a month – before you pay service charges, letting fees and all the other costs. It is not easy to make a profit when buying on a mortgage, but you should at least aim to break even as well as having some rainy day money for unexpected repairs, void periods or building levies in apartment blocks.

Here again are some simple figures. You put down a deposit of £50,000 on your £200,000 flat, and take out a mortgage for £150,000 payable at a rate of 5.25 per cent. This means your mortgage costs you £7,875 a year, leaving you a rental income of £5,125 a year.

When you take off your letting fee of 10 per cent plus VAT, this comes down to £3,597.50 a year. Most buy-to-let mortgage lenders will insist that you use an ARLA letting agent as a condition of the mortgage. And if you opt for the fully-managed service, this will usually cost another 5 per cent. Again, when calculating costs and profits, do not include projected capital growth, just what you can get from rents now. Take off the service charges, estimated at £1,000 a year, and your income now comes down to £2,597.50 a year. And with these mortgage figures, we have not allowed anything for insurance, furniture, fittings, appliances or incidentals.

As you will see, buying to let on a mortgage gives you pocket money, at best, rather than income. BUT, by the process of gearing, where you use accumulated equity in one property to buy another, the figures start to make more sense. Say you have eight properties all with the same yields and costs, you will be getting an income now of £20,780 a year – just about enough to live on.

By this means, you can see that the more properties you have, the more income you will have. Keeping the same figures, if you have 50 such properties, you will now be getting an annual income of £129,850 a year. This is how property millionaires are made. And anybody can do it.

But with a mortgage, it hardly makes sense with just one property. You have to 'gear' to make it worthwhile, bearing in mind that accountancy costs for 50 properties will hardly be any more than for one property. Also, when you are letting many properties, you can negotiate for good deals with letting agents.

In order to make buy-to-let work, you have to do it on a large scale. The more properties you have, the more the exercise becomes worth it – if you can stand the effort of looking after 50 tenants, 50 properties and all the accompanying problems of the combination of human beings and bricks and mortar – often a lethal mix.

So what about the other aspect of buy-to-let investments, which is the capital gain? Don't forget that when you sell any home apart from your principal private residence, you will have to pay Capital Gains Tax, which is 18 per cent of your total gain since 6 April 2008. Changes made to Capital Gains Tax in the October 2007 pre-budget report mean that this tax is now a flat rate, and taper relief after a number of years no longer applies.

In the main, buy-to-let works extremely well, even without significant capital growth, so long as three conditions apply: your properties are always, always fully let; interest rates do not rise too much, or they actually come down; and you don't face massive repair bills.

If you die and want to leave your properties to your heirs, you, or rather your estate, will have to pay inheritance tax.

There are now a number of mortgage providers which specialize in buy-to-let, although most of the main lenders now offer this facility. Most buy-to-let investors take out interest-only mortgages, but it is worth comparing rates as, very often, the interest-only period (or other deal) only lasts for a fixed term. There will also be an arrangement fee, a re-arrangement fee if you change your mortgage, insurance, and a redemption fee if you change mortgages or remortgage.

The buy-to-let mortgage market keeps increasing and there are now many different types of buy-to-let mortgage. For instance, you can get a variable, fixed, discount, tracker, flexible discount, flexible fixed, flexible variable and flexible tracker. Do be careful, though, about mortgage payment protection insurance (MPPI), which some mortgage lenders add on more or less automatically. MPPI is not compulsory, and just means you are paying more each month.

When investing, you have to keep a very close eye on the sneaky little fees and charges which, if you are not careful, can be added on almost without you noticing, especially as arrangement fees rarely appear in 'best buy' mortgage league tables.

Be aware that every time you alter your original mortgage deal, there will be another fee to pay.

Guaranteed rentals

Many developers are now offering guaranteed rentals on new-build properties, usually at 6 per cent. The guarantees are for a specific period of time, typically two years after completion of the development. Then you are on your own.

Many landlord associations are not in favour of these guaranteed rentals, for the following reasons: the 'guaranteed rental' does not guarantee that tenants have been found at this rent, or even at all. In reality, this guarantee amounts to a discount on the property and is not any indication that the property is popular with the tenant market.

To make the equation work and to keep inside the law, during the 'guaranteed rental' period you will still be paying service charges, letting fees, your mortgage and the ground rent. Unless you pay all of these, the developers cannot justify their claim of the guaranteed rental.

What you have to ask is: where am I when the guarantee period ends? What hope do you have of finding tenants yourself at that rent or, indeed, at any rent? Before ever agreeing to a guaranteed rental, you must discover what kind of market exists and what tenants are prepared to pay on the open market. You can only discover this by slogging round letting agencies yourself, and not going on the say-so of the developers and their marketing hype.

How the different tenant markets work

There are many classes and divisions of tenants, and you have to consider in advance what type of tenant you are aiming at. Broadly speaking, they fall into the following categories: students; young professionals (singles, couples, sharers); families; older, divorced or separated people; corporate tenants; in-betweeners (those renting while deciding what to buy) and people on housing benefit.

All of these markets have their own dynamics and a property which appeals to the student market, for instance, would be unlikely to suit a high-earning city type, in terms of either the property or the location.

Students

Brian Palacio, a former detective with the Metropolitan Police, decided to invest in the student market in Brighton and Hove when he was invalided out of the Met with a pay-off of £170,000. He says: 'I wanted to invest my redundancy money in something useful and also have an interest to keep me occupied. Because of the whiplash injury sustained in the course of duty, I am never going to be a hundred per cent and I had to choose something which would give me plenty of time off. A nine to five job was out.

'My doctors also told me I had to choose somewhere healthy and sunny to live, and also to get out of London. I had already studied with the Open University at Brighton and did two summer schools there. I knew that with two universities and many language schools, there would be a big market in Brighton for student accommodation, and this seemed to be the best bet for me.

'So I started looking at four-bedroom houses and began buying on buy-to-let mortgages. I buy houses in bad condition, renovate them and let them through the university housing office, which regulates rents and conditions.

'The big advantage with students is that there is no council tax to pay and I charge them an all-in amount to cover utilities.'

The rents amount to £85–£90 a week each and Brian works on a 40-week year. As a bonus, his houses are often let during the long vacation to summer school students. He does not make a profit from student lettings, but covers his costs. The real profit, he says, is coming from the capital growth in the houses. Brighton and Hove has the most expensive properties in the UK, after London. Brian adds: 'One of the big advantages of going for the student market is that there is always a ready supply of tenants. The universities provide the students so I never have any problem with filling the houses.'

Brian believes that in order to make the student market work, you have to be hands-on: 'You can't leave it all to managing agents and a lot of agents won't handle students anyway. As you have to be prepared to deal with any crises that crop up, it's essential to be near. I don't think it would work to be an absentee landlord hundreds of miles away, with the student market.'

Most landlords insist on tenants paying by standing order, but Brian believes this doesn't really work with students: 'When you have 12 or 15 students all paying about the same, it can be difficult to check through your bank accounts to see whether they have all paid. I take cheques or cash and have had no real problems with rent. I take one month's rent as a deposit.'

Brian says that if you want an income from letting, don't rent out to students as you are really only likely to cover your costs. The universities and colleges set the rent and won't take you on as a landlord if you try to charge more. But as his houses have already made a tidy sum, it works for him.

A number of companies are now offering student homes as investment opportunities. You will find these companies at Property Investor Shows. Mainly, these student homes are brand-new developments which have been designed to cater exactly for student needs. The Warehouse, one such company, can be contacted on: 01772 200949.

Student housing is a specialist sector but one that is growing all the time. As the government aims to get 50 per cent of all young people into higher education, this sector is set to expand even more, and when you factor in the number of overseas students, both undergraduate and postgraduate, studying in the UK, it adds up to a huge and burgeoning market.

There are two main types of student accommodation: new-build properties and refurbished houses targeted specifically at the investor in this very specific market. Newbuild accommodation for the student market only – most commonly four-bedroom, three-storey houses – cannot be occupied by anyone else. It is rather like sheltered accommodation at the other end of the age spectrum; only those who qualify can live there. Most newbuild student accommodation comes with a restrictive covenant, and this is something the investor must bear in mind when buying such a property, as such units can only be sold on to another investor in the same market.

By contrast, refurbished accommodation, typically Victorian terraces or 1930s semis near to a university and adapted for student use, may be sold on to anybody, whether another investor or an owner-occupier. Thus there is an easier exit strategy from ownership of a refurbished student house.

If you buy a student house through a recognized company specializing in this market, such as Assetz, they will handle all the red tape including, for instance, liaising with the university, licensing the property as an HMO and fitting all the rooms with broadband access.

Brian Palacio found that the universities and colleges set the rent in his area, but according to Assetz this practice is dying out as the student population continues to expand and an increasing number of private companies and developers come into the market. In some cases the developers will enter into an agreement with the university. This is something the investor needs to check.

Nor is it the case any more that rents are paid for only 40 weeks a year. In most instances the student rooms will be let for 52 weeks, although some contracts allow for half rent to be paid during the long vacation if the student is not in residence. Increasingly, though, students seem to stay up during the long vacation and get jobs locally, rather than leaving the properties and going home.

Most investors find that student lets achieve a higher yield than ordinary buy-to-let properties, with 7 to 8 per cent being average. This is almost twice as much as rents during 2008 in the ordinary sector.

As a student, Romain Record soon realized there could be more to college life than sex, drugs and rock 'n roll. He could become a property developer as well! So, before his first year was out he had bought his first student house for £69,000 and rented it out.

That was in 2000. By the time he graduated from Loughborough University, where he had read – appropriately – business studies, Record owned six homes. Now a full-time student landlord, he owns 25 terraced houses, which he rents out to a total of 116 students.

How did it all happen? Record, 28, says 'I borrowed £5,000 as a deposit from my dad for my first house and he acted as a guarantor for my mortgage. I later sold that place at a profit, and used this money as leverage to buy-up terraced houses which I then renovated and adapted specifically for the student market.'

They get the complete treatment, Record adds, and there is no problem with choosing, because they are all identical inside. From an investment angle, the main attraction is that he is repeating himself with every student house he buys; 'I know precisely what's required and exactly how much revenue the houses will generate', he says.

Rents start from £65 a week inclusive, and although this includes unlimited hot water, there is a monthly allowance for utilities, 'otherwise the temptation would be to leave every light on in the house for ever'. Each student room has a double bed and broadband connection. 'As students become more financially independent', Record says, 'they are looking for a better product and demanding ever higher standards.' His dedicated website, www.top-lets.co.uk asks: 'Had enough of rubbish accommodation?'

As the student homes come under HMO (Houses in Multiple Occupation) legislation, they require a licence from the local authority. This costs around £500, lasts for five years and is compulsory, with a draconian £20,000 fine for non-compliance. Students have to take the houses for a full 52 weeks, and contracts run from 1 July to the end of the following June.

Romain Record's property empire has grown fast and successfully but he fears he may not be able to expand any further; 'It has become almost impossible to get new mortgages, and lenders will now only take on new licensable landlords with a 50 per cent deposit.'

Now that the combination of falling rents, fast-crashing property prices and stricter mortgage requirements is making ordinary buy-to-let less attractive to enter, investors are increasingly wondering about the ever expanding student market.

Romain Record's houses are so popular that they are all fully let by 1 July each year. But before you eye up that dilapidated terraced house with a view to cramming in half a dozen students and counting up the easy cash, listen to Andrew Menear, an accommodation officer for Brighton University.

He says: 'Because the university has recently built more halls, landlords are experiencing more voids, and some student houses have been vacant all year. This means the private sector is becoming more competitive and rents are falling. Plus, we are planning to build yet more halls. One reason for this is that it is becoming unpopular to have student homes in residential areas, as they lower property values.'

A student house is usually immediately recognizable by its neglected garden, piles of cruddy bikes, curtains tightly drawn all day and – if the students are at home – loud music 24/7. This will put owner-occupiers off buying homes in that area.

Menear adds: 'In Brighton, the student sector is not as good as it used to be and we advise landlords to contact us, rather than trying to let directly to students, as if we take them onto our register, the houses can then be advertised for nothing on our website. Student landlords should certainly not sign up with letting agents, as they charge £160 for reference checks and then take six weeks' deposit and one month's rent upfront, which most students can't afford.'

A popular alternative is for universities to become the tenant, and then sublet to students; 'This means that we will fully manage the property and guarantee rent for 48 weeks of the year. Also, deposit protection is not needed.'

If you are interested in the student sector, don't just buy a property and hope that students will fall over themselves to rent it from you. Instead, talk first to the local university accommodation office and get a clear idea of the type of accommodation and location that is in most demand. Then adapt the house accordingly, bearing in mind that an accommodation officer will inspect it before agreeing to add it to the register, after you have sent six digital pictures to the relevant website. The property must be suitable for three to five students, with a communal room and shared kitchen and bathroom as well as a study bedroom each.

To be accepted onto a university landlords' register, the student home must comply with the following:

▮ it must be licensed as an HMO;

▮ it must have a current (yearly) gas certificate;

▮ it must have an Energy Performance Certificate;

▮ it must have an electricity certificate;

▮ it must have TV points and broadband connection in each study bedroom;

▮ it must have central heating;

▮ there must be lined curtains in bedrooms;

▮ locations must be near public transport;

▮ there must be somewhere to put bikes;

▮ landlords must ensure they are covered for student occupation on their insurance.

So far as mortgages are concerned, there are around 40 lenders that would consider student lets. If parents purchase a buy-to-let property for their student child(ren) they will usually find that the rent from three or four students more than covers the mortgage. Then when the children graduate, the property can be sold or kept as a longer-term investment.

There are, though, some new rules that have to be followed for student houses, of which the most important is the Houses in Multiple Occupation (HMO) legislation. If you are considering buying student properties, it is essential to contact the local council to see whether the property needs licensing, how much the licensing fees would be, and whether any specific criteria or adaptation are needed to conform to legislation. Criteria vary from council to council but the standard HMO rules say that a three-storey property with five or more tenants sharing at least some facilities will count as an HMO. In fact, any house in multiple occupation where there are some shared facilities may well need a licence, so better to be safe than sorry, especially as fines for non-compliance can go up to £20,000.

Licensing fees demanded by local councils can vary from £100 to £2,000, and they are not transferable when a property is sold. Licences have to be renewed every five years. Since HMO licensing came in during 2006, some mortgage lenders have altered their criteria for HMOs.

You will also need to be up to speed with any other areas of legislation, particularly Health and Safety Ratings Systems.

If, instead of buying a student house, you decide to invest in purpose-built student accommodation such as halls of residence, this can be put into a Self-Invested Personal Pension (SIPP) – one of the few remaining residential property areas which still qualify for this, and the tax relief that goes with it. See Chapter 9 for more detailed information on SIPPs.

This is a hands-off type of investment where you just put money in, as with any other type of non-property investment, and it is handled by specialist companies, such as Assetz. To give an example, Assetz is selling student apartment halls in Lincoln where there is a 24-hour management team. An investment of £243,000 will give a net rental income of £14,888 pa, or 6.1 per cent. If you borrow £205,550 on a 5.2 per cent mortgage, you would still come out with a £4,147 profit in the first year. (Note: this is just an example, and figures may vary, although university halls of residence are actively looking for investors as the student population inexorably grows.)

Most people interested in the student market would probably be parents with undergraduate children, but this sector is not, of course, confined to any particular group of people.

Young professionals – singles, couples, sharers

This is by far the biggest tenant pool and is in many ways the easiest to operate, as young professionals are earning a fixed salary and know in advance how much rent they can afford.

The secret here is to discover what the average salaries are in a particular location, and then see if your potential investment works financially. Suppose you rent a one-bedroom apartment to a couple in their mid-twenties each earning £25,000 a year, you know that their combined income of £50,000 will mean they can pay around £250–£280 a week in rent. If you set your rents much higher than this, you will simply not attract tenants.

These days, tenants are used to negotiating and slogging around to find the best deal. They will look at around 15 properties before deciding, usually, on the cheapest.

Although an income of £50,000 may sound a lot, remember that many graduates will still be repaying student loans, which gives them less disposable income for rent.

Young professionals like clean, smart, simple flats, usually furnished and with dishwashers, power showers, internet connection and, if possible, some outside space. Having said that, they are not usually keen gardeners and you cannot expect your tenants to look after a garden. Mostly, these tenants do not have cars and do not need garages, but they have to be very near to transport links, near to their work and also to restaurants, pubs and night life.

Corporate tenants

Corporate tenants want very high-spec properties for which they will pay a premium rent. Rents of £3,000 a week are not unusual with this sector, but for that, these tenants want highly designed properties very near to their work. As they work long hours, they will often look for something in walking distance to their jobs.

Mostly, the corporate market is operated by relocation agents who drive very hard bargains indeed. Only enter this highly specialized market if you can afford the high purchase price of the property and the equally high running costs.

In general, as corporate tenants are thinner on the ground than others, it can take around 13 weeks to rent one of these properties.

Country rentals

Apart from holiday lets, the country market can be difficult. Letting agent Jane Russam, who specializes in country lettings for Knight Frank, says that a £700,000 country house would yield no more than £1,800 a month in rent.

Country homes must be unfurnished – furnished properties are difficult to let, Russam says, and in addition the property has to have something special about it. The average stay for this market is 13–15 months, and the tenants are most often the 'in-betweeners' who are renting while they look around for something suitable to buy in the area.

Families

This sector wants houses rather than flats, with gardens and near to schools and other facilities for young children.

If interested in renting to families, you would first need to discover what, if any, is the family market in your area, what kinds of families they are, and what kind of rents they are prepared to pay.

In many areas the family market is increasing fast, with the main requirement being for a three-bedroom house with a small garden. Some people are discovering that it makes more sense to rent than to buy, with increasing numbers preferring to have money in the bank than struggle to pay an ever-increasing mortgage. They too constitute a growth market for the property investor.

A case in point is writer and father of one, Dan Kieran. He and his teacher wife bought a flat in London, then after a few years decided to move to Chichester and rent instead. The sale of the London flat yielded £90,000 cash, which they have decided to put in the bank rather than use as a deposit on another property purchase. The thing is, says Dan, there are so many lovely homes to rent these days that it seems more sensible to do this than tie yourself into a mortgage for a quarter of a century. The money also gives Dan some security, and a nice financial cushion as a freelance writer.

Renting to recent immigrants

This is a complicated issue for the buy-to-let investor, and many more checks need to be carried out than for ordinary renters. I would say the most important things to know are that they are legal immigrants, that they have proper jobs and that most of all, they have a guarantor who is a UK homeowner with a steady job, who can guarantee the rent if the immigrant defaults or disappears.

Because it can be difficult to carry out ordinary credit checks on tenants from another country, you need to make doubly sure that the rent will be paid, whatever. This may mean that the checks usually carried out on the tenant will have to be carried out on the guarantor instead. The guarantor must sign the tenancy agreement and it should never be an ad hoc or informal agreement.

It is also essential for the immigrant to make sure he or she understands all the legal ramifications of the tenancy agreement before any keys are handed over. This means that either you, or they, may need to engage the services of a bilingual lawyer. The influx of immigrants, particularly those from recent EU member states, has greatly increased the need for rented accommodation, and many investors are now looking closely at this market. I have myself rented out properties to recent immigrants and never had a problem and, clearly, such people have to live somewhere. When first entering the UK they almost always need or want to rent.

A table prepared in October 2006 by London estate agents Ludlow Thompson showed that 13.7 per cent of all overseas enquiries now came from recent EU countries (mainly Eastern Europe, or former Communist countries), 9.5 per cent from Australia and 7.8 per cent from France.

It looks as though the biggest growth in the private rented sector will come from Eastern Europeans, and landlords should prepare accordingly for this. All migrants from EU countries are entitled to work in the UK without the need for a visa or work permit. In fact, the biggest areas for growth in rented property seem to be students on the one hand, and Eastern European migrants looking for work, on the other.

Leasing to the local authority or a housing association

Many landlords go for this option because it takes all the worry away from you. Here, you lease your property to the local authority or housing association for a term of, typically, three to five years during which time they simply take it over and you can forget about it.

They will find tenants, paint and redecorate your property, take over all the running costs (apart from service charges in flats) and pay you the rent. They will also guarantee to return your property to you in excellent condition at the end of the lease period. Not only do they not charge you any commission, they may well pay you a golden hello when first leasing your property. This can be up to £5,000 with some authorities and associations, in certain areas.

Very many landlords find this option works extremely well, but in exchange for all this largesse, the association or local authority impose some stringent conditions. A representative will come to your property and assess it for suitability. You have to pay for this. Funnily enough, health and safety standards are far higher here than in other sectors of the market, and you would have to make sure the property had fire doors, smoke alarms, fire escapes and up-to-date electrical and gas installations. You pay for any upgrading the property may require.

Then the authority or association set the rentals. They will offer you so much for a one-bedroom flat, so much for a house – and there is no deviation from this. If you are interested in leasing your property to this sector, first do research as to what is required. Many housing associations provide landlord packs, as do the universities.

Stadium Housing Association, one of the many such associations involved in private sector leasing, explains its requirements.

Much private sector leasing exists to provide otherwise homeless people with temporary accommodation until they can be permanently housed. Sometimes, this 'temporary' accommodation can last for years. Mostly, the tenants are on housing benefit and the rent is paid directly to the housing association. If the temporary tenant secures permanent accommodation during the period of the tenancy agreement, then a new incoming tenant will be signed up.

Before the agreement is drawn up, any compensation for damage to the property or furniture is agreed. You will need to supply a CP12 for any gas installation and appliances and an NICEIC electrical certificate. Stadium Housing requires the property to be fully furnished, but not all housing associations insist on this; very often with other associations the properties are rented out unfurnished.

Rent will be paid by BACS and rents are paid monthly in advance. Stadium Housing does not redecorate or refurnish at the end of the lease, but again, some associations do agree to do this.

Being a social landlord

In some areas, this is the only tenant pool there is, and you have to know you can handle it. Since April 2008 local authorities pay housing benefit directly to the claimant and the days of paying rent straight to the landlord are over. The idealistic intention here is to give social tenants more responsibility and choice by allowing them to pay the rent themselves, and operate in the same way as private tenants.

Many landlords, however, find that their tenants spend the rent on themselves and fall into arrears. It is only when the tenant is eight weeks in arrears that you can apply to have the rent paid directly to you, and as the money has gone, there is no way of making up the two months' arrears.

Also, because social tenants have no financial resources whatever, they are not in a position to pay a deposit or for dilapidations. Before entering this sector, make sure you know all the ramifications. Some companies in the North of England find, renovate and sell cheap properties to investors, which are intended for rental to social tenants. These companies also offer to find tenants, but in reality, the operation does not proceed as smoothly as it should. Many tenants in this sector default on rent and then disappear without trace.

Most High Street letting agents do not handle this sector of the market, as it is too tricky.

It is also tricky to evict a social tenant who has been housed by the local authority or housing association. Although such tenants will have a tenancy agreement along the same lines as an ordinary AST, they cannot be summarily kicked out. Instead, you have to write to the relevant authority or association, who will investigate the complaint and write to the tenant.

The tenant will usually deny that he or she has received such letters, so the next step will be for a representative to call round and inspect the property. Eventually the matter will come to court and, at this stage, the tenant will usually be speedily evicted but it can take several months for this to happen. The best advice here, if you decide to accept social tenants, is to ask the rental organization what happens when there is anti-social behaviour or complaints from other occupiers in the building.

Local councils and others providing social housing are reluctant to evict tenants who are placed with private landlords as they are then homeless and may have to be accommodated in a B&B, at vast expense to the local authority.

Property clubs

These are offshoots of the heavily-advertised 'Become a Property Millionaire with little or no cash down' ads you see in newspapers and hear on the radio. What happens here is that you buy membership of a property club, usually at several thousand pounds, for the privilege of gaining access to discounted off-plan properties.

There are two types of property club: one where the club itself buys properties in bulk and sells them on to you, the investor, and the other where you pay a membership fee for access to discounted off-plan properties which have not been bought by the property club.

In 2005, five property clubs were wound up by the High Court for fraudulent practices whereby investors paid several thousand pounds but never got their hands on a property. Rogue investment companies charged naïve investors up to £50,000 for newly built houses and flats at discounts without needing deposits. The problem was, these investors never got their hands on the property – the property club just pocketed their cash. The Department for Business, Innovation and Skills (a new name for the DTI) discovered that these clubs were simply helping themselves to the money they had taken off investors – who usually raised the cash by remortgaging their main home – and caused them to be closed down.

So does this mean that property clubs, along with timeshare and holiday clubs, are a bad idea and yet another means of separating the gullible and the greedy from their money?

Not necessarily. Although it is estimated that one in six new flats is now sold to a buy-to-let investor through a property club of one sort or another, there are bona fide operators in the game. But always beware of the magic word 'invest' because this always means that you CAN lose some or all of your money, however low the purported risk.

The investment club is usually tied into a mortgage company, and this is where you start paying as, very often, the mortgage deals are not as good as you could get on the open market. But you are locked into them for ever and the investment club may well insist that you use their mortgage providers.

When buying off-plan through an investment club, there is a danger that all the properties will come onto the market at the same time and there will not be enough tenants to go round.

Here are sample figures from one such club, Viceroy Properties, for off-plan properties:

Market price of property	£175,000
Discount	£26,500
Net price	£148,500
Viceroy's fee	£4,112 (2 per cent of market price + VAT)
You pay	£152,612

Assuming 6 per cent growth over the following year, you have made a gross profit of £33,000. That is without taking into account rental income, which, at 6 per cent of the purchase price, would yield another £9,120, giving you a gross overall profit of just under £42,000 in a year.

The best advice is that until you know how much money you can make from a property, you should not be even vaguely interested in it.

There are a number of property clubs advertising on the internet, and all promise discounted properties. But before signing up, you need to know that the discount is genuine and based on a realistic valuation; also, that you will be able to sell the property, as rental income will frequently not cover costs completely and it can be years before a new or off-plan property comes into profit.

New or amateur investors are often persuaded to buy a portfolio of properties instead of timidly purchasing just one. But be very careful to research rental demand, values and the market generally in the area before signing up to buy, say, 10 properties in a new development.

Would you enjoy being a landlord?

It is very important to ask this question, as much of the hype surrounding buy-to-let gives the impression that there is absolutely nothing to being a landlord, and you can just let agents look after everything for you. In fact, the contract remains between you and the tenant, nobody else, and you are responsible not only for your property but also for your tenant.

Both properties and tenants need a lot of looking after and it is emphatically not simply a matter of money in and money out.

Doing it together

Setting up a buy-to-let business is becoming a popular way for couples to join forces and double their expertise. Lee Grandin, of Landlord Mortgages, says: 'Buy-to-let enables couples to build a small business together with relatively little risk. Couples generally are good at working together with, typically, the man handling the finance and the woman handling the interior design, tenants, check in and check out.'

Nearly half of all borrowers with Landlord Mortgages are married couples, and 90 per cent of their most successful landlords are a husband and wife team. Lee Grandin adds: 'It's in their interests to work together because they hope their portfolio will finance a comfortable retirement.'

David and Linda England own three London buy-to-let properties and four in Blackpool, total worth around £1 million. Their rental income of around £50,000 a year more than pays their interest-only mortgages.

Sherron and Patrick Parris own two buy-to-let houses near where they live in North London, which are home to a total of nine people, mainly vulnerable young men. Both former social workers, they now combine building up their property portfolio with housing youngsters who find it difficult to cope in society. This way, they hope to combine work they love with security in retirement.

Dr Nicholas Bateson and his wife Ameer live in London and own a total of 25 properties worth around £3 million. Mortgages come to £2 million, and the rental income offsets the repayments. They do all the work of finding and vetting tenants themselves, thus saving letting and management fees.

The advantages for couples working together in this way is that there is double capital gains tax relief (each individual has a yearly capital gains tax allowance) and personal assets can be exchanged tax-free, which cannot happen with any other type of partnership.

You have to get on well together, though!

Beware the leasehold trap

By far the greater majority of properties bought on a buy-to-let basis are sold leasehold rather than freehold. Most new developments are leasehold properties as they are flats rather than separate houses and, as we have seen, to buy leasehold means that you are never the owner of the property.

Because you have bought a length of time, you have to be very careful that the capital value of your property does not go down as the lease shortens. This is an aspect of property purchase many investors never consider, but if the lease becomes shorter than 70 years, you will find it difficult, if not impossible, to get a mortgage on it. This means you cannot sell the property as it has no resale value.

The same applies to ex-local authority high-rise flats. These are often sold at what seems like an incredible bargain, until you realize they have no resale value, either because the lease is extremely short or because they are on the 15th floor, too high in the sky to get a loan. If you cannot get a mortgage on a leasehold property, assume it is not a good buy.

The only exception to this rule is if you buy for cash on a very short lease, and the rental income will give you much, much more than you could hope for with a bank account. Once the lease is up, you have nothing to sell and you will lose all your capital, but if the rental yield is high enough, you may still come out on top. It is a high-risk strategy, though.

When buying leasehold properties for investment, always make sure that your purchase comes with a share of the freehold. This is the most important question to ask when considering a buy-to-let flat, as otherwise the freeholder sets the charges and levies and you could be seriously out of pocket.

Whenever serious investors are considering buying a flat, they should always ask about service charges, the sinking fund and whether there are likely to be any big bills in the near future.

Be aware that very few newbuild and off-plan properties are sold with a share of the freehold, and this in itself makes the purchase very tricky. These properties do, of course, come with a shiny new lease, and most of these are for 99 years. New properties rarely come with longer leases than this. If you keep the property for 15 years, this lease is getting dangerously near the 80-year cut-off point for mortgages.

Lease extensions and buying the freehold

Although the leasehold situation is far from perfect, it is vastly better than it used to be in that leaseholders can now improve the value of their property either by buying a lease extension of up to 90 years from the freeholder, or getting together with the other leaseholders in the building to buy the freehold between them, by a process known as collective enfranchisement (CE).

Since 2002, it has been possible for leaseholders to force the landlord or freeholder to sell them a lease extension or the freehold. But beware – both processes are extremely complicated, long drawn out and require valuations by experts. In simple terms, what happens is that a specialist valuer will add up the freehold interest, length remaining on the lease, ground rents and so on, and arrive at a reasonable offer figure. This is then made to the landlord, who can either accept it or come back with a counter – usually higher – offer.

Although the landlord can legally be forced to grant a lease extension or relinquish the freehold to the leaseholders, a fair price has to be offered. If the price is ridiculous, the landlord can simply reject it. Basically what happens is that the landlord has to be adequately compensated for what he will be losing by granting extensions or freeholds to the leaseholders.

With lease extensions, a figure has to be put on the fact that the freeholder will have to wait a very long time before the freehold reverts to him. The shorter the lease, the more expensive it is to buy an extension.

With collective enfranchisement, the leaseholders have to get together and work together to buy the freehold between them. In order to make this work, 50 per cent of the leaseholders in a building have to agree. This can be expensive and time-consuming and needs somebody highly motivated to push it through.

You can get loans and mortgages for this purpose, as after the extension or enfranchisement, the value of each individual flat will be greatly enhanced.

I have been through the collective enfranchisement process twice and would say that it is definitely worth it to own the freehold, whatever the agonies and frustrations en route. Whether it is better to go for a lease extension or buy the freehold depends partly on the attitude of the other leaseholders in the building. It is very difficult, if not impossible, to persuade everybody in the building to co-operate in the collective enfranchisement as, at the very least, they will have to shell out more money. Older leaseholders often take the attitude that the lease will see them out, and if they do not have any heirs or beneficiaries, often cannot be persuaded to see the point of CE. Or, in many cases, they may simply not be able to afford it. But unless you arrive at that magical 50 per cent, CE cannot continue.

There are now one stop shop companies which specialize in lease extensions and collective enfranchisements and it is very much worth everybody's while to contact one of these. One of the best known is Rosetta Consulting, at www.rosettaconsulting. com. This company will arrange everything, from valuation to legal experts and representation at the Leasehold Valuation Tribunal (LVT) if necessary. The LVT is called in to adjudicate at times when the leaseholders and freeholder cannot reach agreement on the value of the lease extension or the freehold itself.

Although it can be a risk to buy a flat with a short lease, it is a much lesser risk than it used to be. In the old days, many people bought flats on short leases, especially in the area known as prime central London, as this was the only way of buying into such a desirable area. There was no thought of investing – just of living in a favoured and central location. But now that most people see their homes and properties as investments, they are increasingly keen to maximize their value, and the government has finally stepped in with laws to help such people.

Buying short leases

Many investors nowadays buy short leases which, in central London at least, can be as short as 10 or 15 years. What happens here is that the investor buys a short lease, usually at a bargain price, and once in residence proceeds either to buy a lease extension of 90 years, thus vastly increasing the value of the property, or clubs together with the other leaseholders to buy the freehold collectively.

A third option is to buy the short lease and then rent out the property for the remainder of the lease, when the property will be worth nothing. This option does not of course give you the purchaser an exit strategy, but you may be able to make a useful profit on the rental income in the meantime.

There are two main types of short-lease property. One is the very high-end prime central London property on, for instance, the Cadogan Estate, and the other is ex-local authority property, right at the other end of the market.

It is possible to get a mortgage on a prime central London short-lease property from a specialist lender, but this can be difficult, if not impossible, with an ex-local authority property. In general terms, the shorter the lease, the more difficult it is to get a mortgage, although it is always possible to borrow money at a high interest rate for such a purchase.

If you are interested in buying a short lease – usually defined as less than 80 years remaining – you will need to know in advance that you can buy a lease extension, and also how much it is likely to cost. If you are buying an ex-council flat on a short lease, you would need to speak to the local authority or the freeholder – which may well be a different entity from the council – and see what the situation is regarding a lease extension.

It used to be very risky indeed to buy a property with a very short lease, but since the laws relating to lease extensions changed, this option has become a much more secure method of buying a property at a bargain price. In effect, you buy the property in two stages: one when you buy the short lease and another when you buy the lease extension. Normally you would have to wait two years before applying for a lease extension, but these days some properties are being sold with lease extension documentation in place. In some cases, especially with very elderly owners who have let the lease run down, the owner either cannot afford a longer lease or cannot face going through all the hoops of the lease extension business, so sells the property with the run down lease.

Short-lease properties very often come up at auction, and you would need to have all your figures worked out very carefully before making a bid. You would also have to know that it is possible to get the kind of rent you would need to make the investment pay, factoring in the cost of refurbishing, advertising, service charges, possible void periods and other running costs such as gas and electrical certificates.

Personal story

I started buying flats to let in 1995, and the exercise has served me extremely well. Because I always bought for cash – initially by downsizing on my main home, rather than releasing equity – the rental income has been all mine. The properties have increased in value and the flats have always been tenanted. As with most people, I have had to learn as I go.

The first flats I bought were very cheap but had extremely high service charges. Also, it was not possible to enfranchise as not enough residents were interested.

I made sure that subsequent investment properties I acquired always came with a share of the freehold, and that the service charges were reasonable enough to allow me to sell the properties if necessary.

The only downside, looking back, is that after a time, your investment flats have to be refurbished as they come to the end of their renting cycle. This usually means they have to be withdrawn from the market as you cannot expect tenants to pick their way around building works.

After refurbishment, you may not get very much extra rent, even though the cost of renovation has been very high. Yet if you don't refurbish, you may not be able to rent the place out at all. These are the figures I was quoted, before and after: one studio flat was being rented out for £300 a month. The refurbishment cost £12,000, after which I could get £410 pcm. Another flat was rented out at £220 a week; again the refurbishment cost around £12,000 and the new achievable rental was £250 a week. Yet another studio flat was rented out at £650 a month. With a new kitchen and bathroom, £8,000 minimum, the rent would be around £780 a month.

A refurbished flat may not, either, sell for very much more than in its grotty state. One of my flats went on the market in its raw state for £170,000; a similar, refurbished flat in the block was on the market for £180,000, but smart as it was, potential buyers considered it too expensive for its size and location. BUT there is a big plus in that the cost of all these improvements can be added onto the cost of your investment, thereby bringing the capital gains tax liability right down when you sell. So, even though a refurbished property may not sell for very much more than an unmodernized one, your eventual profit will be greater because of the lower CGT liability. So – it's even-stevens, one way or another.

The other big plus for me was that a decade after being purchased, all my investment flats were worth far more than when bought and, more importantly, yielded far more profit than a similar amount left languishing in a bank account. Plus, buying, renovating, renting and selling are all exciting activities, whereas just putting money into low-interest-paying bank accounts is boring and frustrating, especially as the interest never amounts to anything.

More than that, the rental on the south coast properties more than paid the running and refurbishment costs of my holiday flat.

Somehow, buy-to-let does work – and the 'property millionaire' seminar organizers know it. Success is a matter of research, research, research, and number-crunching, squared.

A quick sale

There are a number of companies in existence which will buy your property off you, at below market value. These companies are springing up all the time and they specialize in hard to sell properties. They take all the hassle away from you and they will buy any property, whatever its condition, legal problems or drawbacks. The process is quick and simple, as you just sell it to them. You do not have to wait for a buyer, as they are the buyer – and they guarantee to buy anything.

But there is a mighty downside as you will not get the best possible price. What you get is the 'trade price' for the house or flat; a price at which, as with the trade price in used cars, the company can sell on to make a profit. Although you will not get the highest price for your house, at least you will get something, and in certain circumstances, achieving a quick sale is preferable to having the property on the market for maybe years on end. Of course, the more problems the property possesses, the less you will get for it.

There have been several articles in the papers about home buying companies which offer very low prices indeed, so the thing is to contact several and see what they say.

The kind of properties which may be suitable for a quick sale include: very rundown, unmodernized or derelict properties; properties with sitting tenants; properties with unpaid debts; properties which are in unpopular locations; properties which have to be sold quickly after a bereavement to pay inheritance tax. It is not always possible to make loads of money from property and all experts in the game say the same thing: get rid of the dogs – even if you can't get a very good price for them, as it can take too much time and trouble to hang onto them.

4 Developing property

Watching amateur developers trying to make money from doing up derelict properties has become a hilarious television spectator sport, especially as they make every mistake going yet, by some miracle never fully explained, end up making money after all.

I suspect that the reason they appear to make money is because not all the figures are factored in. For instance, we never find out how much they have to pay estate agents, how much the repayments on their mortgage or loan cost, and how much capital gains tax they have to pay. Nor, as most of them seem to give up their jobs to do this developing, how much income they lose while 'developing'.

Not everything on 'reality' television is as real as it appears!

But outside the magic rectangle, how easy or difficult is it to make money by developing property?

Once again, it is all a matter of very careful number-crunching. You first have to discover, by diligent research, how much a property in good condition will fetch in a particular area, compared with a similar property in bad or derelict condition. The difference is not always great enough to make renovation worthwhile.

Then you have to work out the realistic price of developing. Most people completely underestimate just how much it will cost to renovate and how long it will take. You cannot always get builders just when you want them, and often, getting the relevant permissions from the local council takes months as well. Also, councils charge a lot of money (plus VAT) for giving planning permission.

Then there is the cost of the loan or mortgage to take into account, plus the buying and selling costs. Also, when you own a property, you become liable for council tax, service charges if you have bought an apartment, and utilities. These charges continue right up to the day you complete your sale.

Apart from this, you have the always unknown factor of house price fluctuations. There may be a sudden collapse in the market which will adversely affect the sale price of your development, however lovingly you have restored it.

Before ever developing a property, you have to consider how long you could keep it going if it took a year or more to sell. Sometimes you just have to hang in there until the right buyer happens along.

The other aspect to work out is the lowest possible price you could accept for the property and still make a profit. At times when the property market is static or falling, many people decide to rent out their newly-developed property until such time as the market picks up. So it is always worth checking out the rental market in your chosen area, to see whether this might provide a sensible fallback position if for some reason you are unable to sell on completion or for a price that will realize a profit.

Getting started

The first thing you have to do is target an area just starting to come up. This is identified by at least a few houses in the street having smart front doors, tidy front gardens, and expensive curtains, blinds or shutters at the windows. Another sign of regeneration is late-registration cars parked in the road.

One way of discovering a hotspot is to look at areas just next to those which have already come up. When I first bought a house in Richmond, Surrey, the surrounding suburbs such as Twickenham, East Sheen and Teddington were much cheaper and vastly less desirable. Nobody who was anybody would dream of living in Twickenham. But now, Twickenham and East Sheen are just as expensive as Richmond, although in my view nothing like as glamorous. Barnes, also in the borough of Richmond, has become ferociously expensive, as well.

To take another area I know well, when I first bought a flat in Worthing, West Sussex, nobody wanted to know. This dull, dismal town, Brighton's poor, plain sister, was full of decrepit old people and nursing homes. But then Brighton and Hove became a city and prices there soon went out of the price range of ordinary buyers. They came ever further along the coast – and discovered Worthing. Now, although it would be an exaggeration to say that Worthing rivals Brighton for style and flair, it is certainly getting there. Professional developers have targeted the town and are building high-spec new developments there; the first high-spec residences for 200 years, since Worthing first became a resort in the reign of King George III.

As a result, trendy shops are coming to the area, restaurants are opening up and, so I am told, the night life is improving.

Why is this all happening in Worthing? Simply because Brighton, apart from its high prices, is full up. There is nowhere for future developers to go in Brighton, and they are being forced further afield. Even Bognor Regis, long a joke town, is finally getting high-spec new apartments, for the same reason. When expensive areas are full up, or too pricey for the ordinary buyer, the place next door starts to be colonized by the people who would have bought in the trendy place, if they could have afforded it.

Spotting the next hotspot

Estate agent Lucy Winfield, who has been investigating future hotspots for the UKTV show *Property Prophets*, says: 'The first thing to look out for is skips in the street. This indicates that the regeneration process has at least started, and incomers are spending money on their properties.

'Then, when window boxes are being installed and plastic windows and doors are being replaced by wooden ones, you can be sure the area is coming up. Even if only one or two houses have been comprehensively gentrified in a particular street, you know that money is beginning to move in. Another unmistakable sign is that local newsagents are starting to sell more upmarket publications than before.'

The next thing to look out for is upmarket shops and supermarkets, such as Waitrose, Starbucks and M&S Simply Food coming to the area.

In London, after Clapham came up, buyers who couldn't afford Clapham bought next door in Balham. Now Balham is smart and becoming expensive. In other parts of the country, areas subject to government schemes, or where major developers are moving in, are sure signs of regeneration.

When developing for profit, be wary of houses that have been on the market for a long time, say a year, as this indicates there is not much profit, if any, to be made from developing. Houses and flats that can be turned round quickly for profit are snapped up very quickly indeed. There are a lot of people in this game, looking all the time!

If you are new to developing, it is better to go for something that simply needs updating, without incurring planning permission, rather than a total wreck which will need the whole complement of planners, architects, project managers, building trades, interior designers, landscape gardeners and the entire professional team.

The thing to look for when renovating or developing is rarity. Pretty Victorian and Georgian houses will always be worth renovating, as no more will be built, and they were the last attractive type of bulk housing to be erected. Edwardian, thirties and subsequent housing tends to be extremely ugly. But not all old housing stock is well built. The Victorians and Georgians were well used to jerry building, to putting houses up quickly, and in any case, the kind of building materials used in those days is no longer available.

Then areas ripe for regeneration or rapid growth have, in themselves, to have something special. Obviously in Britain there is a limited amount of coastline, and figures from the Land Registry show that seafront homes have increased in value far more than any other type of housing, since 1990.

Otherwise, an area has to have natural beauty, or be very near offices, factories or other significant places of work. Or it has to be an area specifically targeted for regeneration such as Gateshead, next to Newcastle on Tyne. When I lived in Newcastle, most of Gateshead was extremely run down. Now it is vibrant, attractive and buzzy.

Areas next to existing hotspots will also never be the next big thing unless they can offer facilities such as good schools, good transport links, good shops, good restaurants and lack of crime. Particularly lack of crime. In fact, high crime rates are probably the biggest reason nowadays for areas to be shunned by people with money and taste – the sort you need to attract to your newly developed property. People will only buy in a surrounding area if that area can offer a good lifestyle in itself – not just because it is next door.

The next thing, again before you buy or even make an offer, is to get some ballpark figures from builders as to renovation costs. Mainly, these estimates will not involve painting and decorating. It is not worth doing a place up cheaply and badly, as it will always lose out on survey if it has serious damp, subsidence or needs a new roof. If buyers cannot get a mortgage, they will not be able to buy, and they will only be able to get a mortgage if the lender approves the property for the loan in question.

Then there is the garden to think about, plus presenting the house to your target market. Everything costs, and adds up, and when time is important, costs can soon mount up. When renovating your own home, you can get things done gradually; when developing for profit, you do not have the luxury of time.

When doing costing, always round UP the figures rather than down. Also allow for council tax, utilities, interest on the loan and incidentals such as new windows, a new front door or new locks, plus, as always, service charges if buying a leasehold apartment.

It is also worth going into some local agents and finding out how quickly places are selling, how long they hang around, which kind of properties are the most popular, and whether designed properties go for significantly more than those in their raw or dingy state.

The only way to property develop, on an amateur scale, is to undertake meticulous research. You have to know for sure that you can add significant value.

Finance

Unless you have the money sitting in the bank, you will have to get a loan or mortgage and the most obvious way of raising the money is to release equity in your main home and remortgage. If you do not already own a home you will have to buy the property on an ordinary mortgage, which might be difficult if you do not ever intend to live there yourself and are just developing. You will almost certainly have to find a large deposit.

And do not forget that remortgaging comes at extra cost. You have to pay a fee to remortgage and may also have to pay a penalty for withdrawing early from the original mortgage.

The television property finance expert Alvin Hall advises against borrowing from family or friends, which is often recommended on expensive property seminars for people with no cash resources of their own. It is never a good idea anyway to borrow the deposit to buy property as the interest repayments are too high to make it worthwhile financially.

You can now get specialist loans for bridging, investment and refurbishment; in fact, finance for all types of property improvement such as developments, conversions, buy-to-sell and buy-to-let. Again, it is a matter of working out the interest payable and adding this onto the other costs, before making an offer. You also need to discover how much it costs for a short-term loan such as a bridging loan. Mostly, short-term loans for investment and refurbishment have much higher interest rates than ordinary mortgages, which are payable over a long period, usually 25 years.

The reason short-term loans are more expensive is that, over 25 years, you pay an enormous amount of interest on a mortgage. Although it seems a cheap loan, interest adds up over such a long period, and mortgage lenders, peculiarly enough, do not like to forgo any tiny bit of interest due to them.

So expect that borrowing will be much more expensive for developing or investing than when buying to let or buying your own home.

Which improvements add value?

In any street or any area, there is always a ceiling, a maximum that people are prepared to pay. If you are selling one house and buying another, it may not matter too much if you take a low offer on the house you are selling, and make an equally low offer on the one you are buying, as the two things even out.

When developing, this doesn't happen. You have to maximize your profit in every way you can, and do not want to put yourself in such a position that you have to accept a low offer. In areas of low wages, that ceiling may be very low, so it makes sense not to decorate or refurbish it beyond what the market can afford. If considering developing in a particular area, it is worth finding out beforehand what the average wages and salaries are, and what the average mortgage is, as well. When my son Will and his family were looking at three-bedroom houses in Peckham, London SE15, with a view to buying, they found that they were all on the market at around £250,000. At prices between £245,000 and £250,000, they were soon snapped up; a house on at £275,000, much larger than the others and with a big garden, lingered on the market for many months. When Will offered £250,000 the offer was gratefully accepted right away. From that, you can learn that £250,000 was the most buyers were prepared to pay in that area – mainly because although targeted for regeneration, Peckham and Nunhead still have a very long way to go before they become expensive and chi-chi.

One reason for the prices sticking at this level was that the only interested buyers were young families and first-time buyers who were very limited in the amounts of money they could raise. And the significance of the £250,000 limit was that stamp duty thresholds increase at this amount. Where the upper price limit nudges dangerously close to a change in stamp duty thresholds, there is little chance of buyers offering over the amount where they would have to pay more to the Treasury.

Where prices are way above these thresholds anyway, the stamp duty amount is not a decisive factor. Buyers interested in a £1 million-plus house are not that concerned about stamp duty levels.

But where there is no hope of attracting higher-level buyers to an area, there is little point in developing to beyond the limit – as nobody would pay it. Richer people would seek out trendier areas anyway.

Note: if an area gets a bad reputation for having a high crime rate and street violence, this will damage its reputation for many years after this is no longer the case. A bad reputation sticks to areas for very many decades, and it is hard to reverse it, whatever the reality.

Where there is a profit margin, the following improvements will add value: power shower, central heating (essential – NEVER put in horrible storage heaters to save money), new kitchen and bathroom and, most of all these days, off-street parking. People will pay a lot, do a lot for off-street parking, especially now that most built-up areas have restricted parking and in any case, very few urban areas have allocated parking. In Brighton, for instance, it has become almost impossible to park, and in some areas of London, garages and off-road parking spaces are changing hands for £100,000 or more, so valuable have they become.

Gardens are an asset for some sectors of the market. They are essential for young families, but very optional indeed for singles, young couples or even older couples.

Renovating and developing are great fun, which is why so many people like to do it. I find renovating totally addictive and just love it. But sometimes I have to be aware that, by renovating, I am actually pricing the place out of the current market, and there is actually no way of making a quick profit.

The real problem with amateur developing is the need to sell on quickly, as the only real way to make money is to be able to hang on until the market is at its peak for selling. Some people worry that by the time their property has reached its ceiling price, the décor will no longer be so fresh and new, especially if they are forced to rent it out in the meantime, to cover running and loan costs. In an ideal world, you would buy a wreck and then just sit on it until the market was ready, then renovate. Most ordinary people could not afford to do this, but it is how big property developers make their money.

Many very rich property developers I know buy sites, or derelict developments, then wait years before putting them back on the market.

Buying land

The plethora of television programmes about property development has made many people imagine that the only way to 'develop' is to buy a tatty old home that you turn into something wonderful. The great majority of shows have concentrated on this aspect of developing because, again, it is something everybody understands, and it is visually interesting.

But property development can also be about buying land for development; land on which nothing has yet been built. Here, you buy a stake in the land which then increases greatly in value when houses are built on it. You as the investor do not buy the actual houses, or plots on which they will be built, but only the land.

Over the past few years, a number of companies have sprung up offering land investments, but as with any other investment, you are taking the risk that the land will eventually be approved for building on; otherwise, it is not likely to increase greatly in value, especially if there is no profitable use to which it can be put in the meantime.

The way it works is that the original landowner takes investment advice before a sale is made, and makes sure they sell at a profit. They will also try to seek a slice of future profit when the land is used for building.

Land with development potential is usually sold with uplift. This technical term means that the original landowner receives a proportion of any future increase in land value if planning permission is achieved. The value of residential land has increased by 926 per cent since 1985, and presently, over 3.2 million new homes are required in the UK over the next 18 years. There are companies who buy tranches of land and then try to interest investors in theoretical parcels of it. You buy a 'share' in the land in much the same way that you might buy a share in Marks and Spencer, for instance, in that you do not own an actual slice of the real estate, the clothes or any of the retail goods, just a share in any profits the company might make.

Such companies also make the point that the richest people in the country are usually landowners or property developers. Well, you can't argue with that as it is demonstrably true!

Here are some figures: in 1983, land in Inner and Outer London cost £759,000 per hectare; 20 years later its value had risen to £5,493,000 per hectare. Land in Wales in 1983 cost £85,000 per hectare; in 2003, its value had risen to £980,000 per hectare.

But it is all a complicated matter. You cannot just go somewhere in the UK, buy a field off a farmer and then guarantee to make a huge profit when houses are built on this land. Although the UK is undergoing a massive residential expansion, and new housing seems to be going up everywhere, it is not quite what it seems. The focus in many parts of the country is on affordable housing, and providing homes for key workers at rock-bottom prices. Areas on which building is likely to take place can only be in those places that can sustain significant increase in population. Brighton, for instance, is 'full' and there is a serious problem with water shortages. This in any case limits the amount of new housing that can go up in the area, whether it is 'full' or not.

There also have to be good enough roads to take the extra traffic, schools, hospitals, public transport and other facilities.

Katherine Lewis, senior partner at Hayden James Land Acquisitions, believes that buying land as an investment can be very difficult if you are doing it on your own. She says the secret of successful investment in this daunting sector – hedged in as it is by political considerations, protests by residents and pressure groups, vested interests by local councils and possible shortage of essential facilities such as water, gas and electricity (or the difficulty of laying pipes) – is to use a land banking company which offers land plots for sale and releases freehold title deeds to the plots. You as the investor need to know that all the necessary services will be laid on, as well as planning permission for profitable building.

'Land-banking' is the term given to the strategic acquisition of land parcels in advance of expanding urbanization.

These are some of the things you need to know if interested in investing in land (which saves you all the hassle of actually buying or building a house for investment).

In the UK, it is now law that on many, if not most, sites, around 28 to 32 per cent of a development should be allocated to affordable housing. The idea also is that no specific development should become a cheap housing ghetto, but the prime-price housing should be mixed in with the 'affordable' or cheap housing. New developments in future must consist of mixed housing and not just detached four-bedroom homes with beautifully landscaped gardens.

So far as location is concerned, the land must be next to an existing development, as this is how new developments work. As an investor, you need to know that the land is highly likely to be developed for proper residential use.

You also have to know that the roads and highways will be able to cope with increased volume of traffic. Also, how is the site being sold – for investment, or self-build? In the main, self-build cannot be considered primarily an investment. Although you may make money, you must not be seen to be self-building primarily for profit.

Buying land as an investment only works when the entire site is sold to one developer, rather than dozens of individual self-builders.

You must also know what the projected timescales are. Although these are notoriously elastic in the building trades, experts in this business advise that timescales vary from 8 to 20 years in the future. So you could be looking at a long time before your investment pays off.

Then, before signing up with a land company, you need to know that the projected returns are based on true market values rather than land values. The market value is the value once the affordable housing, services, roads and so on have been deducted from the return.

It is also essential to know whether the local sewage works can cope with the extra population in the area. If the capacity is considered insufficient, the projected development will not be allowed to proceed until the plant is upgraded and expanded. The costs of upgrading the sewage plant will also affect the final market value.

So – a lot to think about, especially for amateur part-time investors.

Other questions you must have answers to include: does the development company use a local planning team? Local knowledge is important when trying to build a rapport with local departments.

Are you provided with an individual freehold deed for each plot of land purchased? If the land company only registers your interest in their books, you could end up with nothing if the company goes bust.

Is each project self-funding? You need to know who is going to pay for planning consent, at £200,000 minimum.

Financing the investment is also complicated. Most land companies retain financial experts who will advise on the best means of financing the investment. Options include a fixed-term loan and remortgaging.

As we said earlier, when one type of investment has reached its peak, the smart money goes on to another type of investment. Investing in land, rather than the actual housing, is relatively new, at least so far as the ordinary, small-time investor is concerned, and definitely worth considering at times when it is becoming increasingly difficult to make significant profits from ordinary developing, given the very high cost of purchasing developable properties in the first place.

Caution!

Very often, huge returns are promised when buying agricultural land for future housing developments. A large field that costs £100,000 in its raw state can be worth £2 million-plus once planning permission is granted, say promoters of these schemes which, typically, parcel up a couple of acres into small plots for investors putting up between £5,000 and £10,000 each. Exhibitors at property shows are currently pushing this investment option hard.

But unless you know for sure that planning permission has been, or soon will be, granted, you are advised to stay away from the hype. Otherwise, this is the most speculative type of property investment of all, with a very high failure rate if permission is not granted, or not likely to be granted within your lifetime. Without such permission already in place, the land remains virtually worthless.

The Campaign to Protect Rural England (CPRE) has issued a very stern cautionary note to anybody considering investing in 'land-banking'. They say that hundreds of pieces of English countryside are currently being sold directly to the public as a 'supposedly sure-fire' way of making large amounts of money. The operators, continues the CPRE, sell the land in tiny plots on the basis that its value is bound to rise one day. The thing is, 'that day' may not be in the investor's lifetime.

In the meantime, the sites in question are often divided up into plots by stakes and fencing, which look unsightly and so long as the land is undeveloped, there is no incentive to look after the land. The CPRE also points out that even if planning permission for new homes is eventually obtained, the developer would then have to negotiate with dozens of small plot owners, and it could be difficult to trace them all.

The CPRE says that land-banking operators typically buy farmland or woodland that is not zoned for a change of use, and then divide it up into small plots only large enough for a single house. Then they sell the land using the internet, at a much higher price than it was originally purchased. The CPRE also maintains that high-pressure sales techniques are used, and recommends that the Office of Fair Trading should investigate all sales claims of these operations. There is, it says, no documented case of any plot sold by a land-banking company ever receiving planning permission.

Land-banking schemes are not illegal but they are not regulated by the Financial Services Authority, which makes them even more risky. This means that if you put a deposit down on a rural plot, you have no right to a refund or statutory cooling-off period of 28 days.

Some land-banking operations have been closed down by the Department for Business, Innovation and Skills as they were found to be operating illegal collective investment schemes. As a result, land-bankers nowadays state in their brochures that they do not operate collective investments.

If you are interested in investing in land-banking, you need to make sure that planning permission either has been or will be granted. For this, you would need to do intensive research with the relevant local authority planning department, rather than just go by the say-so of the land-bankers.

Land-bankers tend to sell greenfield sites, when it is official government policy to use previously developed land within urban areas for rebuilding wherever possible. Although there will obviously be some green-belt land used for housing, is there any guarantee that your plot will fall into this category? You need to know that there is before putting your £10,000 (a typical sum) down on a land-banked plot.

It may also be worth considering agricultural land as an investment. Prime agricultural land is, at the time of writing, worth between £5,000 and £8,000 an acre. The way to invest here is to buy the land, then hang onto it until the price goes up. There is little money to be made from leasing agricultural land to a local farmer and yields are as little as 1 to 2 per cent. Andrew Shirley, Knight Frank's expert on farmland, explains: 'This is an investment you would buy for capital growth, not yield. You are certainly not going to lose when buying land, although it may take a decade or more to realize a reasonable profit.

'The land is bought freehold and the major advantage is that no inheritance tax is payable on this kind of investment. You could also buy amenity land in the expectation that it will be built on one day, although this strategy can be high risk for the small investor.'

Loans and mortgages are available for land purchase, whether agricultural or amenity land.

Another option is to buy a farm with a sitting tenant, as you will be paying below market value, in exactly the same way that you would buy a house or flat more cheaply if it contained a sitting tenant who was a controlled tenant and therefore could not be evicted.

As Andrew Shirley points out: 'With land, as with a house, you would gain an uplift of at least 100 per cent when the tenant leaves, although you could have a long wait.'

Buying at auction

Ever more people are buying investment and development properties at auction, especially as there are now a number of mortgage companies offering specialized 'auction finance'. The usual offer is of 70 per cent of the valuation or purchase price, whichever is the lower, or 100 per cent finance with proof of additional security, such as a large amount of equity in your main home.

Cash deposits are not allowed in auction sales, because of the risk of money laundering, and all finance must be in place beforehand. The time between making a successful bid and having to complete the deal is usually 20 working days, and as most mortgage lenders take far longer than this to process a deal, you would need to find out in advance whether you can borrow the amount of money needed. And don't forget that most auction properties need work after purchase, and you would have to find the finance for renovation as well as the purchase.

You have to hand over 10 per cent deposit of the hammer price immediately after the sale, plus the auctioneer's fee of, typically, £175.

By far the greatest majority of properties bought at auction are those which need some work – usually a lot of work. Either that, or they are repossessions, or contain sitting tenants paying a peppercorn rent, who can never be evicted. There is usually some significant reason why a property goes up for auction, which is that it cannot easily be sold any other way.

Very many professional builders and developers buy at auction, so you are competing against skilled and wily operators.

Again, on television, we have seen amateur property developers buying at auction who then find they cannot make any real money at all once the property is theirs. You need to know just how much you can get on the open market for a developed property, as costs can easily run away with you. Also, people get carried away by bidding at auctions, where the 'guide price' given on the catalogue is usually the starting, rather than the finishing, price. Very often there will be a reserve on the property, which is about the same as the guide price. So always expect to pay more than the price listed in the catalogue.

Most catalogues have a little 'plus' sign next to the guide price, which is your indication that the hammer price is expected to exceed the catalogue price. If the hammer price wildly exceeds the loan or mortgage you have secured, you will have to find the finance in another way, usually by a horribly expensive bridging loan. There will also be another arrangement fee to arrange any extra finance.

Example: Robert bought a totally derelict studio flat at auction for £46,000. It was so derelict it did not even have an electricity supply or a working toilet. The flat was in a listed building, so required listed building consent as well as ordinary planning consent.

Although the studio looked easy enough to modernize and renovate, in fact it turned out to be a terrible job. Robert was prevented by the council from starting work until all the listed building consents were in place, and this took months as the applications had to be sent round to every resident in the block and also posted on lamp posts in the area.

Another complication was that wiring and cables for the whole building ran through the flat. Instead of boxing these in, Robert cut through them, thereby cutting off the entryphone and telephone systems for the entire building. BT charged £3,000 for repairs.

All the time work was not proceeding, Robert had to pay service charges on the flat plus interest on his loan. In the end, the work cost £15,000, excluding decoration, furnishings or appliances, bringing his total outlay up to £61,000. Add on another £5,000 at least for other costs and we are up to £66,000. Such studios, in good condition, fetched between £75,000 and £80,000, so for all that work and effort – by the time the permissions were through and the flat was finished – Robert had owned it for six months, and would get, at best, a clear profit of £10,000.

If he rented it out, at, say, £400 a month, this would bring him in a gross rent of £4,800 a year. Take off service charges (£800), letting fee (£564) and mortgage or loan repayments, and it is hardly looking like a good investment.

Don't forget either, that council tax becomes payable on an empty or uninhabited flat after a period of time. Councils vary in their time limits but eventually you will have to start paying, even if the property is still unfinished.

By contrast, John and Diane Edwards, featured on the television series *Homes Under the Hammer*, have successfully bought two properties at auction, both in Wales. The first one cost £24,500 to buy, and they spent £5,000 on materials for renovation. Two years later, the property was valued at £70,000. Their second auction property cost £32,000 and they spent £8,000 on renovation. That was valued at £50,000 a year later.

The secret of making money from cheap properties bought at auction is, the couple believe, to do most of the work themselves and treat it as a business. John says: 'We will take on projects only if the figures add up. When buying at auction, I ask the agent for the "out" price – what the house would be worth when renovated. I then work out how much it would cost me to do it, and that fixes my limit.'

Buying at auction is always fun and exciting, but seasoned operators in the game stress that it is not a soft option. The competition from other bidders, the need to work out very specific figures, including interest payable on short-term loans and the cost of renovation, all have to be carefully calculated before making a bid. It is always a good idea, if you are new to auction buying, to attend a couple of sales as a spectator, before attending for real.

Also, always view the property before making a bid. Auction sales do have viewings, but they are usually block viewings, for a couple of hours or so only. It is rare that agents will take time to show you individually round a property coming up for auction.

When buying at auction, you will need to provide identification, such as: current passport, full UK driving licence, HM Revenue and Customs Tax Notification or Firearms Certificate (!). You will also have to provide evidence of your permanent address with a council tax bill valid for the current year, original mortgage statement from a UK lender, a utility bill issued to your address within the last three months, or again, a full driving licence, although you cannot produce the driving licence for both requirements. You need two separate acceptable documents.

So what can you get at auction? There is, nowadays, the whole range of property, from houses with vacant possession, to flats with and without vacant possession, to land, with or without planning permission, garages, flats above shops, commercial property, sites for development, ground rents, freeholds, property both in the UK and overseas, timeshares, newbuilds, and land with planning permission for use as holiday homes.

It used to be the case that only terrible properties were sold at auction, but now sellers have realized that they can often get MORE at auction, either from bids on the actual day, or sealed bids beforehand, than they can on the open market.

A friend put his garage, sale value through estate agents around £7,000, up for auction, where it went for more than double as a result of fierce bidding for this very rare product in a built-up area.

Personal experience of buying at auction

In June 2006, I bought a piece of land for £12,000 at auction. It was a truly terrifying experience. The auction, held at Eastbourne Town Hall, was absolutely packed, with standing room only. I soon realized that many people were there simply for a day out, not to bid for lots.

We bidders had to register in advance of the sale and were given a card bearing a bidder number, which we had to raise up high in the air when bidding. When my lot came up, I was shaking with fear and fright but I finally managed to secure it against two other bidders. The land in question was an area of 'amenity land' behind our apartment building, and was advertised as being suitable for five or six car parking spaces. My job was to buy the land for the building, on behalf of the residents, to prevent this use.

The minute the hammer came down, the land was mine and I had to go straight away to a table where the estate agents sat, and put down a 10 per cent deposit. I also had to produce two different proofs of identification, my passport and a recent utility bill, and sign the document which meant that contracts had been exchanged. I walked away in a dream.

Later, when I spoke to auction specialists Andrews and Robertson, they said this shaking was common, in fact so common that often, successful bidders could not legibly sign the documents. Make no mistake, auctions are highly stressful events – for everybody.

I would now advise anybody interested in buying at auction to attend a few such sales first, as a spectator, to see how they operate. The auctioneer is usually something of a performer and entertains the audience at the same time as trying to get the highest price for each lot. At the sale I attended, I would say that 75 per cent of the lots were withdrawn as they did not come up to the guide price. I later learned that it is extremely rare for all lots to be sold at auction.

When trying to buy at property auction sales, you have to be prepared to lose the property you set your heart on, as until bidding starts, you have no idea who might be bidding against you, or how far rival bidders will go.

Nowadays, there will be auction finance and mortgage specialists in attendance at such sales and they will be able to arrange bridging or other suitable loans for buyers. But the 10 per cent deposit has to be available and paid there and then. I paid £2,000 to secure the land and the rest of the money had to be paid within three weeks.

Distressed assets

It's an ill wind that blows nobody any good, as the old saying has it.

Since the credit crunch of 2008, when many heavily geared property investors, developers and others were unable to pay their mortgages or loans went under, a vast amount of properties known as 'distressed assets' have come onto the market. These are, typically, properties bought as investments where the rent has nowhere near covered mortgages and other outgoings, and which have been repossessed by the banks or other lenders who wish to offload them as quickly as possible.

Distressed assets are defined as those assets that have to be sold at much less than their actual market value in order to be sold at all and, in fact, 'assets' is completely the wrong word for them as they have become utter liabilities.

There are now a number of companies specializing in offering distressed assets for sale, allegedly at prices of up to 50 per cent below market value. These properties, which are sourced and bought by these new companies, are then sold to investors who have the cash resources to make a killing. In order to benefit from a distressed asset, you must put down at least 25 per cent deposit of the purchase price in cash and be able to service interest rates of at least 5 per cent.

One such company, www.uk-property-repossessions.com says that it looks for a minimum of 30 per cent reduction in value, only buys properties which are already in good condition and ready to rent out, and will only buy if the gross rental yield works out at 8 per cent or more. In fact, unless the gross yield is at least 8 per cent you will lose on the property as by the time you have factored in lost interest on your 25 per cent or more cash deposit, the commission to the distressed asset company and the ongoing costs of your purchase, your outgoings will exceed your income. You also need to know for sure that the distressed properties actually will produce the advertised rent, and that you will not be left with long void periods where you have no income at all.

Some companies are also offering 'distressed assets' seminars around the country and these are replacing the highly expensive property seminars that focused more or less exclusively on new-build and off-plan properties bought supposedly at a discount – but which were then frequently found to be worth much less than the purchase price, and in many cases, could not be resold at anything like the amounts promised by the developers or property clubs.

Let's hope the burgeoning distressed assets industry doesn't go the same way!

Of course it is always possible to buy a distressed asset yourself, usually at auction but sometimes sold by high street estate agents, although the big question always is: how do you know it is 'distressed'? The usual definition of a distressed asset is one that has to be sold below its actual value because the owner can no longer afford to keep it. The expectation is that distressed property assets will start to rise in value as soon as somebody buys them – although that cannot be guaranteed.

But there are also opportunities in a financial downturn to buy a bargain that is not exactly a 'distressed asset' but which the owners are desperate to sell. During 2009, vendors who were prepared to slash up to 25 per cent off the asking price of their property, compared with its estimated value in 2007, found ready and willing buyers. Here are some examples: a property originally on the market at £600,000 in West Hampstead, London, eventually sold for £390,000. The owners had no choice but to keep slashing the price as they had already moved from London to Derbyshire, where they had taken up new jobs. They could maybe have rented it out but, in this case, preferred a lump sum of cash rather than the drip-drip of monthly rents and all the hassle of renting out a property at long distance.

Another property, in Holloway, North London, was originally on the market for £530,000 and eventually went for £450,000. At the higher end of the market, agents were seeing properties valued at £1.5 to £2.5 million, go for 25 per cent less than the original asking price. In most cases, these vendors were also able to buy their next house at a similarly reduced level, so it came to the same thing, but if you were an investor with cash sitting in the bank, this was clearly the time to pounce.

If you are tempted to sign up with a company specializing in acquiring properties at bargain prices, make sure you add up all the figures before deciding whether or not any particular property constitutes a bargain, and do not allow yourself to be beguiled by such empty inducements as 'offered at 50 per cent below market value'. The market value is nothing more or less than what you can get for it. If its market value is 50 per cent more, why is nobody prepared to pay the extra 50 per cent? That is the question you must always ask.

Sometimes, the property is sold at a reduced rate because it has to be sold quickly to realize whatever sum of money it can, and its owners simply cannot afford to keep it on the market any longer than absolutely necessary. But even when this is the situation you as the new purchaser need to know that it represents a bargain for you.

Extra costs involved in buying a distressed asset may involve a big fat fee to the sourcing company, a mortgage arrangement fee, service charges on the property if it is an apartment, legal fees, agent's fees for letting and managing the property, ground rent, council tax and utility bills during void periods and also refurbishment and furnishing costs. Sometimes these costs and fees are higher than for ordinary properties, and the mortgage arrangement fee for a distressed asset can come to 5 per cent of the entire loan, as it is seen as a higher risk than usual to the lenders. This means that on a mortgage of £80,000, you would be paying an arrangement fee of £4,000 – money right down the drain and irrecoverable.

You may discover that once all the nasty sneaky figures have been taken into account, the property does not look such an unmissable bargain after all. Plus, if the property is in an area unknown to you, make sure you visit the place yourself and snoop around, rather than just taking the acquisition company's say-so that it is in a great location where renters are fighting to pay over the odds.

Some investors are tempted to buy-up properties in areas completely unknown to them because they seem cheap but, always, things are cheap for a reason and this applies to properties as much as any other commodity.

Sealed bids

It is becoming ever more common to buy property via sealed bids. But is this a good idea for investors?

Nicola Oddy, of Stacks Property Search and Acquisition, who is based in Cornwall, a popular place for sealed bids, has this advice: 'With sealed bids, buyers are effectively buying blind. Because of the existence of the sealed bid, they are tempted to put in an offer much higher than the asking or guide price, simply so that they can secure it. This means they risk paying way above the true value.

'The risk for vendors is that a couple of days after the potential purchaser puts in the sealed bid, he gets cold feet and withdraws, usually because of rumours that there was a huge gap between the top and runner-up bid.

'So this means that vendors have to go back on the market, and all the initial excitement has fallen away. By this time the original bidders have fallen away as well and are no longer interested. This means other purchasers think there is something wrong with the property as it has been on the market for a long time.'

Nicola's advice for anybody tempted by a property that has gone to sealed bids, is:

▌ Try to get the vendor to accept an offer before it goes to sealed bids.

▌ If not, make your bid the top price you would be comfortable paying, rather than what you think you need to bid to secure the property.

▌ Dress up your offer in terms of a quick exchange and flexibility of terms (this is always a good investment strategy anyway).

▌ Get a survey done before the date for sealed bids so that your offer is not subject to survey.

▌ Try to get as much information as possible from the agent, such as how many other bidders there are, what else they have been looking at, and how much interest there is generally in the property.

▌ If you do make a sealed bid offer, drive it to the agent, obtain a receipt and if possible, sit there while they open it.

Conversions and change of use

Many people, on seeing a large derelict property on the market, immediately think: conversions. Although there is certainly a lot of money to be made from turning a large derelict house into flats – professional builders are doing it all the time – it is difficult for the first-time amateur to work out all the costs involved. Also, such projects almost always go over schedule and over budget.

In general, big conversion jobs are something best left to established firms of builders, as you not only need planning permission, but have to assemble a professional team who will, between them, be able to do everything required and also work their way through the maze of planning requirements. Then you have to liaise at an early stage with a firm of estate agents, who can start to market the conversions, starting with the show home, and proceed to sell the rest off-plan. It is a daunting prospect for the well-meaning but inexperienced property investor. The best advice is: start small, and if you are successful and discover a flair for this hands-on type of investing, proceed from there.

The first thing you have to think about is how you would fund such a project; second, and vitally, is there already outline planning permission?

A good tip is that you should never buy a derelict property such as an old pub, or farm outbuildings, with the idea of turning them into apartments or habitable homes, without knowing for a certainty that planning permission has been, or will be, granted. Do not ever expect that permission will automatically be granted. Councils are peculiar animals, as I know from my long fight with Richmond Council to get permission for two parking spaces – which were already there – in front of my own house.

Tip: whenever trying to get planning permission for a project, always make an appointment to see the council official concerned. Do not try to do everything by letter. Once the council planning people actually see and meet you, they can change their minds, particularly if you have good plans already drawn up – NOT scrawled on the back of an envelope – and can put a good case for permission being granted. It's often assumed that local councils are just faceless organizations, but this is not true. Once you get a human being on your side, it's amazing what they will agree to.

This is particularly important if you are considering turning former business or commercial premises into residential dwellings or holiday homes, as it can be a long, hard struggle to persuade councils that you are going to turn a former eyesore into something beautiful and useful.

Listed buildings

There are around half a million listed buildings in the UK, which are subject to special rules and planning consents that make them more difficult to develop and renovate than other properties.

To address the specific problems of listed buildings, Peter Anslow founded the Listed Property Owners' Club in 1994. For a fee of £55, members can access information sheets, legal and specialist advice, specialist insurance and a bi-monthly magazine. The Club will also advise on grants and matters such as VAT, which is zero-rated on some aspects of renovation, but not others. For instance, if you want to put in new alterations in a listed building, this is zero-rated for VAT, but repairs and maintenance – an ongoing task with listed buildings – attracts VAT. It is the other way round from what it should be, but there you go.

There are grants available for improvements to listed buildings; we, the residents, managed to get two improvement grants for a listed building from the local council, and there are also lottery grants available. But they are rare, hard to come by, and you have to be able to put forward a very good case indeed.

The Listed Property Owners' Club can help you round the maze of improving these buildings. They can be contacted on 01795 8449398; e-mail: info@listedpropertyownersclub.co.uk.

If you like the idea of a listed building, you must be certain that every alteration and addition was authorized by the local council's conservation officer. If not, you would be liable for the cost of correcting them, regardless of who commissioned them, or when. There is no time limit on the enforcement of such repairs or alterations.

Advice from the Listed Property Owners' Club is that you should, wherever possible, use a solicitor who has specific experience of listed buildings. At the very least, you should inform your solicitor that the building you are buying is listed and it is up to the solicitor to make sure you are aware of any potential liability for what previous owners may have done to the building.

New rules on home extensions

If you do not own a listed building, you may be glad to hear that the rules have been relaxed for homeowners wanting to add a conservatory or extension to their property. In many cases, you will no longer need planning permission although you should always contact your local authority to see whether permission is needed in your case. As planning permission can cost up to £1,000 and involve an eight to 16 week wait, this is good news. It is also the case that householders will no longer need special permission to put up solar panels or wind turbines. This does not, however, apply to listed buildings or conservation areas.

However, if you want to construct a loft extension, you could find this harder as these will be decided in future on their position in the roof rather than the actual size of the planned extension.

Note: if using a reputable conservatory or loft extension company, they should be up to date with all the new rules and regulations on home extensions. If they don't seem to know, walk away and contact another company.

An interactive guide prepared by the Department of Communities and Local Government has been designed to help people who want to improve their home and to discover whether or not they may need planning permission for their extension or other improvement. The government's website, www.planningportal.gov.uk/uploads/hhg/houseguide.html guides people round the new rules and covers everything from driveways, garages, hedges and conservatories to lofts and other planned extensions.

Click on the part of the house you are thinking of changing and a pop-up explains all the new rules.

This information is extremely useful for investors as extensions and conversions are usually cited as the best way to increase the value of a property, and the new rules are particularly helpful when it comes to extending and improving smaller properties such as terraced houses, which are the most popular types of property bought by amateur developers. Relaxation of the former draconian rules may also encourage more people to develop and improve existing properties.

5 Holiday lets

Holiday cottages and holiday lets are very different from buy-to-let in that they are considered a commercial business, rather than unearned income. Also, there are very different arrangements concerning tenure, since holiday lets are not considered housing, as such.

Holiday lets, tax-wise, fall into much the same category as having a car-hire or boat-hire business.

With buy-to-let, you are entering into complicated landlord and tenant regulations, which do not apply with holiday lets. Even so, there are stringent tax, insurance and letting considerations; most holiday let companies issue fat books of rules and regulations to owners which must be complied with before they will take your cottage onto their books. Some of these are legal requirements, such as health and safety matters, while others are simply operating rules to ensure the smooth running of the business.

Some people find that it is easier to invest in holiday lets than buy-to-let, since the considerations of unpaid rent, evicting bad tenants, problems on return of tenants' deposits, whether to furnish or not, simply do not arise, as you are providing somebody with a holiday, not an essential roof over their heads. You could, theoretically, let the same property as a holiday let or an assured shorthold let, but the two types of stay come under completely different rules. Holiday lets are a specialized business and it is rare for the same agents to handle both types of business, although this is now starting to happen.

Holiday lets are always fully furnished, all the rent plus deposit is taken upfront, and the length of stay is clearly spelt out in the letting agreement. Once the letting period has expired, the holidaymaker simply leaves. You, the owner, provide everything and the guest hands over a wodge of money in return. Obviously, there are rules regarding breakages and damage, and these are set out in the agreement, but when damages occur, the deposit, or part of it, is simply not returned. It is unusual for holiday lets to get into long wrangles and legal disputes, and this is another reason why some people prefer the quick turnover of holiday guests to the hassle of long-stay tenants.

In order to count as a holiday let, a property cannot be let to the same person for more than a month, it must be available for holidays for 140 days a year, and actually let for at least 70 of these days. The same tax and investment rules also apply to caravans, mobile homes and park homes let out on a holiday basis. The main difference between holiday cottages, and caravans or mobile homes, is that the former increase in value over time (you hope), whereas the latter depreciate fast. As such, with caravans, recreational park homes and (static) mobile homes, or immobile homes, all the value of the investment is realized in rentals; with bricks-and-mortar cottages, you have two possible investment streams.

For most owners, there are two ways of playing the holiday lets game: you either buy purely as an investment, or you buy the place as your own holiday home and make it pay for itself when you are not in residence yourself. Because it is difficult to make a good income from lettings alone, most owners take the attitude that the lettings will enable the cottage to cover its costs, be available for their own use, and appreciate in value. But if you go through a letting agency, which most cottage owners do, you will find it is not available for your own use during high season – the very times you might want to use it yourself. Many agencies will even not take your cottage on if you want it yourself during high season, as that is when they, as well as you, make most of the yearly income.

Some agencies may even charge you for using your own cottage! In general terms, if an agency takes over your cottage, it will not be available for your own use between May and September.

Many people imagine holiday cottages to be sweet little secluded hideaway gingerbread houses, with thatched roofs and roses round the door. But these days, the holiday lettings business includes designer apartments, modern bungalows, terraced houses in towns and almost any kind of property – so long as it is situated in a place where people want to take holidays.

The term 'cottage' is used very loosely, and can encompass grand mansions and huge farmhouses as well as studio flats suitable for one or two people.

In recent years, the holiday lettings business has become extremely sophisticated and streamlined and if you are interested in this kind of investment, you can get advice on where to buy, how to finance the purchase and how to furnish and equip it for maximum return.

Marsdens Cottage Holidays have been operating in North Devon since the early 1970s and have the whole holiday lettings business down to a fine art. They will advise on every aspect of the business, including what to purchase – so long as you are interested in North Devon, of course.

Director Janet Cornwell said: 'We can advise on the best areas to concentrate on, depending on whether you want the cottage purely for business or partly for your own use. We are in touch with most local estate agents, and can say whether a particular property is likely to prove a good holiday let. Once we take on a cottage, we take it over. We can find housekeepers, gardeners, plumbers and other tradespeople, as we all live in the area ourselves, and we also give a star rating to your cottage depending on how it is furnished and what facilities it offers.'

As with hotels, the more stars, the more expensive the cottage.

The star rating, from one to five, does not depend on the size of the property, but how coordinated, comfortable and 'designer-y' it is. For instance, a cottage awarded one star will be in good condition, but there may be signs of wear and tear and the furniture will not necessarily be new or coordinated. Crockery and cutlery may not match. A five-star property, by contrast, will have new, expensive and coordinated soft furnishings and carpets. With a one-star property, guests may not be met personally but will be told where to find a key; with a five-star property, guests are personally greeted on arrival and there will be a welcome pack consisting of fruit, flowers, groceries and possibly wine or champagne.

Most reputable holiday cottage agencies in the UK belong to the VisitBritain (VB) organization, which was formed in 2003 by the merger of the British Tourist Authority and the English Tourism Council. Their officers will come to inspect holiday cottages and give them the appropriate rating, using standard tests applicable to every cottage.

The idea of VB is to 'build the value of tourism by creating world-class destination brands and marketing campaigns'.

Janet Cornwell says that the more beautiful parts of the UK remain highly popular with tourists and also families who do not want the hassle of travelling abroad. Another huge advantage of holidaying in the home country is that you can take your pet. Most UK holiday cottages allow pets, so long as they are well behaved, and this is a major plus for pet lovers. Because schools do not now allow children to take time out for holidays during term time, school holidays are almost always fully booked. Holiday cottage owners who do not want children in their cottages have to buy properties which are unsuitable for families. There is a lot of emphasis in all the brochures on what type of cots, bunk beds or other equipment for small children is provided – and if you want to discourage families with small children from staying in your cottage, you simply do not provide these items. But it may be more difficult to exclude pets, especially if the competition allows them.

Purchasing and financing a holiday cottage

You first need to ask yourself whether you are interested primarily in investment, or in purchasing a cottage for your own use. Second, are you mainly concerned with rental income or capital growth? It is not always possible to obtain both from a holiday cottage. Some investors like to break even, and pin their hopes on capital growth, while others do everything they can to maximize the rental return.

As with other property purchases, there is a wide variety of mortgages you can take out for your holiday cottage, and buy-to-let mortgages are available, provided you are not going to use the cottage yourself, as a second home. You just need to make sure the place can be self-financing through rentals.

The other thing to bear in mind is that there is an increasing market for high-quality cottage accommodation, to let primarily to couples rather than families. These people are normally interested in short breaks, maybe as short as two days. The upmarket holiday cottage is becoming ever more popular, although agents say that high capital value and fabulous furnishings are not always reflected in extra rental yields.

Marsdens, for instance, can provide income projections for cottages in their area once they inspect a potential purchase. They point out that the more individual and unique a property, the more likely it is to let well. As with everything else concerning property investment, successful holiday lets are all a matter of sussing out the market, and then buying appropriately.

Most holiday letting companies advise borrowing money rather than using your own capital to purchase. The reason for this is that you can get tax relief on mortgage interest payments, repairs and replacements – even losses. And if the rentals cover costs, why use up your own money, which then becomes unavailable to you? You will, of course, have to find a cash deposit of, typically, 20 per cent of the purchase. Marsdens say that many of their owners and potential owners are suspicious of mortgages and like to own the place outright, if they have the capital available. But this is not always advisable for tax reasons.

Holiday letting income is treated as investment income but, unlike buy-to-let, it is treated as earned income for income tax and certain capital gains tax purposes.

In order to count as income, the lettings must be on a commercial basis and carried out with a view to making a profit. Losses may be set against other taxable income and certain capital expenditure also qualifies for tax relief. Loan or mortgage interest payments are allowable in full, and you can also use capital gains tax rollover relief and business relief on a property let for holiday purposes. You cannot do this with ordinary buy-to-let.

Holiday lets are treated as commercial property by the taxman, which means that 75 per cent of your profits are completely tax-free. In order to qualify for this tax relief, you must have owned the property for at least two years. Rollover relief means that you can sell one property and postpone paying capital gains tax by buying another for the same purpose.

The way this relief works means that if one holiday property is no longer popular, you can buy another in a more desirable area without losing profits to the taxman. You cannot do this with ordinary buy-to-let, as this is not considered commercial, or a business, but unearned income.

You will, of course, encounter all the other costs in buying property such as estate agents fees', legal and surveyor's fees, and mortgage arrangement costs. As with all property investments, it is a matter of adding up the figures to see whether the tax relief makes financial sense to you.

You are also allowed to use the holiday cottage yourself occasionally, although this may affect the income tax and tax relief claimable. In order to count as a holiday let, the property must be run as a commercial proposition, and not let out to friends or family for next to nothing.

Another bonus is that holiday lets may be exempt from inheritance tax. This is a complicated area, though, and may not be clear-cut if you are also using the holiday property yourself. It is essential to get expert tax and inheritance tax advice before entering the holiday let market, as rules are always subject to change and, in any case, everybody's personal circumstances will differ.

Note: the term 'holiday let' is used loosely and does not necessarily mean that the property has to be in a designated holiday area, just that it is used for no more than a month by the same person, and is not considered somebody's main home.

Because holiday lets are treated differently from other types of property investment, it is advisable to take advice from a specialist accountant before proceeding with a holiday lettings business. You would need to know, as an investor, whether it would be more profitable to go for holiday lettings than ordinary lettings. Because it is a specialized business, accountancy fees may be higher, as you are now running a bona fide business, even if you only have one modest little holiday cottage in your portfolio.

But obviously, as with any property investment, all rental income receivable has to be set against the costs of purchase, agency fees, refurbishment fees, council tax and utility bills. In most circumstances, you as the owner will be responsible for all bills, and you must also provide not only the television, satellite and cable services where applicable, but make sure there is a valid television licence covering the property as well.

The rental income from holiday lets is an all-in fee, minus the agency charges of around 20 per cent. In most circumstances, the tenants do not pay any extras apart from their rent, although in some circumstances, they may pay for extra cleaning or house-keeping.

Investment pointers

When buying a holiday cottage for investment purposes, the matter of supply and demand is all-important. Obviously holidaymakers flock to the popular spots, where there are already likely to be lots of holiday cottages available, and where there is fierce competition, prices may come down. On the other hand, if buying in a remote, little-visited area, you may find it hard to attract enough visitors to make the investment worthwhile.

Many developers are now concentrating in holiday areas, and are building high-spec apartment blocks, often right on the sea-front. While these make wonderful holiday apartments, you must check first to see whether holiday lets are allowed. Most residential leases do not allow holiday lets, as these are considered a business, rather than housing. So before ever buying a beautiful high-end apartment for holiday lettings, make sure you do not fall foul of the lease.

It is up to the owner to make sure holiday lets are allowed in apartments, as public liability insurance will be required before holiday accommodation can be taken on by agents. Public liability insurance, insisted on by holiday letting agencies, indemnifies you the owner for up to £2 million, and is applicable only to businesses.

Estate agent Sarah Wood, of Humberts Group plc, started a holiday cottage agency in 2005 in East Sussex and Kent, and has seen it grow and grow.

Her belief is that the holiday cottage business is going to grow faster than ordinary buy-to-let as demand is increasing all the time. Not only that, but recent changes in planning laws are making it difficult to get permission to convert a barn, say, to residential use. But it is possible to obtain permission for commercial use – and holiday cottages count as commercial.

Sarah says: 'This is all part of trying to encourage rural businesses, and holiday cottages can provide a lot of work for local people such as estate agents, cleaners, painters and decorators, handymen and so on. Another big factor is that because of a big drive towards protecting the environment, people are becoming increasingly reluctant to fly, and are considering taking their holidays in their home country instead.

'We started to become aware of a changing market, and decided to promote holiday cottages as property, in the same way as estate agents promote other properties, rather than with a traditional holiday cottage-type brochure.'

Sarah believes you can make much more money from a holiday cottage than from ordinary buy-to-let, so long as you are prepared to be hands-on and make sure everything is working and immaculate week to week. 'Holiday cottages are more work than ordinary buy-to-lets but the advantages to the investor are the tax advantages from running a business, and also because you can charge more. With holiday cottages you are basically selling a dream, rather than a roof over somebody's head and this makes the market very different indeed. You do not have to come to terms with complicated and ever-changing rules of tenure, or grapple with legislation regarding deposit or illegal eviction.

'But you may have to wait a while for your cottage to take off. We estimate it takes two years for any cottage to become really popular. Once this happens, you can normally get year-round bookings, even in the depths of Kent! In the winter, we can fill up the cottages with winter break visitors.

'We are in the middle to upper market and my criterion for taking on a cottage is that it has to be somewhere I would like to stay myself. First and foremost a holiday cottage has to be pretty. Then it has to be clean and comfortable, have nice linen and be in a location people actually want to come and visit.'

Sarah's experience is that the most popular cottages are the bigger ones that will take family groups. 'These days we are getting more mixed family groups, say a granny with a mum and couple of kids, or two families wanting to holiday together. Smaller cottages which sleep only two are more difficult to let.

'My view is that the holiday cottage business in this country is set to grow hugely. In the main, our cottage owners do not live in the properties themselves and so are able to let them out all year round.'

Interior design

Thanks to all the makeover programmes on television, even holidaymakers, let alone buyers, are now expecting a far higher standard of comfort and design than in the past. Many items considered 'luxury' at one time, such as dishwashers, power showers and en suite bathrooms, are now expected as a matter of course, even in a one-star property. Marsdens insist on a minimum three-star rating before they will take a cottage onto their books.

VisitBritain has compiled a comprehensive, not to say virtually indigestible, guide to star ratings for holiday accommodation, which even lists the type of cutlery and level of cleanliness a property must possess to be awarded a certain rating. For instance, a cleanliness rating of 68 per cent achieves a three-star rating, whereas for a five-star rating, the cleanliness level would have to be 90 per cent or above. Assessors, says the VB brochure, 'ignore their own individual personal tastes and judge the quality by way of benchmarks'.

Here are the current standards for the average three-star rating, just to give an idea of how detailed VB is in its assessments:

▮   All double beds must have access on both sides (ie, not to be pushed against walls); the exterior must be well-maintained but can have some weathering; there must be easy access to parking with a well-maintained surface (ie, not up a muddy track); there must be a good first impression with no noise level discernible; there should be evidence of attention to detail regarding cleanliness, clean and fresh surfaces and soft furnishings and carpets cleaned on a regular basis; there must be six coat hangers (not wire) for each guest; kitchens and bathrooms must not be carpeted and laminate or wood floors in living areas should have rugs on them; toilet brushes must be provided; all kitchen equipment and appliances must be thoroughly cleaned and smell fresh when guests arrive.

▌ There should be a 'good range' of pictures on blank walls in living areas, good quality flooring and underlay for carpets. Tiling should have clean grouting and wooden floors must be in good condition. Curtains should be lined and 'not water-marked'; furnishings should be coordinated and furniture be of good quality. There must be a table large enough for all guests to dine comfortably. There must be a range of sofas and chairs and a general fresh and airy atmosphere.

▌ There must be plenty of table lamps and floor lamps, and automatic, thermostatically operated heating. Beds may be of 'older style' but in good condition and all mattresses firm and not saggy. Bedding must be coordinated and pressed. The bathroom(s) must have coordinated sanitaryware, a shower, good shelf space for guests' belongings, a fixed razor point and light adjacent to mirror. Finally, all items in the cottage must be free from damage or marks.

Phew! But that's not all.

So far as introductions and management goes, a three-star service would include a picture of the cottage to be sent before-hand and a letter of introduction; welcome beverages must be provided, such as tea and coffee set on a tray; where bed linen is provided, beds must be made up before guests arrive. Tourist information and places of local interest should be provided, plus lists of places to eat. There should be a 'good range' of up-to-date magazines provided, also games and detailed guest information such as local churches, shops, chemists and pubs.

If a cottage is also your own holiday home, many items may not be 'compliant'. As with buy-to-let, they have to meet certain minimum standards by law, never mind the appearance of the cottage. Upholstered furniture must comply with regulations concerning flammability, and any furniture manufactured before 1988, when the new regulations came in, may not pass muster. So don't be tempted to furnish your holiday cottage with hand-me-downs from aged relatives; at least, not if you want to rent it out for income. All furniture and bedding in the cottage must have a permanent label on it stating that it complies with 1988 Fire Safety Regulations. Fire blankets and fire extinguishers must carry the appropriate British Standard; smoke alarms should be fitted and fire extinguishers serviced annually.

These regulations become even more stringent when it comes to children's equipment such as bunk beds, high chairs, cots, pushchairs, or play equipment in the garden. If you are not sure about any equipment you can ask your local Trading Standards Officer to inspect; in any case, agencies will not take your cottage onto their books unless it complies in every detail with current regulations.

Obviously, as with buy-to-let, it is all a matter of catering for the right market, depending on the clientele and what they are prepared to spend. There is not much point in designing and equipping a holiday cottage way beyond what the market requires or can afford. If you over-design it could frighten some people off, as they will be terrified of marking or soiling the plush furnishings.

Case study

Marion Mathews and Renske Mann bought a holiday cottage in bad condition in the quaint North Devon seaside town of Appledore. They bought it on a mortgage which was covered by rental income on an existing buy-to-let property in London.

However, as usually happens, the renovation had cost far, far more than the original estimate and by the time it was finished Marion and Renske were out of pocket. They reluctantly decided to try letting out as a holiday cottage, which was not their original intention, and were pleasantly surprised to discover that their holiday home, which sleeps five, was in great demand.

'At first I was not keen on the idea of letting it to strangers,' says Marion. 'But after we had let it, through a local agency, for a couple of weekends, we got used to the idea and realized we could easily use it ourselves and let it out to holidaymakers. Now it is fully booked for much of the year, and we book ourselves up a week or a couple of weeks between holiday bookings.'

As Marion and Renske are now both retired from work, they can visit the cottage out of season. 'The agency don't like you to book it up yourself during the high season, but obviously if there's a cancellation, or a gap between bookings, we can use it ourselves or lend it to friends.'

The cottage is about 200 years old, right on the sea wall and so has a stupendous view overlooking the harbour. There is no garden, just decking outside, so no garden maintenance. The cottage has three bedrooms, one with en suite, a very large open-plan living room with picture windows looking out onto the sea, a large dining area, and small kitchen at the front. It is fully furnished (all from Ikea!) and has wooden floors downstairs. The cottage is trendy, designer-y, fully equipped and everything is new. It lets out for around £500 a week in high season, and is booked for about 20 weeks a year.

Marion says: 'The rental income is paying the mortgage and the cottage is now entirely paying its way. I wouldn't say we are making a profit, but we are certainly covering costs and the good thing is that the cottage is occupied for much of the year. We thought we would mind strangers using it, but find it is no real problem at all.'

One thing Marion and Renske were certain about is that they wanted to use an agent which did everything. 'Some agents just put your property on their website, which doesn't work if you are not around yourself. The local agents we found do the whole thing, down to cleaning and making the beds, and we just leave it to them. They did insist on public liability insurance and would not take on a property without it.'

The other aspect to be aware of, says Marion, is that competition is hotting up with holiday lets and most holidaymakers have plenty of choice. Therefore, standards have to be high in order to get bookings.

'We would not do holiday lets as a pure investment,' Marion added, 'as the returns are too low. The awful climate in the UK means that there is a short high season, and the competition in popular areas keeps the prices low.

'On the plus side, we are covering the costs of a beautiful holiday cottage which we expect to appreciate in value as it is very old, very special and right on the seafront.

'We are looking at a 10-year time span, by which time, with any luck, the property would have increased significantly in value. You have to own a property for that long before the investment pays off. In the meantime, we are getting a lot of pleasure from it and enjoying our jaunts down to Devon between bookings.'

However, Renske had this to say in 2009:

'We were doing extremely well until 2007, taking about £10,000 gross per annum, which gave us a small profit (probably about half), which was good for us, because after all, we were not looking to make money. We wanted to have a holiday home for ourselves that didn't cost us anything and the little profit was a bonus.

'However, we then had two diabolical summers in a row! Our takings went down to £7,000 in 2008 and were even lower in 2009. We're always hoping for some really good weather to persuade people to come back again, as so many of our lets are "repeats".

'At the same time, our costs for the property are huge. We have it repainted every three years (inside and outside, too, because of the sea air), and we also have to maintain the sea wall, which needs to be tarred every three years at a cost of about £600. So any profit is out of the window and we'd be lucky to break even now. However, as we (especially me!) love staying there ourselves, we have no plans to sell until there is a glimmer of hope and change of government.

'We use a local letting agency. They do everything and we don't do any marketing ourselves, as they do it (not terribly well, but we can't be bothered).'

Nobody should imagine that holiday lets are an easy option. The wear and tear on your property is enormous and there's always something breaking down, a shower leaking, the boiler not working, the washing machine needing replacing and so on. After every use, the place needs to be cleaned professionally, too, and you shouldn't even think you could keep an eye on it remotely.

Tip: Keep up appearances!

In order to attract – and keep attracting – holidaymakers, cottages have to be maintained in tip-top condition. Most bookings happen by word of mouth, and if a cottage always looks in show-home condition, it will automatically attract a high level of bookings.

When Marion and Renske first started renting out their holiday cottage, bookings were slow and sporadic. But after only a year, their cottage was so booked up, year-round, that they could hardly squeeze in a week for themselves. They believe that the secret is never to let it start getting tatty round the edges, bearing in mind that holiday cottages soon deteriorate if left to their own devices, and most particularly those on the seafront.

Another tip is to keep a close eye on the cleaning levels. Many holiday cottage owners discover that although the cleaning is good enough at first, cleaners often get lazy after a time and skimp on the cleaning. Unless the place is gleaming clean, it will not attract repeat bookings. Items also have to be replaced more often than you would probably do in your own home. This applies especially to plastic goods such as buckets, sink drainers, scrubbing brushes, bins and dustpans. Some holiday cottage owners reckon these items have to be replaced every six months, at the most.

Investment extra

Marion Mathews and Renske Mann own three properties which are all producing income: a five-storey house in Holland Park, London W11, which they restored from a wreck; a modern two-bedroom apartment in Brook Green, London W14; and the Devon cottage.

The Holland Park house has an art gallery downstairs, let on a commercial rent to an art dealer; the modern apartment is rented on an Assured Shorthold Tenancy; and the Devon cottage is available for holiday lets.

Marion, formerly editor of a beauty magazine and Renske, a PR director, can now enjoy a civilized and comfortable retirement. They have also taken advantage of the Civil Partnership legislation, meaning that they can leave the properties to each other without incurring inheritance tax. For this, same-sex partners have to formally declare that a Civil Partnership exists.

Advertising your cottage

If you have a holiday cottage for rent, you need to make sure it is advertised properly. The easiest way to do this nowadays is to have a smart, dedicated website showing pictures of the cottage(s), a map of the location, prices and amenities. There are many web designers specializing in this kind of design and a website is essential for anybody with a holiday cottage, as this is where people usually look nowadays. A very smart, well-designed and (most important!) up-to-date website will attract guests to your cottage. To get an idea of how a holiday cottage website should look, go to www.earlscroftfarm.co.uk.

Never doubt the power of the web for advertising. In fact, many property investors are increasingly doing away with print advertising in favour of websites. Here is what property investor Dominic Farrell has to say about print advertising:

> Personally, I'm not a great fan of general print advertising. I don't think the effect justifies the expense. You have to do a considerable amount of it to get a return. I also think that the industry has moved away from general print advertising onto the internet. (From *The Jet-to-let Bible*)

Debbie and Trenter Ellis have two seafront flats in Worthing, West Sussex, which they let out as holiday apartments. The properties are beautifully furnished and presented and the Ellises have paid great attention to a professional, attractive and easy to navigate website. They have also registered their properties with the local council, who have come round to inspect and awarded the apartments a star rating. This means they can be advertised in the town's holiday brochure.

Debbie says: 'We find that holiday lets work better than ordinary lets. For one thing, you never have full occupation, so the properties get much lighter wear and tear than if people are in them all the time. We work on having four to six months occupation a year, although often we get more than that. Also, as your guests are on holiday, they are out most of the time. We find also that they hardly cook, as they tend to eat out.

'Because they pay a big deposit and all the charges upfront, they look after the places, whereas long-term tenants may well trash them.

'As we only have holiday guests, we can book ourselves a week or so if we want to, especially at short notice when we have a clear week.'

Debbie's experience and attitude differs somewhat from that of Marion and Renske, but there are good reasons for this. Debbie and Trenter own holiday flats in apartment buildings which, although they are directly on the seafront and, as such, receive much buffeting from the elements, get lighter wear than the Devon cottage. This is partly because more people can be packed into the cottage, and families often stay there, whereas the Ellises' guests are mainly quiet retired couples.

This brings us to another point, which is, if you are interested in investing in holiday lets think very carefully about the kind of people most likely to book up your place. Some holiday lets are suitable for 12–14 people and clearly, the more people who can stay at any one time, the heavier the wear and tear. The way most owners make a profit is to pack the let with as many holidaymakers as possible, so that a one-bedroom apartment can be advertised as 'sleeping six'.

Debbie and Trenter chose Worthing for several reasons: 'It's a very easy and quick drive from London and near to both Gatwick and Heathrow. Our apartments have a wonderful sea view, and it's easy to park right outside. Brighton is only ten miles away, and the South Downs, with their wonderful walks, are also near at hand.'

The Ellises' apartments are fully furnished with washing machines, television, cookers and microwaves, and are also dog-friendly. (Note: if buying in an apartment building, check whether the lease allows pets and children; also whether it allows holiday lets at all.)

Many holidaymakers specifically choose properties where well-behaved dogs are welcome and if you can admit dogs, this widens your appeal. Mostly, guests will bring their own sheets and pillowcases, but duvets and pillows are provided. However, usually, linen can be provided if necessary, and this is essential because if guests are coming on the train or straight from an airport, they might not want to lug bedlinen and towels as well as other luggage.

The real challenge with holiday lets comes with cleaning the apartments, as they have to be thoroughly cleaned between guests, and sometimes there is only a two-hour turnaround before one lot leaves and the next guests arrive. Debbie and Trenter, who live in Guildford, cannot always come to clean the places them-selves, so they have hired the caretaker to do it for them. Otherwise they would have to use a local cleaning firm, and although some cleaning companies specialize in holiday lets, the standards can be variable. And the level of cleanliness is vital to the success of such a venture, both for repeat bookings and word of mouth rec-ommendation.

To get an idea of how a holiday lettings website should look, visit the Ellises' website at www.worthingbeachapartments.co.uk.

Holiday lettings overseas

More or less the same strictures apply to holiday lettings in other countries, where you can either try to make money from dedi-cated holiday accommodation, or cover some or all of the costs of your home overseas by renting it out when you are not there yourself.

By far the greatest number of homeowners overseas finance their home in the sun by borrowing against their UK home, and then try to cover the running costs and mortgage with rental income.

The problem here is that nowadays so many people have homes in the sun that fewer people want to rent other owners' villas or apartments than used to be the case. Increasingly, people have their own homes, which they are also trying to rent in high season. There are also so many new homes being built in popular places such as Portugal, Spain, Greece and Florida that it is becoming ever harder to break even, let alone make money. When the market has been flooded with new properties, everybody will inevitably get a smaller slice of the cake.

Also, in most overseas locations, as with the UK, you will not be able to get rental income all year round. In Portugal, for instance, you might get 22–26 weeks a year once your property is well known and you have started to attract repeat business.

Just to give an example: a three- or four-bedroom, three-bathroom villa with a pool in the Algarve, Portugal, might bring in up to £2,000 a week in high season. Outside July and August, you might need a heated pool to attract guests, and this means extra costs.

On average, if your villa is popular with guests, you might make around £10,000 a year from lettings, with about £5,000 left after expenses. You will also, in Portugal and most other countries, have to pay extra insurance and pay extra to maids and other staff during high season.

In Portugal, most owners will be banking on capital appreciation, although in Greece in 2005, house prices actually went down. But over the long term, these fluctuations usually correct themselves upwards.

With buy-to-let, the uppermost consideration in every investor's mind is making money. But with holiday lets, the pure investment side may take second place to being able to afford that place in the sun, or that place to retire to one day.

Caravans, mobile homes and park homes

These cater for a different kind of clientele from the holiday cottages business, given that caravans and mobile homes have to be situated in parks, rather than being hidden in secluded valleys. In most cases, they cannot be regarded as permanent homes and in any case, as they are all on sites, agreements have to be entered into with the site owner who may provide facilities such as toilets, shops, restaurants, bars or leisure activities.

As such, you would have to obtain permission from the site owner to keep your caravan or park home on the site and enter into a legally binding agreement. Insurance cover is also different from that for holiday cottages, which can, if necessary, be used as a permanent residence. If you intend to rent out your caravan or (static) mobile home to holidaymakers, you will need public liability insurance as well as contents insurance and rebuilding insurance should the home burn down.

Caravans and park homes have always had a more downmarket image than holiday cottages, due to their being situated on sites, but in recent years, this element of the tourist industry in the UK has grown faster than any other.

Are caravans and park homes good investments?

There are two kinds of park homes: holiday homes and residential homes. In general the holiday homes would depreciate in value in much the same way as a car, and the only investment angle would be from the income you receive from letting the place out. Not all parks allow lettings to others, so when thinking about a park home from an investment point of view, you would have to check with the park owner to make sure lettings are allowed.

Some park homes are built to withstand the British winter, while others are for summer use only, and the park would be closed down in the winter. Park holiday homes are not considered 'property' in the same way as other homes, but are intended for recreational use only.

The other type of park home is the residential home, which is intended as a home and not meant for holidays. In most cases, you would not be allowed to rent out a residential park home for a holiday. Most residential parks are 'age exclusive' and there is usually a lower age limit of 50 or 55. Children are not allowed to live in these parks, although they may come to stay for short holidays.

Both holiday homes and residential homes on parks are prefabricated, in that they are built in their entirety at the manufacturer's and then deposited on the site, where they will remain. Both types of homes have to be licensed by the local authority, and both types will incur a yearly pitch fee.

But whereas the holiday homes decrease in value over time, residential park homes follow exactly the same pattern as other types of residential property in that they can appreciate in value, and follow booms and busts just like property not on a park site.

John Buston, spokesperson for the British Holiday and Home Parks Association, which was formed in the 1950s, says: 'Residential park homes act just like ordinary bricks-and-mortar homes, except that they are primarily intended for retirement. Owners like them because the park provides a semi-secure environment and there is also a social life available in the park.

'These homes intended for permanent living are following an American pattern of retirement living, and for the individual they can definitely be an investment, as you can sell your park home in exactly the same way as any other home. These homes are built for permanent use and many these days are extremely luxurious. There is also security of tenure with the residential homes.

'Where the homes are intended only for holidays, parks do their utmost to discourage permanent residence. You would pay council tax on the residential home but not on the holiday home. Local councils make stringent checks to make sure nobody is illegally using the holiday home as their main home.'

The third type of park home is the timber lodge. These look like log cabins, and many are built for permanent residential use. Timber lodges tend to be more expensive than other types of park home and the residential ones can easily cost as much as a bricks-

and-mortar home as they are built for winter conditions to Scandinavian standards.

Although holiday parks and park homes have a lingering 'trailer trash' image, those in the industry assure me that this is way out of date and there is now a distinct cachet attached to the more luxurious park homes on beautifully designed parks. 'On some of the best parks, there is a long waiting list,' says John Buston.

VAT

In theory, holiday homes attract VAT as they are considered a business. In reality, your turnover would have to exceed the VAT threshold of £68,000 (in 2010) before this applies, and it is very unlikely that one or two holiday cottage rents would ever come up to the VAT threshold. You would have to be charging over £1,000 a week and guarantee to have the holiday let fully booked all year round to rake in this amount.

But if you have a large number of holiday homes, VAT might apply. It is an investment consideration if you are thinking about building up a large holiday let portfolio. A VAT registration for holiday homes cuts both ways: on the good side, it means you can reclaim VAT on agency charges, repairs, renewals and anything else pertaining to the business which attracts VAT; on the bad side, you would have to charge your guests 17.5 per cent more for their stay – and this might put you out of the competition as far as other, similar or identical holiday cottages are concerned. The government introduced a 15 per cent VAT rate in 2009; however, this finished at the end of the year and the following are the current rates (at the time of writing).

The standard rate is:

▌   17.5 per cent up to and including 30 November 2008;

▌   15 per cent from 1 December 2008 to 31 December 2009;

▌   17.5 per cent from 1 January 2010 until further notice.

The rates of VAT may change from time to time. These changes are usually announced in the Budget, so if you are running a holiday letting business which is at or near the VAT standard rate, you will need to check regularly to make sure you are using the correct rates.

Very many holiday home owners and holiday let companies work to very tight margins, because of the fierce competition. One holiday home owner in Devon told me that he was having difficulty making ends meet because so many of the local farmers were now offering holiday accommodation at cut-price rates.

HM Revenue & Customs produce a leaflet: Hotels and Holiday Accommodation (VAT notice 709/3), which you can download from their website: www.hmrc.gov.uk, and which gives useful information on the ramifications of VAT for this particular type of business.

Taxation

Holiday lets used to be vastly more advantageous, tax-wise, than long lets, as they were considered a commercial proposition rather than as somebody's home.

For instance, if you made a loss on your holiday lettings, you could write this down as a trading loss, especially if you were otherwise employed, and you would therefore pay less tax. All capital costs such as replacement items, painting and decorating, cleaning, advertising and agency fees, were also allowable against tax.

Then when you wanted to sell, you could reinvest in another property without paying Capital Gains Tax (CGT) in the meantime and continue to reinvest in this way until you stop, at which point the CGT will be payable.

It used to also be the case that you could claim business asset taper relief, a measure introduced by the Tories in 1983 to boost the tourist industry and encourage people to holiday in Britain. By this measure, holiday cottages were given a special 'trading status', which meant they could claim the taper relief allowable on purely commercial property. Since April 2010, this taper relief on holiday cottages has been abolished.

Other tax changes were introduced, to take effect from 6 April 2010, and these collectively remove most or all of the previous tax advantages of holiday lets. From this date, income from holiday lettings will be treated in the same way as any other rental income, rather than as a fully commercial venture. This means that losses on the property will only be available against rental profit rather than set against general income as before, and the Capital Gains Tax advantage is also abolished.

If you already own any holiday lets, it is essential to speak to your accountant to understand how and whether these tax changes will affect you. Obviously for any holiday properties bought after 6 April 2010, the new tax changes apply straightaway but whether anything can be backdated to your advantage, for holiday properties already owned, will depend on individual circumstances and need expert advice from your accountant, who should be up-to-date with all the changes.

In the past, inheritance tax (IHT) business property relief was also available on holiday lets where the lets were very short term, say of one or two weeks' duration. In some cases, 100 per cent of the value of the property was exempt from IHT. But from April 2010, this relief is also withdrawn, as HM Revenue and Customs seeks to bring holiday lets more in line with ordinary lets.

Again from 6 April, holiday lets owned within the European Economic Area (EEA) will also be included in the new UK tax rules.

How to flip like an MP

In 2009, the UK electorate was sent reeling by the revelation that many MPs had been flipping on their first and second homes to avoid paying the capital gains tax levied on a second home.

The current situation is that everybody is allowed to buy and sell one home free of capital gains tax, if this is designated their principal home. Every other property is considered a second home and liable for CGT when sold. But many MPs had – quite legally – been flipping between one home and another, saying first that one was their main home and then the other, to avoid paying this tax – a tax THEY had invented for other people to pay!

So how does this flipping work? People who own two – or more – homes can elect which one is to be their main residence to attract the tax-free status. If an MP buys a London flat, he or she can elect that their constituency home in the country is their main home.

So, an MP buys a London flat and it is designated a second, rather than a main home. But then, after three or more years of continuous ownership, this flat is put up for sale. Normally it would attract CGT, but once an offer is accepted on the property, the MP can then elect to 'flip' the tax-free relief to the London flat a week before the sale. This means that for one week and one week only, the London flat has suddenly become their main home.

Then, a week later, once the sale has been concluded, the main residence is flipped back to the country, or constituency, home. Although the London flat may only have been the main residence for one week, the 'time to sell' rules kick in and the whole ownership of the flat, for however long a period, acquires enviable tax-free status. A property has to be in the same ownership for a minimum of three years for this flipping to be legal.

It is true that the country home does lose this tax-free status in the meantime but no matter, in a long ownership this is likely to be insignificant and that property will not attract CGT on resale either.

Although this rule was used to their advantage, as we now know, by MPs who were advised of such a tax dodge by their accountants, it could of course be used by any property owner.

So if you, as a property investor, are interested in flipping – something that would never even occur to most of us honest souls – ask your accountant what is permissible and legal under the rules.

Note: if you rent out your second home on an assured short-hold tenancy, it becomes somebody else's main residence, and therefore these tax rules would not apply. In fact, this becomes a problem where a homeowner who is unable to sell is forced to rent out their home to pay the mortgage. The property becomes somebody else's home for the time that it is rented out, and therefore CGT kicks in.

But when it comes to holiday lets, where they are emphatically not the short-term guests' main homes, flipping may indeed work in your favour.

Another factor is that if you are a married couple, you are only allowed one main home between you. The same applies to those in civil partnerships. But if you are living with a partner of the opposite sex in unmarried bliss, or have not signed a civil partnership with a same-sex partner, you are each allowed one main home.

The tax rules here are that a married couple or those in a civil partnership are seen as traditionally 'one flesh' whereas unmarried couples are regarded as separate entities.

6 Commercial property

The prospect of investing in commercial property used to frighten off the averagely timid residential investor.

In fact the very word 'commercial' was off-putting in itself, reminding potential investors of boarded-up shops, dismal business parks on bleak sites and grim offices with dirty windows, stained grey carpet tiles and vertical blinds.

But we are all getting braver now, investing in all kinds of property, and commercial property is the latest such product to attract ordinary, everyday investors who are looking to broaden their horizons and, with any luck, make more money. Also, the fact that commercial property has been allowable for inclusion into a Self-Invested Personal Pension plan (SIPP) since 1989 has made ever more people who want to avoid paying tax consider this option.

Around 75 per cent of those who have already invested in residential property are now looking at commercial properties with a view to diversifying their portfolio, expanding their skills base and also, giving themselves another interest. Long-term investors are starting to get tired of residential buy-to-let as they think: been there, done that. In general terms, commercial property is less hassle than residential property, requires less commitment of time and energy and often has higher returns. In addition, these returns are guaranteed for maybe a 10-year period, during which time there will be several rent reviews in an upward-only direction. Some commercial leases are for as long as 25 years, which saves the problem of having to find new tenants every six months or so.

Other attractions of commercial property are that there is no work for the landlord once the premises have been bought and rented out. There is no maintenance, no decorating, no looking after the tenants and their problems, no renovation or updating. The tenant, not the landlord, is responsible for the upkeep and decoration of the premises. Most commercial leases stipulate that even if the property is let in dreadful condition, it has to be returned in excellent condition, under the terms of the 'full repairing lease' the tenant signs at the outset.

Some people believe that commercial units are more predictable in their yield than houses and flats, which are driven by supply and demand. But yet, there are many empty shops, empty office premises and abandoned business park units which once housed thriving businesses. So – there are no absolute certainties.

It is true that, in the past, small-time investors hardly ever considered commercial property, as it was more difficult to understand, and just did not have the attractive vibe of residential property.

But now, just as overseas property has come within the scope of the average person, so has commercial property. Both types of investment have been made easier in recent years by the availability of suitable mortgage products for business or investment purposes, aimed at the small-time investor or purchaser.

One of the major reasons people rushed to invest in residential buy-to-let in the first place was because housing was something they all understood. After all, everybody has lived in a house or a flat, maybe both, and everybody has had experience of renting or buying. Therefore, to make the leap into investing in residential property was not all that strange or unknown. Also, in buying their own homes on a mortgage, everybody had in some sense invested in property, even if they were not doing it primarily for financial gain.

But commercial property – necessarily less appealing than a lovely new flat where you have seen the beautifully designed show home – was, for many, a foray into *terra incognita*. Would we be reduced to letting out our retail premises to a charity shop? Would we be buying office space nobody wanted? Would all the businesses housed in our premises suddenly go bust, leaving us with a white elephant? And whereas with residential property we could pick and choose our tenants, with commercial premises we might not have a choice as to what kind of business would be carried on within.

There is also, with commercial property, none of the potent satisfaction of renovating, decorating and presenting the place to appeal to renters or buyers. Tenants of commercial premises are usually themselves responsible for doing up the shop, office or business park in their own way.

However, more investors are now overcoming their initial distaste and taking the plunge, typically starting with small offices and retail shops, and if all goes well, expanding into small business parks or light industrial units. Such investors are attracted by the capital appreciation and usually higher yields of commercial property, without all the accompanying baggage of thousands of years of landlord and tenant law to grapple with.

Case study: Mike Taylor

Computer expert Mike Taylor invested in commercial property many years ago and believes it has several advantages, not least of which was that when he got divorced, he gave one of these properties to his ex-wife! He had two commercial units off the Uxbridge Road in West London for many years, and now has one.

He says, 'In the main, industrial property does not rise in value at quite the same rate as residential property but the advantages are that you as the owner are not responsible for repairs and it is also very easy to get somebody out if they are not paying rent or looking after the place. The main problem with investing in residential property, as I see it, is that you are providing somebody with a roof over their heads and cannot just make them homeless. But you can just turn somebody out of an industrial unit as it is not a home and the same rules of tenure do not apply.

'The other thing is that in London at least there is an enormous demand for industrial units, especially as many councils have squeezed out small messy businesses such as car repair workshops. For me, commercial property makes sense as I am receiving income at the same time as the asset is rising in value, but I don't have to put any money or effort into maintaining it.

'Your biggest potential problem is that the business renting your premises will go bust, so you do have to choose your tenants carefully, and go for established businesses. Both of my units are 3,000 square feet, and one is used as storage for a Far-Eastern supermarket, whereas the other contains bathroom fittings. Not very glamorous, maybe, but necessary to modern life. The other thing to look for when considering a commercial unit is that there is easy car parking. A unit without car parking is virtually useless these days.'

But first of all, what is the definition of commercial property? For the purposes of this chapter, it is defined as any premises which are used solely for carrying on a business and are not used or intended for any kind of residential purpose. A guest house or hotel, for instance, where you are living on the premises yourself, comes into a slightly different category which will be discussed in Chapter 7.

There are three main types of commercial property: retail, such as shopping centres, retail warehouses, shops, supermarkets and department stores; offices, such as ordinary offices and business parks; and industrial, such as industrial estates and warehousing.

A report on commercial property by the British Property Federation (BPF) said that London and the South East are the most dominant areas in terms of the number and value of commercial investment possibilities. In particular, the office investment market is heavily skewed towards London, which alone accounts for 60 per cent of the market value of offices.

The main advantages of investing in commercial property, according to the BPF, are that tenants typically stay far longer than in residential property, these same tenants are liable for repair and upkeep of the property, and most of the profit arises from income rather than from capital growth. This means that commercial property tends to provide a reliable and secure cash flow with leases typically lasting eight to 12 years. There are noises that the government is looking hard at commercial property leases and is seeking to control the upward-only rent reviews, but at the time of writing (2009) no legislation has come in.

Commercial property, in common with other asset classes, particularly property, is always liable to be affected by legislative change. There is no way that you as an investor can protect yourself against it.

This is why, although most experts advise investing in property for the long term, a close eye has to be kept on any legislation or tax changes in the short term. Very often, the government brings these changes in suddenly without warning or, alternatively, decides at the last minute not to legislate. This happens far more with investments and particularly property investments, than any other government concern. They try to tinker around and then eventually realize that such tinkering isn't going to work.

The BPF report concludes by saying that investing in commercial property is not always as easy as in other asset classes because of the large lot size, illiquidity of the asset and the uncertainty of the market business.

There are four ways that a commercial property investor can invest: personally, in your own name; using a company; indirectly through an ISA; or through a SIPP. If you are interested in the more indirect ways of investing in commercial property, you would need to seek the advice of a tax adviser conversant with this highly specialized sector.

David Whittaker, founder of Mortgages for Business, which arranges mortgages for all kinds of non-domestic purposes, explains all:

'The typical new entrant to the commercial property sector is an experienced buy-to-let investor who has been in the business for about a decade and now wants to diversify.

'This kind of person is nervous of investing in greenfield sites, for instance, or multimillion-pound new office developments, but has become thoroughly versed in residential buy-to-let and has maybe started looking at flats over shops, then started thinking: why don't I buy the shop as well?'

When first venturing into commercial property, it is important not to stray too far from your existing skills base or your geographical base. 'If you have a couple of residential buy-to-lets on the south coast, you might think about diversifying into retail shops. After all, you know the area already, you know which types of shops succeed and which ones don't last and you know the kind of people who live and shop in the area. You might not know much about these things in a totally unknown area.'

It is also important, at first, not to stray too far outside your financial comfort zone. 'If you have been used to buying rental properties for £150,000 each, it is not too far out of your orbit to buy a commercial property for £200,000. You should always buy within your existing comfort zone as once you step outside your range of skills and enter an unknown world, you stand to lose money. As a general rule, you should never buy into assets you know nothing about, as they have a habit of turning into a nasty liability.

'You should not invest in anything which feels totally unfamiliar.'

David Whittaker emphasizes that as residential buy-to-let is not a get-rich-quick scheme, nor is investing in commercial property. 'As with residential investments, you are looking at a 10–15-year time period for your investment to pay off,' he says.

There are very many advantages of commercial property investment over residential, not least the fact that with commercial property, you are not taking on board complicated laws concerning tenure, some of which go back to the Domesday Book. When a tenant moves into rented residential accommodation, that tenant has rights, simply because they have now been housed and you cannot just make a person homeless. Also, residential tenants can only move into a property which has already passed all the health, safety and fire regulations, which has an up-to-date gas certificate, and where the furniture must be compliant with the latest regulations.

None of this applies to commercial property. It is up to the tenant to make sure the premises comply with any health and safety rules. And all you as the commercial landlord do is to collect the rents, quarterly in advance.

Also, you will insist on a deposit of, typically, three months' rent. Plus, you the landlord are not responsible for maintaining the property.

But all through 2009, we were treated to the depressing spectacle of retail outlets closing and often they were whole chains that had been around for years, such as Woolworth's and MFI. The result was that many high streets became wastelands, and not even charity shops were able to fill the gaps. At the same time, many units on retail parks stood empty, as did office blocks as, one by one, apparently rock-solid businesses collapsed.

Reports in the media were suggesting that commercial property values in many sectors had fallen by up to 40 per cent and that even the Duke of Westminster, one of the richest property owners in the world, had lost huge sums on the Liverpool shopping centre in which he had invested heavily. Several commercial investment companies went out of business during 2009. We also read that the profits on Gordon Ramsay's restaurant business were down by 90 per cent.

So if big important people have been losing money on retail businesses and commercial property investments, is this still a sensible sector for the small investor?

Again, it's the same story as with residential property; if you have the cash, you can pick up some real bargains and as with the residential sector, the commercial sector is bound to recover. It's just that the current financial downturn has been so all-encompassing, nobody knows how long it will be before new businesses take the place of the old, outdated or unviable ones.

It is also worth bearing in mind that, in the commercial property sector, many of the concerns that went out of business were still trading, and still popular. Their demise came not because there was no demand for their products, but because they could no longer service their loans owing to the collapse or near-collapse of so many banks and financial institutions.

So how do you get started? First of all, you get the particulars of a commercial property up for sale, in exactly the same way as with a residential property. If the premises are already occupied, you ask to see the business accounts. If the business is a limited company, you can search records at Companies House, as company accounts are then in the public domain.

Otherwise, you get on to the accountants. If the business is not a limited company, they may refuse to let you see their accounts.

'Then you have to look at the general appearance of the business, the cars of the directors and employees, and judge for yourself whether it is a prosperous concern that can pay the rent,' says David Whittaker.

The next step is to look at the lease. If you are very new to buying commercial premises, it is essential to take the lease, which will be part of the vendor's pack, to a suitably qualified commercial lawyer who will give it an expert reading. You need to know from the lease who pays the rates, and whether the rent is an all-inclusive amount or excludes certain rates and other costs.

The lease, in this instance, will not be the lease on the property, but the lease issued to the tenant of the business premises. In normal situations, the lease will be for a period of 10–15 years, as opposed to the six months of an Assured Shorthold Tenancy.

If, on the other hand, the building is empty, you need to know how long it has been empty and what the usual rent on the premises would be. If there is only normally a six-week gap between tenants, then you can expect to be fairly certain that it will rent out again. If, on the other hand, the shop or office premises have been boarded up for many years, there may be a problem with renting these premises out. If retail businesses blow up and blow down within a year, and nothing lasts very long, you may be best advised to walk away.

There may be no passing trade, there may be too much competition in the area, the location may be crime-ridden or too far away from the town centre. There may be all sorts of reasons why businesses in those premises do not succeed and, as with residential buy-to-let, a lot of preliminary research is required.

Supposing you decide to buy a particular retail shop or suite of offices. You now need to know the percentage yield in rent that you can expect. 'The more blue-chip the company, the tighter the yield and the harder they negotiate on leases,' says David Whittaker. 'If you are renting to a new interior design company or wine bar, for instance, you would expect a yield of 10 per cent, at least, and for the tenants to sign a lease of 10 years. But if you rent to Boots, for instance, who are unlikely to go bust in the near future, your yield may only be 5 per cent, and the lease they agree to sign may also be only five years. But you can be pretty sure they are not going to go out of business, and you have much more security than with, say, a new and untried restaurant.

'As a landlord, there is much less hassle than with residential property, but negotiations can be more protracted when there is a rent review. The tenant may have 10 years' security of tenure, but they may negotiate hard to keep the rents down, even though they will go up by a certain amount. The tenant agrees to ever-upward rent reviews, but can argue about the actual amount.'

One major advantage of investing in commercial property is that, unlike buy-to-let or holiday cottages, it is more or less a hands-off investment, where little or no work is required by you, the investor, to maintain the property. Once you have made the original investment, you do not need to expend further energy, time or money, as the lessee will look after the property for you under the terms of a commercial lease.

However, here again an eye has to be kept on legislation. During 2008 there was speculation about rent reviews being discontinued. For decades these have been an automatic assumption in commercial property investment, promising ever-upward rental income. But the main reason why some commercial enterprises like retail shops go out of business is not lack of trade; it is because the lessee cannot afford to pay the increased rent. It is in the light of this fact that rent reviews may in the future become subject to negotiation by both sides.

Mortgages

Mortgages on commercial property are no different from buy-to-let mortgages on residential investments. Typically, you the landlord would have to find 20–25 per cent of the purchase price in cash, and then get a 20-year mortgage on the rest.

As with residential buy-to-let mortgages, the repayments come from the rent, and the mortgages are granted on the ability of the tenant to pay rent, rather than your own income or assets. Commercial mortgages tend to be at a slightly higher rate than residential mortgages, typically 2.5 to 4 per cent over base, compared with 0.9 per cent over base for residential mortgages.

A commercial mortgage can be used for more or less any business purpose, such as acquisition of business premises, commercial or even residential investment and property development.

Specialized commercial mortgages are available for the leisure industry, retail, industrial, care homes and agricultural use, for instance. As some businesses and ventures are considered more risky than others, so the terms of the commercial mortgage will vary. For instance, a commercial mortgage for a doctors' or dentists' surgery will carry more favourable terms than one for a leisure venture, which is considered notoriously high risk.

For the buy-to-let investor moving into commercial ventures, the best kind of mortgage would be the semi-commercial mortgage, This covers flats above shops, living accommodation over a fish and chip shop or restaurant for instance, living accommodation over a pub or other leisure activity, where the mortgage would cover both the residential and the business aspect of the premises.

It is also always worth enquiring whether a specialized commercial mortgage may be more advantageous than an ordinary mortgage; for instance, if you are investing in holiday lets, which seem to come halfway between commercial and residential in the taxman's eyes.

Most lenders will place restrictions on the kind of business allowed and some types of business – for instance a sex shop – may be excluded by certain lenders. It may also be the case that some lenders do not want to be associated with certain kinds of businesses, and in any case, the terms vary considerably according to the kind of business carried on and how risky it is seen to be. A local pharmacy, for example, would be considered less risky than an avant-garde art gallery.

Nowadays, most ordinary mortgage lenders will offer commercial mortgages and most of them, particularly since 2008, will be looking for a positive credit rating. People with an adverse credit rating may not be eligible for a commercial mortgage, and a commercial lender will be looking to fund a business that is stable and profitable. Obviously there are no absolute guarantees and, as with residential mortgages, lending criteria have tightened up a lot since the end of 2007.

But the market is now becoming competitive, as commercial mortgages aimed at the small investor are getting more streamlined, so as ever, it pays to shop around.

In most cases, you would have to present a business plan, as the lender needs to know that the money is safe. Domestic mortgages are relatively easy to determine as you are going to be living there, but with commercial property, there are a lot of considerations that need to be addressed, such as: what kind of retail outlet or business will rent these premises, and how much profit/turnover will they be able to guarantee? Some mortgage lenders exclude fast-food outlets, restaurants or any business operating anti-social hours.

Mostly, a lender would have to have a fairly clear idea of the type of business envisaged in the premises before agreeing to lend money to purchase. They are naturally keener to lend when there is already a blue-chip tenant in situ than with a new, untried and uncertain business.

Much commercial property is now bought at auction, and you can get fast-track loans for these, as well. There is usually an arrangement fee of around £500, and there may be other costs involved in buying at auction.

So why do users of retail outlets, office premises or business parks not buy the property themselves, rather than renting from an outside landlord?

David Whittaker explains: 'For a shop owner, their money is tied up in stock. If they have £100,000 to spend on their new business, they are going to want to buy wine, clothes, furniture – whatever they are going to sell – rather than wanting to tie it up in the real estate. Similarly, in the case of business parks, where there are many little outlets trading in what I call Janet-and-John businesses, where there are one or two employees manufacturing teddy bears, for instance, they do not want to put their money into a building where it becomes unavailable to them to run their business. Such people do not want to put capital into the premises, but concentrate on selling their goods. All profits and assets will be ploughed back into the business. In most cases, it makes more financial sense for them to continue paying rent to a landlord.

'Many people renting office space, similarly, do not want to put capital into the premises, but into the business.'

Tax implications

Rental profits from commercial property are taxed in the same way as any other rental income, whereby you pay income tax at either 22 per cent or 40 per cent, depending on overall income level. If you set up a company, you pay corporation tax at rates ranging from 0 per cent to 32.75 per cent, with the average that most people pay coming in at 19 per cent.

You do not get an annual 'wear and tear' allowance of 10 per cent on commercial property as on residential property that is rented out but instead, you become eligible for a series of capital allowances. These can be set off against your other income if you have not made a rental profit in that year. These capital allowances are usually available only on the fittings, rather than the main fabric of the building.

With commercial property, you are taxed as with holiday lets, where you are assumed to be in it for profit. Therefore, it is not considered unearned income as with residential buy-to-let, even though in most cases it is far less work than renting to residential tenants. But there you are.

Capital gains

Under new rules announced by the Chancellor in October 2007, business asset taper relief has been eliminated and replaced by a flat rate of 18 per cent. Formerly it was possible to gain a 75 per cent exemption from capital gains tax after letting out a property for certain types of business for two years. This was a major tax advantage which no longer applies.

Because of this vastly increased potential tax liability, expert tax advice should be sought before considering buying commercial property. As this property currently attracts regular upward rent reviews (but see comments above about these) and is usually subject to a full repairing lease by the lessee, the rents in themselves should create the profit. Capital gains liability on commercial property is no longer subject to income levels or the length of time the property has been owned.

Stamp duty

This is much the same for commercial property as residential property, except that (at the time of writing) exemption for commercial property transactions is £150,000 rather than the £125,000 for residential property.

VAT

You have the choice as to whether to charge VAT on top of your rent. If you do, you can recover VAT on costs and expenses which incur this tax, such as building, renovating and redecorating costs.

Charging VAT on commercial property rent is usually known as 'exercising the option to tax'. If your tenants themselves are registered for VAT (which in a business, they almost always are) then everybody can recover this tax. The problem comes when tenants cannot recover VAT, either because their annual turnover is too low or, more likely, because their business or profession does not attract VAT, such as an NHS medical practice.

The stumbling block here arises when you do not initially charge VAT on the rent as you cannot change your option, once it has been exercised, for another 30 years. One way round the complicated VAT option is to charge a higher rent – say 15 to 17.5 per cent above what you would normally charge – to include VAT, rather than charging it on top. This always assumes, of course, that you will be able to get the higher rent.

Lease premiums

This is a lump sum payable to you in consideration for granting the lease and only applies to commercial property.

Clearly, in order to start investing in commercial property you need the services of a good accountant conversant with this type of investment. It is more complicated initially than residential investment, but once up and running, should not cause day-to-day concerns.

Flats above shops

The government has been trying to interest people in buying flats above shops and been successful, up to a point. Flats above shops are usually cheaper than dedicated residential property, and investing in a flat of this type is very often the starting point for investing in commercial property. Sometimes you have no choice but to acquire the commercial premises at the same time as the flat.

Flats above shops are often in excellent locations, and are usually cheaper because you have no say in what type of shop sets up below the flat; if it is an Indian restaurant, a betting shop or off-licence, your residential flat may continue to be worth less than other flats of the same or similar specification.

Many people buy flats above shops in the belief that eventually they will be able to turn the shop into a dwelling, and thereby make a killing. But beware – in most cases you would not be allowed to do this. It is one reason why shops below residential flats often stay boarded up for years. Nobody wants to take on the shop because they cannot see how to run a viable trade there, yet the council will not give permission to turn the shop into another flat.

Note: If a property has a commercial lease, or part commercial lease, and you do not use the commercial part for carrying on a business, you could be liable for enforcement action from the local council. In some cases, leases state the kind of business which must be carried on in the commercial part of the premises, such as a café, general store, grocery, chemist, or whatever. Take advice before attempting to deviate from the provisions of any commercial lease.

Case study

Many years ago, a couple I know bought a totally derelict house in London W11. The upstairs of the early Victorian terrace was a residential flat on two floors, and the downstairs was a disused dairy. They said: 'Originally the big advantage for us was that buying the property enabled us to live in an area where we probably could not have afforded a whole house, as commercial properties are usually worth much less than residential ones, and it's easy to see why.

'Having commercial premises below a flat spoils the look of the residential property and also means more people are coming and going. In our case, we have a reliable tenant who runs an upmarket art gallery and who pays us a rent which covers all of our overheads for the entire property.

'Commercial tenants are far less hassle than residential tenants, and our tenant does all the repairs and paints the gallery regularly, so it always looks good.

'So far as change of use is concerned, you are unlikely to get permission to convert to residential use. When we put our house on the market once, we tried to get permission for change of use from the Royal Borough of Kensington and Chelsea but were refused. Local boroughs get more money from business rates and also like the idea of shops, art galleries and restaurants to bring people to the location. Our advice is: don't ever bank on getting permission to convert to residential use as you are more likely than not to be refused.

'Our property would be worth around £400,000 more and be much easier to sell if we could convert, but we can't. When we tried to sell, most of the people who were interested wanted to convert the place back to a whole house, like the others in the row. But they kept coming up against blank walls. It can also sometimes be difficult to get a mortgage for a part-residential, part-commercial use.

'But it works both ways. Because our place is partly commercial, we did not pay as much for it in the first place.'

As with holiday lets, owners of commercial premises have to take out public liability insurance. You may also have to present a business plan. One of the problems that my friends faced with buyers when they tried to sell their West London house was that there were restrictions on what type of business could be carried on there, as any new venture could not be in direct competition with existing businesses. There were already enough restaurants, antique shops and interior design shops, so a new business had to offer something different. It would have been possible to rent the place out as an alternative health clinic, hairdresser's or similar service, but the premises were deemed too expensive for this kind of business to succeed.

The art gallery presently run on the ground floor and basement is obviously ideal and here my friends have been lucky. But anybody buying commercial premises or, in particular, a unit consisting of a flat and a shop, might find it difficult to let the shop as a going concern. The shopkeeper has to be certain there is enough of a profit margin from having premises in any particular area.

Commercial premises abroad

Increasingly, British people are seeking ways of buying property abroad which generates an income, and living over the 'shop' while renting out the retail premises to shopkeepers or office workers is one way of doing this. It can be difficult to acquire business premises abroad, especially where local laws differ from those of the home country.

In Spain, for instance, if you buy a business you take on the tax debts, if any, of the previous owner; in France, buying commercial property may involve purchasing shares in a holding company.

It can also be difficult to raise finance as British mortgage lenders are not keen to lend money on commercial property in other countries. You can of course – in theory anyway – get a commercial mortgage in the country where you wish to buy property.

British people have started to invest in commercial properties in other countries, but as with residential property, it can be difficult to establish title and also understand laws concerning foreign investment. This has not prevented British investors who already have holiday homes overseas from investing in shops, cafés, wine bars and other concerns which they do not intend to run themselves, but just take the rents from the tenants. Although it sounds risky, mostly it seems to work, but you would need a good bilingual commercial lawyer to help you through the process.

Syndicated property purchase

As I know from experience, it can be extremely bleak going it alone when buying investment property. This bleakness is intensified a million fold when buying commercial property, for although it can be quite interesting going to look at office blocks or retail enterprises with your friends, it is depressing going to look at these unpromising edifices by yourself.

As investing in commercial property is also something of an unknown factor for many ordinary investors, the sensible thing can be to purchase commercial property through a syndicate. Here, a group of people, say between 5 and 15, each pool their resources to invest together in commercial premises. The syndicate (often successfully formed through a group of friends who already know and trust each other) can then purchase a single property or a group of properties, which may be offices, retail, warehouses, industrial buildings or leisure centres.

Each person would invest, say, £50,000 minimum. Then the syndicate can jointly borrow up to three times the amount invested; the loan is secured on the property and the rental income receivable. In a typical syndicate, each property is bought with a 7- to 10-year time span in mind. There must obviously always be an exit strategy and properties bought in this way must have resale value.

Once the properties are sold, the profits are returned to the syndicate. There should also be protection for any member who needs or wants to exit early.

There are companies that specialize in this kind of thing, or you can go it alone and manage the whole thing yourself. One huge advantage of buying commercial property in a group is that you can amass pooled expertise; clearly, you would need to team up with people who are all equally dedicated and who can all put some expertise into the pot. One member may have previous experience of running a retail business, another may know the area well, another may have links with local councils and planning departments, another may be a qualified accountant or lawyer.

Whether you decide to have your syndicate professionally managed or whether you believe you have enough expertise to do it yourself, it is vital to have a legally binding document drawn up before you proceed. Sounds obvious, but very often friends just think they can trust each other and then, a long way down the line, discover this is just not so.

Property unit trusts

This is a way of investing in commercial property at a distance and may suit those who do not want all the hassle of coping with this type of property themselves. The trusts invest in the shares of commercial property companies listed on the Stock Exchange, as well as investing directly in offices, retail and commercial premises such as business parks.

There are three main funds: Aberdeen Property Share, New Star Property and Norwich Property. These funds have in the past given investors spectacular returns of 15–60 per cent, and believe that even with a downturn, annual returns of 7 to 10 per cent can be expected.

Property unit trusts are managed for you, so you lose personal control over your investment. During 2008 many of these funds performed much less well than in previous years, owing to nervousness in the retail trade and the fact that the slowdown in consumer spending left many retail outlets standing empty.

New Star is an example of a leading fund which has invested heavily in this sector: 80.2 per cent of its assets went directly into property during 2007/08. Its retail outlets include Staples Corner in north-west London and retail stores such as Halfords and John Lewis.

You must expect ups and downs in the market. But even with the downs, you are still investing in a tangible asset which will always have some value.

Property unit trusts are becoming more popular all the time and it is possible to invest in commercial property funds with as little as £5,000. Rather than invest directly in properties, you put money into a spread of investments that are managed for you. Advocates say that this creates better risk diversification and you have experts to manage the money for you.

Against this, of course, you lose control over your investment and it becomes much like any other stock or share. There are also fees to pay for this kind of investment, on top of the actual money that you invest. However, many funds have performance-related fees, which supposedly gives the fund advisers incentives to buy well and perform well.

Most financial experts continue to believe that investing in commercial property is generally less risky than residential property, but if there is a crash, can you get your money out quickly? The funds, believe City analysts, are generally well managed and may suit somebody who likes the idea of the gains possible on commercial property, but is not keen to get their hands dirty themselves. Analysts also advise investors not to put all of their faith – or money – into these trusts, but only a proportion.

7 Setting up a B&B

It is becoming ever more popular for people who are tired of living in cities or going to their stressful jobs to 'retire' to the country or a popular tourist area with the intention of running a B&B or small guest house to give a desirable lifestyle as well as earning enough income to keep body and soul together.

Of course, the secret of lifestyle success when running a B&B is to choose a lovely house in a lovely area which is not absolutely overloaded with cheaper competition and which has a steady turnover of polite, well-behaved guests.

So, if the idea of buying and running a B&B or small guest house attracts you, what do you need to know?

Hugh Caven, managing director of Walbrook Commercial Finance, which has been arranging finance packages for the B&B industry for 20 years, says: 'The B&B industry is thriving and a lot of people want to get into it. But in order to make it work – and before ever making an offer on a place where maybe you have had a wonderful weekend – you need to do intense research.'

First, you need to find a location that appeals to you and where you can envisage living. The next thing is to discover the typical occupancy rates of B&Bs in that area, and the kind of market available. 'Ideally, you would need 75 per cent occupancy all year round to make it work financially,' says Hugh Caven.

'If you choose a place where there is only holiday trade, you might find yourself without bookings for most of the year, and then you are hectic for about two months in the summer.

'Our offices are in Tunbridge Wells, where there is both tourist and commercial trade. This means that a good B&B will have occupancy all the year round, and if you choose somewhere like this, you have a head start on somewhere that has only summer holiday trade. The trick, when assessing whether a particular place is a good buy, is to link occupancy and room rates. Obviously, if you are only charging £10 a night, you will have your work cut out to make it pay.'

Unless you are a cash buyer, you will have to go to a specialist mortgage broker, such as Walbrook, for the finance. They will want to see existing profit and loss accounts for the past three years of the place you are considering buying, plus a detailed business plan from you as to how you are going to achieve or increase existing turnover.

The main way that a B&B goes up in value, when you come to sell, is if you can improve its profitability. And how do you do this? There may be too much competition around to put room rates up very much, so the only thing is to concentrate on increasing the occupancy, by making your B&B irresistible and head and shoulders above the competition. (BUT – beware the VAT trap, see later.) Running a B&B can be a fabulous business, but you have to get it right. The B&Bs that survive are those that attract year-round trade. This means that the business can survive a poor holiday season because of bad weather, for instance.

'Many people coming to us for finance say they will improve the profitability by doing evening meals,' says Caven. 'In my view, this is a mistake and almost always leads to disaster. Most people don't like to have dinner in the same place they have breakfast and if you've ever watched three lone guys having dinner in an otherwise forsaken guest house dining room, you will know there are few bleaker scenes imaginable. It's horrible.

'Unless you have a master chef and can offer gourmet meals in a proper restaurant you open to the public, you won't be able to make it work. Then you would need a restaurant licence and may have to attend a catering course.

'The only way that offering evening meals works is with the coach trade, where old age pensioners buy a package that includes the coach travel and guest house, with virtually nothing else to buy. And that really is at the very lowest end of the market.'

If you are interested in running a B&B, you should buy an existing business rather than trying to start from scratch, as the chances are you will not be able to get proper finance for a start-up where there is only potential, and not actual, trade. This is apart from any planning permission considerations, and in conservation areas, or national parks, it is difficult, if not impossible, to obtain planning permission for yet another B&B.

There is also the fact that B&Bs change hands very quickly indeed, and the average stay in one place is three to five years, when they are on the market again. So the chances are that it would not take you long to find an existing B&B for sale in your chosen area. The rapid turnover is not, Hugh Caven points out, because the businesses have failed, but rather because the couple running the place are retiring or splitting up.

Around 99 per cent of people buying B&Bs are couples, either same-sex or heterosexual. It is very rare for a single, lone person to be interested in this kind of investment.

Another factor favouring couples is that one partner can be mainly responsible for the B&B while the other continues their existing job. This means that the turnover can be kept below the VAT threshold because there is another source of income.

The couple trap

The vast majority of B&B businesses are bought by couples who believe they would love to work together. But after a few months of being joined at the hip, they often discover they are unable to work together after all. They may start working together at 5.30 in the morning, and are still together at 11 at night.

Another reason why B&Bs frequently come back onto the market is because of illness. There is a high level of illness in the industry, mainly because the couple running the B&B drain themselves by working too hard. They may think they can't afford staff, or they can't find staff, and so do all the work themselves. They discover that running a B&B is not the doddle they imagined it was going to be.

It is also very common, so I am told, for one half of the couple to fall in love with a member of staff, where staff are employed, and go off together.

So – as with establishing a buy-to-let business, you need to be reasonably certain, if you are a couple, that you will be able to work together day and night, and enjoy never, ever being separated. Working together in this way can also be stressful when you are trying to establish a new business, especially in a brand-new area.

Almost all of Walbrook's customers are first-timers and almost all are couples. And it is the ending of the relationship, rather than the failure of the business, that brings the B&B back on the market after a very few years.

Markets and buyers

There are several distinct markets in the B&B industry, and in many cases, they would not overlap. The places of outstanding natural beauty and the national parks attract mainly holidaymakers who want a high standard of accommodation – apart from the hikers, who are happy to bed down in a dormitory-type overnight place.

Then there is the commercial B&B which caters for workers away from home who, again, need somewhere quick, easy, simple and cheap to bed down for the night. This type is not dependent on holiday seasons.

Finally, there is the upmarket B&B catering for people going to a wedding or other big party, or having a quiet weekend away where they need en suite, hairdryer, ironing and other hotel-type facilities. This type of B&B would also attract year-round trade.

Another market is coming to the fore, and that is in putting up grandparents who want to visit, but not stay with, their children and grandchildren. Increasingly, grandparents are booking into a guest house instead of staying with their families, either because they have got used to peace and quiet, or because their families have no spare rooms.

Depending on number of rooms, an establishment designated a B&B can cater for one or two guests, or up to about 20 people. They can be in beautiful places or right in the middle of busy towns. You as a potential buyer have to think hard about the way you want to enter this market, and what kind of guests you would be happiest to accommodate. B&Bs can also be basically overnighters, or places where people stay for up to a couple of weeks.

Research

The first thing is to research the chosen location, to establish that there is a year-round, or at least, good enough trade available or potentially available. If there is a very tight season and no real way of attracting guests outside these times, you are probably not going to be able to improve the profits significantly. It is also a good idea to visit both the planning department of your local council and the tourist office, to establish how many visitors the place gets each year, and whether there are any big businesses either coming to the area shortly, or about to close down, which might affect potential trade.

Improving profitability

This is the first thing any lender will want to know, when they study your business plan. As we have seen, most first-timers believe they can increase the takings by serving evening meals, but this is unlikely as, apart from the dismal prospect of guests eating by themselves in an otherwise deserted dining room, most towns with any substantial B&B trade are full of pubs, wine bars and restaurants anyway.

There are several ways of improving profitability when taking over an existing business: updating the décor, introducing mini-bars (and other bars), having a professional-looking website, and putting en suites in every room.

Hugh Caven reckons that, of these, improving the website is one of the most fundamental. 'In today's world, a professional, up-to-date website is vital, but many B&B proprietors have amateur, home-grown websites that may be three or four years out of date.'

It can be expensive to update the décor and for this reason, many new proprietors leave this as it is until trade picks up and establishes itself. Very many people buy with very tight cash flow and there is simply not enough left over for renovation and updating. Mostly, as B&Bs are bought as a going concern, you would have to work out how much you could increase profitability by renovating and upgrading the appearance of the place. Could you charge more for rooms? Could you get more occupancy?

The next thing to consider is the bar – or serving alcoholic drinks. Many B&Bs do not have liquor licences but again, this is not only a potent source of profit but also a way of attracting more guests. Hugh Caven recommends mini-bars in each room, and a bar in or near the dining room which is open, say, from five to seven in the evening. 'Many guests, especially those working during the day, like to get back to the guest house, have a drink at the bar, then have a shower and change before going out in the evening. I advise my customers to buy a B&B where there is already an established bar, rather than buy without one. Again, it is what guests want these days.'

An important task is to make sure that every single bedroom has an en suite. Again, Hugh Caven says: 'This is absolutely essential. If rooms do not have an en suite, you are going to have to charge much less, which means you tend to get the backpacking trade.'

Most existing B&Bs have some, but not all, guest rooms with en suites. Here, if you find a place that interests you, discover whether it is possible to put an en suite in the rooms without one. Otherwise, walk away as the rooms without en suites are going to be difficult to let year-round. Obviously, they can always be let when everywhere else in the area is full.

So these are the main considerations. If, after a few years, you want to move on from the original B&B and you have increased trade, you will be able to sell on at a profit. If profit has declined during your occupation, you may find it difficult to sell at all.

Here are a couple of ads for B&Bs taken from the monthly magazine *Bed and Breakfast News*:

Cross Lanes Cottage, four star Silver award B&B at foot of the Chiltern Hills, Oxon/Bucks border. Accommodation comprises: 2 double and 1 twin room all en suite, luxurious lounge and well-stocked garden with fruit orchard. Owners' accommodation includes 2 large bedrooms with bathrooms, office and sep. family/TV room. All B&B rooms to be sold intact to include: carpets, curtains throughout, china, bedlinen, towels, everything needed to begin immediate trading including dining room, fully furnished with antique furniture. Price £780,000.

Fordside, four star. Semi-detached Edwardian house, situated in Buxton, very close to attractions, Peaks and Dales. Comprising: 4 guest bedrooms (3 en suite), owner's bedroom and private lounge. Private parking. Fire Certificated. The house has not been run as a B&B for three years but would take very little to establish as a thriving business. Price £410,000.

These two highly typical advertisements are aimed at owner-occupiers who need to know that there is private accommodation as well as guest accommodation. As such, you can expect that the sellers will already have complied with all existing regulations concerning hygiene, health and safety, and have all permissions and licences, including television licences, in place.

Information you would need from the seller would include: price of rooms in high and low season, cost of business rates, if applicable, plus any extra insurance needed, such as public liability insurance, and whether the place can be run by, say, a couple, or whether you would need to employ extra staff. You would have to pay any staff the minimum wage, at least.

You would also need to know about laundry arrangements, as these are easily the most potentially problematic areas of running a typical B&B with a quick turnover of guests. Who does the ironing? How many sets of bedlinen do you need for each bed? Is there a commercial laundry available nearby?

The two ads above do not state that the B&Bs are licensed to sell alcohol; so the assumption is that they are not. This is something you might want to alter straightaway.

Before making any kind of offer, you would also need to know how the price of the property compares to other, similar sized properties in the area just used as a private residence.

In general, private houses are more expensive, so by taking on the B&B, you should be getting something of a bargain. You would also need to know how long it has been on the market, and what sort of interest there has been from other buyers.

Case study

In 2003, Jill and John Hitchins decided to set up a small B&B in their beautiful home, a former rectory, near Totnes, Devon. Jill, a TV producer, and John, a college lecturer, felt this was a better option than moving to a smaller place now that their family had grown up and gone. Their B&B, The Old Rectory, Diptford, (www.oldrectorydiptford.co.uk) has four letting rooms.

Jill, a Leith's trained cook, says: 'We felt the house would lend itself as it has six bedrooms and a two-acre garden. There are two staircases, so we did not need fire doors. We charge £85 per couple per night, £60 for a single occupant and £25 for dinner. The business does not make enough money to live on and so John is continuing with his lecturing job at Plymouth. I am also working as a TV producer from time to time. We do turn in a profit, though, and could not afford to live here without the B&B.

'We had to offer disabled access and we must also have a food hygiene inspection each year.

'We applied for, and got, a liquor licence, as this is essential when serving food. I made sure the bathrooms were of top quality and I have beautiful cotton sheets. We have year-round occupancy and also do weddings and special events.

'I love cooking, and our speciality is our fabulous food.'

Jill and John employ one full-time member of staff. Jill says that when setting up a B&B, little things count for a lot. 'For instance, it's essential to have airtight jars for tea, coffee and biscuits in the bedrooms, and these are hard to find. Then I like to have embroidered tablecloths; in fact, I am always buying these tablecloths on eBay and they have become a feature of our B&B.

'It's very important to pay attention to detail, as these are the things that guests remember, mention to others – and the things that get you recommendations and repeat bookings, so long as they are positive, of course.'

The specialist magazine *Bed and Breakfast News* offers some advice on keeping up-to-date with what you offer when it comes to breakfast, as today's guests may well be expecting something special from a time-honoured institution specializing in the first meal of the day:

Sustainable practices are appealing to today's consumer, in direct response to media hype surrounding our declining environment. Experiment with a mouth-watering menu, without breaking the bank or losing the traditional homestyle warmth B&B accommodation is famous for. Do some research into locally sourced produce and negotiate an affordable price on food that remains fresh from plough to plate. Be remembered by your guests and stand out from your competitors.

If you are intent on keeping breakfast simple with tea and toast, market this on the basis that your bread is home-made or delivered fresh and daily from the local bakery. Don't keep it a secret: shout about your support for Third-World producers by serving quality Fairtrade teas and rich-scented filter coffee. Not only is this helping a good cause, it reflects a readiness to respond to consumer trend and conscience.

Loosely categorize your guests into 'destination travellers' (those looking to your accommodation to provide privacy and a relaxing environment) and 'convenience travellers' (those using your B&B as a base from which to explore the surrounding area). Consider rotating the breakfasts you serve based on the purpose of the stay, the time of year and time of day. It may be profitable to offer two sittings to cater for both category of visitor – the early versus the late risers – which operators could determine upon booking. Destination travellers will certainly be prepared to pay a premium for the option of a lie-in, as it's rare to find a B&B that accommodates beyond the two-hour fixed breakfast sitting.

Present the choice of a substantial brunch-style breakfast, serving a selection of hot and cold dishes, from appealing winter warmers, such as smoked salmon and Poached Eggs Benedict on warm butter-toasted muffins, to light, early morning preferences, such as wholesome cereals and croissants. In the summer, when the weather is warmer, you may want to tailor your menu by including healthy five-a-day, vitamin-packed fresh fruit smoothies. Not everyone wants a greasy full English fry-up at 7 am.

Finance

Assuming the place is nicely ticking over, the next step would be, before putting in an offer, to go to a finance company which specializes in mortgage packages for B&Bs and guest houses, and see what they have to offer. Even if you have enough cash to buy outright, it is probably preferable to go for finance, as with this option you have to prepare a business plan and let the lender have sight of all accounts, plus you hope that the B&B occupancy will mean the premises are self-financing. Finance is arranged on the basis of income from the B&B rather than your existing salary or cash at the bank.

In general terms, you would need to find 30 per cent of the deposit minimum in cash before any mortgage offer could be made. The lender would then determine whether the offer would be mainly residential, or mainly commercial. This depends on the proportion of space used for the owners as compared with that set aside for guests.

In general, if 40 per cent or more of the accommodation is used by the owners, you would obtain a residential mortgage, but if the percentage favours the guest accommodation, you would be offered a commercial mortgage.

Supposing the place needed a lot of updating, you would have to negotiate a mortgage similar to that used by self-builders, where you would get stage payments until the place was ready for occupation. Throughout this period, you would typically go for an interest-only mortgage, after which the capital repayments would start. Ideally, as with any other accommodation provider, the yearly turnover would more than cover the mortgage, meaning that you are living rent- and mortgage-free in a beautiful house in a fabulous location.

You should also go and look at the competition, maybe staying in a similar guest house yourself, to get a feel for the way the business works. You will also have to think about whether or not you welcome children, and if so, whether you are going to provide family rooms or any particular facilities for children or babies such as high chairs or cots. Also, would you welcome pets? There are 'pet-friendly' hotels, and if you would welcome a well-behaved cat or dog, you can certainly charge a premium, as it is always difficult to get your pet looked after for a few days.

There are many more issues to consider when setting up a guest house, however small or modest, than renting out a self-catering holiday home. For instance, you may well have to get planning permission for change of use; there may be parking considerations; you may have to provide some kind of disabled access; and if you want to serve alcoholic drinks, you will have to go through a lot of legal hoops to be granted a licence.

For purchase and renovation, the Cumberland Building Society, for example, will lend up to 70 per cent of the market value at any one time. Money for renovation can be drawn down in stages, as with self-build projects, and for extending or improving existing premises. Then you would have to provide a business plan, with projections of occupancy level and takings for the next 12–18 months.

The Cumberland Building Society, which specializes in finance packages for guest houses and hotels, says that although very few new guest house and B&B businesses are being created, there is a very active market in purchasing existing places and renovating or improving them. By far the greatest number of requests for finance is to increase the number of en suites, ideally so that there is one to each bedroom.

Most lenders will offer mortgages for bed and breakfast establishments, and these are known as commercial owner-occupier mortgages as they fall into both the residential and the commercial category. By far the great majority of bed and breakfast owners themselves live on the premises and for this reason, a B&B is considered a hybrid entity, neither 'house' nor 'hotel'.

Investing in a B&B will always require a sizeable cash injection, and when you talk to a mortgage lender, all your assets will be taken into account, as well as considerations as to whether you have another job outside the B&B.

There are specialist inn brokers who are expert in every aspect of B&B finance, and it may be useful to talk to these before making any expensive commitment.

The financial downturn could prove to be good news for B&B proprietors as throughout 2008 and 2009, there has been a move towards building and converting cheaper hotels and overnight accommodation, rather than concentrating on the luxury end. Some four-star hotels are being downgraded to three-stars, for instance, and many old-fashioned traditional hotels are being turned into Travelodges, which offer clean but extremely basic accommodation for overnight guests. Although there will always be a place for the luxury hotel, there is increasing scope for those prepared to offer cut-price accommodation.

VAT

This is a highly problematic area which stymies very many B&B proprietors. Briefly, the situation is this: if your turnover (not profit) is £68,000 or more (in 2010) you become liable for VAT at 17.5 per cent. Estate agent Haydn Spedding, of Colliers Robert Barry, who specializes in selling B&Bs in the Lake District, says: 'Maximizing income is not always the criterion, as if you go over the VAT threshold, you will have to charge more for rooms and services and this may put you above the competition, without necessarily being able to offer anything better. You are up against people who are not charging VAT.

'The trouble is that in the B&B industry, there is very little you can claim back on VAT, which makes it a tricky tax to deal with. There is no VAT on food, for instance. If your turnover is between £64,000 and £150,000 a year, you can opt for the flat VAT rate of

9.5 per cent, and this can come in handy if you have a renovation or upgrading programme on which you can reclaim VAT.

'For this reason, a lot of buyers like to keep their turnover just below the threshold, which means they will probably have six or fewer guest rooms. If you have 14 to 20 rooms, you will almost certainly go over the VAT threshold.'

Haydn Spedding recommends talking to an accountant about the VAT and turnover situation in advance of making an offer or drawing up a business plan.

Legislation issues

VisitBritain's Pink Booklet – the highly detailed bible for existing and potential 'accommodation providers' – states that even if you are only intending to offer simple bed and breakfast in your own home, you may still need 'change of use' planning permission. It is also very likely that any house will need at least some adaptation or alteration before it becomes suitable for guests, and whenever you admit strangers to your property, you have to abide by health, safety and fire rules, and make sure all furniture complies with existing regulations.

You may also be required to take out extra insurance, and in any case, mortgage lenders must be informed, as the home is now being used partly as a business and to make money.

You must also inform HM Revenue and Customs. It is simply not worth taking the risk of just offering accommodation and breakfast without invoking officialdom.

Business rates

If you are offering accommodation in return for money, you may have to pay business rates instead of council tax. Naturally, business rates are higher. In some cases you may not have to pay business rates, if the premises are very small and can only accommodate up to six people at a time, and you are yourself living full time on the premises. But before ever advertising for guests, you must speak to your accountant.

Just to make matters more complicated, it is possible you will have to pay business rates on the part of the house used for guests, and council tax on the part you use for yourself.

Business rates are calculated on the possible rental value of your property, the way old-fashioned 'rates' used to be calculated. Again, you would need to contact your local council at an early stage to discover what these business rates are, and how they might affect what you are thinking of charging for bed and board.

Fire safety

This is of the utmost importance and can never be ignored. The best thing to do, at an early stage, is to ask the Fire Brigade to come round and advise on fire precautions, unless there is a fire certificate already in place, as you will need a valid fire certificate in order to run the premises as a guest house. This regulation does not apply if the guest house can take a maximum of six guests, excluding those living there permanently as family, but including any residential staff.

Current legislation means that you are allowed to burn six guests, but not seven. If buying an existing business and considering extending, or adding to the number of guest rooms, a fire certificate would be needed.

You will also, as with holiday lets, be required to take out public liability insurance, and insurance companies may interpret the 'six bed space' rule very strictly. Ordinary household policies do not cover use of your premises for business purposes.

It is as well to wise up on all these aspects before ever advertising for guests and, if buying an existing business, ask about insurance matters. In any case, your mortgage lender will need to have sight of these documents before arranging the mortgage.

Catering

It can be a much more complicated matter to offer meals in your establishment than to set up self-catering units, as you will need licences to operate your business. Just about all premises which offer food and drink to outsiders for profit will have to register with the local authority. The only exception to this rule is if you have no more than three bedrooms for the use of guests, and are offering tea and biscuit-type refreshment only.

In any case, you should contact your local environmental health department for advice when considering offering catering services, however basic. There are very many regulations which must be complied with, and you never know when an inspector may call, especially if you are operating under the auspices of local or national tourist organizations. Recent scares concerning food poisoning, for instance, have meant that the Food Standards Agency has now issued strict guidelines for handling cooked meats, and preventing cross-contamination from raw foods. There is a 10-point hygiene plan for ensuring food safety in catering establishments, available from the Food Standards Agency, Ref: BEL.

Liquor licensing

If you would like a bar area or are offering evening meals, then you must have a liquor licence in place. In general terms, it is worth going for a suitable liquor licence as you will attract more trade and may also be able to charge more for accommodation. Places with drinks licences are vastly more popular than those without.

There are several different types of licence available: full-on licence; restaurant licence; residential licence and restaurant and residential licence; occasional licence; and occasional permission. Here, you have to decide what type of service you would want to offer regarding liquor, then go to your solicitor to handle your application, as it is a complicated matter whereby procedures must be followed to the letter.

In general, licences are granted to a named individual by the liquor licensing department of the magistrates' court. The licence, once granted, allows the licensee to sell alcohol in named premises. If you have not had previous licensing experience, you may also be required to attend a one- or two-day course run by the British Institute of Innkeeping at a local college.

You have to apply to the relevant licensing session in writing (known as Brewster Sessions), giving 21 clear days' notice. If applying for a new licence, you will need to attach plans of the premises and the location, plus display a notice at or near the premises where the application may be seen by passers-by. And don't forget that neighbours may object.

A notice also has to be placed in the local newspaper. You may be granted, or refused a licence, or, in the case of new premises, you may be granted a provisional licence by the licensing justices. If you are setting up a new guest house, it is best to apply for, and obtain, the provisional licence before you start on renovations or adaptations.

Your local court should have all the papers and documentation you need, and the clerk there may well give advice. But as this is a complicated legal procedure, it is worth using a solicitor conversant with licensing laws. There are also strict regulations about selling liquor to children, or allowing children in bar areas, so if you are setting up a family guest house, this also has to be taken into account.

Television licences

Most overnight guests want television facilities, and here you would need a special Hotel and Mobile Units Television Licence. You should always take out a hotel licence if providing television sets for the use of guests. The fee for the licence is determined by the maximum number of guests and if no more than 15, the licence fee is the same as the standard licence; this goes up for each additional five rooms. In most cases, this covers television watching by owners and staff.

If you want to play music as entertainment, you will also need a Performing Right Society Licence.

Regarding use of guest telephones, there are no regulations concerning how much you are allowed to charge guests for telephone calls. These days, as most guests have mobiles, telephones in bedrooms have become less necessary. Many small guest houses nowadays just have payphones in the hall where you can make outgoing calls but not receive incoming calls.

Unless the guest house is very large, it is probably no longer worth bothering with telephones in guest bedrooms. You may have to think about whether you want to provide internet access for guests, especially if you are catering for commercial trade.

So far as the law is concerned, your guest house is considered either a 'hotel' or a 'private hotel'. Most often, a small guest house will be the latter, and it means you can pick and choose your guests – you do not have to accept just anybody – and people have to book in advance. If you run a 'hotel', by contrast, you are not allowed to refuse a guest unless you believe that person will be a nuisance to your other guests.

Disabled access

This is a bugbear for all who wish to offer rooms to guests on a profit-making basis. In general, the Disability Discrimination Act applies to you if you provide any sort of accommodation in return for money. The best thing here is to contact your local council to see what, if any, adaptations you may need to make to ensure your establishment is usable by disabled people. In most cases, you would have to make the place wheelchair-friendly. Even when buying a going concern, it is worth checking with the council to ensure that your disability provision meets current requirements.

If running a small guest house, obviously the disabled facilities you may be required to provide will be less stringent than if running a five-star hotel. If you are offering bed and breakfast with only two bedrooms, you would not be expected to carry out extensive building work to provide wheelchair access to these rooms.

Furniture and fittings

As with finance packages, there are specialist companies offering 'everything' for the B&B proprietor. Out of Eden, for instance, is a mail-order company specializing in everything for the guest-house proprietor from soap and toiletries to beds, bedlinen, signs ('Do not disturb'), and menu holders and wine lists. Catalogue from sales@outofeden.co.uk.

Those with high aesthetic standards have to bear in mind that furnishings suitable for your own home may be completely inadequate for a guest house, which gets much harder wear. Also, guests staying for only a night or two may not be so choosy as for a permanent residence. Because you are running a business, you may have to go for brighter colours or more lurid patterns than you would ideally like, as these are harder-wearing and do not show the dirt. In particular, carpets in common parts must be extremely hard wearing and resistant to marks.

Starting from scratch

Many property investors would like to turn a private house into a B&B but this is fraught with difficulties, particularly when it comes to getting a mortgage, as you could not get a commercial mortgage for a business which does not yet exist, and a residential mortgage would not be forthcoming for purchase or renovation of a building which will have a change of use from residential to commercial.

If, however, you already own the property and would like to turn part of it into a B&B, you would first have to contact the local council to see if planning permission is likely to be granted. The next step would be to submit detailed architect's plans and get in some quotes for the work. But raising finance for this would be difficult, so the only real way is to have the money to do it yourself. Obviously, expensive loans can be raised, but before ever entering on such a project, see whether planning permission would be granted in the first place.

Very many councils are not keen to give planning permission for new B&Bs or small guest houses as this increases parking difficulties. There might also be problems with neighbours, if the area is mainly residential.

It is becoming ever more difficult to change the use of any building, whether this was originally residential or commercial. Obviously I would not recommend this course of action, but, there is nothing to stop you doing the conversion secretly 'on the black' and then applying for retrospective planning permission, as one way round the restrictions increasingly being used.

Ratings

All B&Bs are now liable to have a diamond rating, going from one to five. This rating means that the establishment has been inspected, and is also regularly inspected. Briefly, a one-diamond rating means that the establishment is acceptably clean and tidy and offers a full English or continental breakfast. Two diamonds indicate a greater emphasis on guest care; three diamonds indicate comfortable, well-maintained bedrooms and quality items for breakfast; a four-diamond establishment has high quality furniture and excellent customer care; and a five-diamond place has very high quality furniture and outstanding customer care.

Those who are just starting out can gain an 'entry level' rating, which can be upgraded when the business is more established.

And finally...

Estate agent Haydn Spedding says that the B&B industry is intimately affected by politics and government policies. 'In the 1990s, people were getting out of B&Bs because they realized they had made a huge gain on their premises, so they were selling them and pocketing the proceeds.

'Most people buying into B&Bs sell their existing house to do so, and the business also becomes their home. But now, people coming up to retirement are buying B&Bs to give them a few more years in employment whereby they can build up their pensions.

'All sorts of things are likely to affect the business, such as charging for roads. If this comes in, are people going to pay £500 to drive up to Ambleside for a £100 holiday? There will always be a market for the B&B but it will always keep changing. The B&B market is far more liable to change and fluctuate than the hotel market, so buyers have to be very sure about what they are getting themselves into.'

8 Buying property abroad

I often used to see a neighbour of mine outside in the street cleaning his car. One day, after a few years of briefly acknowledging each other, we got into conversation, as is the British way.

'Terrible weather, isn't it?' my neighbour offered, looking up at the unrelieved grey cloud blanket overhead in what was supposed to be the height of summer. 'Still, doesn't worry us much. We're off to Cyprus for a fortnight at the weekend.'

'That sounds nice,' I said. 'Have you got a villa or apartment there?'

'Not yet,' he said. 'A few years ago I bought some land...' My hitherto taciturn neighbour became expansive. It turned out that he had bought a large tract of land in Northern Cyprus for £2,000 and eventually hoped to build four villas there. Like any professional developer, he was biding his time, and waiting until Northern Cyprus joined the EU. He did not seem concerned. 'It could be five, seven years, even longer.

'Still, it's only a couple of grand. Worth taking the risk. The thing about Northern Cyprus, the Turkish part, is to make sure of the title. In many cases, the title is disputed and you never know who really owns it. We bought the land through a friend of a friend, and we shan't start building until the Turkish part of Cyprus is harmonized with the rest of Europe.'

Southern Cyprus, of course, joined the EU in 2004 but, at the time of writing at least, no date has been set for the Northern, Turkish part to do likewise. My friend also pointed out that Famagusta, on the border, is littered with abandoned and derelict hotels built in the early sixties in the expectation of a tourism rush which never came when the Turks invaded Cyprus in 1974.

My car-cleaning friend knows he has taken a risk but it is one that may eventually pay off handsomely. In the meantime, as he nudges towards retirement, he has an exciting project to keep him occupied.

At one time I would have been flabbergasted, not to say Famagusted, at this ordinary-seeming middle-aged man being a property expert on Northern Cyprus. Not any more. As we talked, my new friend told me about people he knew who had been snapping up apartments in Bulgaria for £10,000 each, investing in Croatia, buying up car-wash franchises in Poland, investing in safari parks in Africa, and other such exotica.

At one time, people bought property overseas mainly for the purposes of realizing a dream, and to have an exotic bolt-hole. But increasingly, property investors are looking abroad to expand or even start their investment portfolio – and the name of the game is profit, rather than enjoying a leisurely lifestyle in the sun.

The expectation is that much of 'abroad' offers greater long-term capital growth prospects than the home country, and when looking to invest, as with anything else, there are many options to choose from.

These include: emerging markets; beach destinations; existing or mature markets; long-haul destinations; golfing properties; European cities; and ski destinations. Some overseas markets may offer more than one of these possibilities. For instance, an emerging market such as the Czech Republic also offers skiing; other such markets may also be beach destinations, long-haul destinations or golfing locations.

At the time of writing, existing or mature markets include Florida, Spain, Portugal, Turkey, France, Italy and Ireland. Emerging markets include Bulgaria, Croatia, the Czech Republic and Shanghai, and long-haul destinations include Australia, the Caribbean, South Africa, New Zealand and Phuket.

Bill and Hilary Jordon-White bought a two-bedroom off-plan apartment near Bodrum in Turkey for £37,000 in September 2006 and before they even completed on the transaction, similar properties in the same complex were going for £55,000.

So, why Turkey? Bill, a train driver, says: 'We were too late for Spain as you need a minimum of £100,000 to have even a toehold there, and at our age, didn't want to have a mortgage. We wanted somewhere we could buy for cash, especially as it is not easy to get mortgages in Turkey, and we did not want to take any equity out of our main British home. We did have to get permission from the military before we could buy, as does every foreigner buying in Turkey, but for us it was just a formality as they could easily see we were nice, respectable people. But, it has to be done and nobody can buy in Turkey without getting this written permission.

'We have bought into a development of 200 apartments which is being built by a local firm, but the developers are British with, we hope, British standards of hygiene, pool care and general maintenance. There are five swimming pools in the complex, mini-golf, tennis and other sports and we are right on our own private beach.

'We will be hugely improving the local economy as we are all buying furniture and kitchen and bathroom equipment from local shops, using local restaurants, shops and transport. The plan is that when I retire, we will winter in Turkey and spend the summer in our main home. The complex is designed to be let out to families, so we would always be able to get an income and, already we could sell at a profit.'

Bill's advice to anybody considering such a purchase is: 'We would never do it unless our main home was rock-solid. Some people have been pouring money into their foreign apartments and putting their main home at risk. Nor, at our age, would we buy unless we could do it for cash.

'It is also essential to look at the infrastructure of any emerging market and in Turkey, roads are being built along the coast and a motorway is under construction. For us, it was the place to go.'

But here is an example of what NOT to do when buying property abroad. Heather and Simon, a middle-aged couple with adult children, decided to invest in property abroad as their pension. They downsized on their main house, freeing up £150,000. Simon then went on a fly 'n' buy trip to Turkey and, seduced by the extremely clever and persuasive marketing team there, put down a deposit on three off-plan properties, imagining that he would easily be able to 'flip' – that is, sell them on to someone else before completion.

After that, he and Heather went to Bulgaria, where they did the same thing and bought two more properties off-plan. Heather admits: 'My brain left me.' The upshot several years later is that they cannot flip on any of their properties. The developer cannot even sell all the units in the apartment blocks: only 60 per cent have been sold, with little chance of the remainder finding buyers. So Simon and Heather are stuck with five properties that are going to cost them, rather than making them money, and which they cannot afford to maintain.

Any hope that the developer might buy back the properties will come to nothing. The company will take the properties back only at a vastly reduced rate. In the meantime, the couple face not only ongoing running costs but also somehow have to pay for the five properties they have bought.

The moral of this story? Never, ever go on an inspection trip unless you have already carried out all the research necessary and are 99.9 per cent certain you want to buy into that particular development, in that particular country. The research involves going into every little aspect of the finance, running costs and mortgage availability; most of all, it means carefully considering your exit strategy.

There are many companies advertising off-plan developments on the internet. Naturally, all are going to hype up the location, the return on investment and the capital gain. But few, if any, of these companies will give a guarantee of buying the property back from you at more than you paid for it. Some may offer guaranteed rental for a number of years, but even when this happens, do not imagine you are necessarily home and dry. You need to know that the rental will cover your costs and more and that the property is likely to increase in value in the meantime.

How can you know this? Well, you can't, for sure, but at the very least you need to carry out careful research into the country where you are thinking of buying. Turkey is popular and the properties sound cheap but investment expert Gary Festa says that Turkish properties are marked up by 60 to 70 per cent for the tourist market, and that Turkish nationals cannot possibly afford them. This means that the properties have value only for the foreign market and depend more or less completely on the tourist trade for income.

When investing in property abroad, what is the main purpose of the exercise these days? According to a survey by the Homebuyer Show in 2005, just over 25 per cent of investors were after long-term capital gains; 21.24 per cent wanted a holiday home; 20.35 per cent were interested in short-term holiday lets; 15.93 per cent wanted a possible retirement home; and 7 per cent were interested in renting out their property to local residents. Only 2 per cent were considering short-term corporate lets.

So how can you tell whether your desired spot has investment potential? One obvious appeal is a budget airline, although these are notoriously subject to going bust or cancelling routes at short notice. Property experts maintain that wherever there is a low-cost airline, the property buyers soon follow. Another is existing or potential membership of the EU and yet another plus is a wide range of leisure facilities such as sport, children's entertainment and water activities. And of course, good weather is always a prime attraction.

But beware! The most popular overseas locations, at least for Brits, are hot, dry places. Coming from a cold, wet country, we long for reliably hot, dry weather. But any country which is both hot and dry is also very liable to have a chronic water shortage. In Spain, for instance, where there is an insatiable demand for private swimming pools and golf courses – which of course have to be watered regularly – there are also often severe water shortages. Desalination plants, which are used in places where it virtually never rains, are extremely expensive.

Investing in property abroad is always risky, but many overseas property experts believe that the only real way of making a profit, either with existing or mature markets, is to buy off-plan or newbuild apartments or villas in places that are on the up and up. It is almost impossible to make money from buying a romantic wreck and then lovingly restoring it yourself.

Case study

A friend bought two off-plan apartments in Bankso, Bulgaria, on a fly 'n' buy trip. She said, 'I bought one to flip and the other to rent out as a ski apartment. You have to be aware that these trips are very high-pressure and I don't know anybody who left without buying an apartment. You are totally hassled all the way and if you fly out with them you have to go to the meetings they arrange. It all happens so quickly and people were even fighting over the units.

'The people who arrange the fly 'n' buy trips can organize everything for you including renting and managing the apartment and selling you a furniture package. It is a very smooth operation and you have to be very careful when adding up the figures to make sure you come out with something. I think that with the first apartment I will be lucky to come out with £4,000 profit when I sell.'

'The other thing is that if you buy to flip, which is that you sell on before you pay the last tranche of money, you have to be very sure that this will actually happen, otherwise you will be left with a large debt on a property you didn't really want to own in the first place. The last e-mail I got, on 17 May 2007, said that the market had now changed and they could not guarantee a buyer in the necessary time frame. This means that if I don't find a buyer I will have to pay the last lot of money to the developers.'

One reason for the market suddenly changing could be that Bulgaria was bidding for the Winter Olympics but was unsuccessful. 'As an investor, you have to be on the alert for this kind of thing happening all the time, and keep hearing in your head the old proverb: don't count your chickens before they are hatched.'

My friend continued, 'It seems to me that the developers and companies who are selling off-plan apartments and villas in other countries are very clever indeed. If you don't manage to sell before the property is completed you may have to get a mortgage, and this means you have then locked yourself into a long-term loan with very severe penalties for early exits. I certainly didn't want a mortgage on my buy-to-flip property but if I don't manage to sell before completion, I will probably have to arrange one.

'It can all be a big trap if you don't have the ready cash. My apartments cost around 38,000 euros, which sounds very cheap but there are all sorts of costs along the way, which inexorably add up.

My legal fees were over 500 euros on each purchase and then there were other fees, such as the notary fee and other costs, plus you have to pay stamp duty of 2 per cent if you complete on the purchase and don't manage to sell before completion.

'I wanted to buy somewhere in a town rather than a development miles out but there is a lot of pressure to get you to buy in a gated development away from it all.'

You also need to be very sure, if you are being sold a 'front-line' apartment or villa in a development, that your views will not be blocked by another development being built in front of it in the future. Many investors have been very disappointed to learn that what they imagined would be wonderful views will be blocked by another development being built in front.

Also, if you are buying ski apartments, as my friend was doing, you must make sure that skiers will actually be coming to the place. The property investment business talks all the time of 'due diligence' but it is very easy to be swayed by high-pressure salespeople, most of whom rely totally on their commission. Unless they sell you a unit, they don't earn anything, so they are extremely hungry people.

After my friend's ski apartment was finished and furnished, she advertised it on several websites. But – nobody booked it at all! Although she received several enquiries, none of these led to a booking. At the same time as she started advertising her ski apartment in Bansko, news came that 33 per cent of Bansko's foreign-owned properties were back on the market, often at 50 per cent below purchase price.

Clearly nobody could have seen the credit crunch coming or money drying up all over the world, but whatever sales and purchase prices might be doing, if nobody wants to book your ski apartment, wherever it is, you have got yourself a very expensive liability. The probability with my friend's apartment is that it was competing with so many others on the market, and maybe not enough people went skiing to Bulgaria to take up all the apartments on offer.

As with UK property, there are two main ways you can hope to make money: from rental income and from resale.

Most investors would hope for both types of gain, although this may not always be possible. If you are mainly interested in rental income, you would need to determine the popularity of the place as a holiday destination or resort, and what attractions, including weather, are on offer. You may have in mind a beachfront property, a ski chalet, a golfing villa or apartment, or a place with huge attractions for children. But there has to be something that makes people want to flock to the area.

You would also need to know how long the rental season lasts. In some countries or cities, there may be year-round letting potential, but in other locations, the season may be extremely short.

Then there is the vexed question of competition. If there is huge competition, this will inevitably bring down prices, and you may discover that your wonderful villa or apartment is either empty, or will only rent out at a rate far too low to cover costs, let alone make a profit.

To give an example, many investors who snapped up cheap-seeming properties on Sunny Beach in Bulgaria, where many developments are going up, managed to rent their apartments out for just six weeks in the year, at around £200 a week. Therefore, although they may have only paid £30,000 for their apartment, the gross rental return was just £1,200 a year, or 4 per cent. The net rental return, after advertising, cleaning and management costs, would be about half this – hardly enough to cover the mortgage and service charges on the apartment.

It's not that I have anything against Bulgaria; I am just using it as an example of how careful you have to be when considering investing in somewhere that seems not only exotic and sunny, but cheap. At the time of writing, Bulgaria is being talked up as an investment hotspot, but there is massive development going on, at the same time as the tourist industry is not well established. Some investors have already had their fingers burnt in Bulgaria, and got out.

Cheap is cheap for a reason; it is high risk. And the newer the market, the longer you would have to hang on to your investment before it produces the hoped-for returns.

Beware also the 'guaranteed rental' trap. One company advertising new and off-plan apartments on the Black Sea in Bulgaria was offering a 7 per cent guaranteed rental – for six months. Guaranteed rentals are also a feature of many new developments in Portugal.

Before enthusiastically signing up to a guaranteed rental scheme and imagining that all your financial woes are over, you need to check out exactly what is being 'guaranteed'.

The Florida Mortgage Corporation advises that many guaranteed rental schemes on holiday investment properties are exaggerated, untested and flawed, and also take an extremely optimistic view of continued growth in the holiday market.

What will happen if there is an enormous downturn in tourist trade after the guarantee period ends? During 2008, many people were cutting back on foreign holidays, partly because of rising airfares driven by increasing fuel costs, and partly because of having to cover increased mortgage costs on their homes.

You also need to know that the company or the developer has adequate reserves to meet the guaranteed rental. If it all goes belly-up and the rental money is not paid to you, what are you going to do? Will you sue the company? Will you do so in the UK or in the country where you bought the property? Have you even thought about it?

Because you are still liable for management fees during the period of the guaranteed rental (otherwise the scheme cannot count as a rental), you also need to check how much these cost and whether there will be anything left over after the guaranteed rental is paid to you.

Note: almost all off-plan developers now offer inspection trips, guaranteed rentals and discounts for early buyers. It all sounds good, but never forget that developers are all in the business of making money from you, the investor. Never buy unless all the figures stack up, and there is not just a genuine rental market, but a guaranteed resale price as well.

You particularly need to know, as with the home market, whether there is a real rental demand, and whether you could get that 7 per cent (or whatever is offered) on the open market when the guarantee period finishes. Not all these 'guaranteed rentals' mean that the place is actually rented out.

As a general rule, it is not easy to make a profit on rentals from holiday apartments anyway. You would be lucky even to cover your costs in most places, simply because there are so many similar apartments, and very many companies offering huge discounts you may not be able to match. The only exception to this is Italy, where there is little speculative development, and many beautiful, tastefully restored villas which appeal to the upmarket lover of Italy.

The bog-standard family wants somewhere sunny, cheap and easy to get to for a holiday – and this market has a great deal of choice.

Other questions you must ask yourself (or ask an objective overseas property expert with nothing to sell you) include:

- How easy or difficult is the buying process?

- How easy is it to get a mortgage?

- What are the costs of buying?

- Are there any local taxes to pay?

- Are there restrictions on UK nationals owning property in the country?

- Do you have to form a company in the chosen country?

- How easy or difficult is it to establish title?

- How long would you realistically have to wait to see a good return on your investment?

- What is the situation with paying tax on rental income?

- What about inheritance tax and capital gains tax?

All countries have different rules, even within the EU. And, as ever, when investing in property, the eventual profit you may make is not just a matter of looking at the purchase price and the selling price, but how much it costs you to buy, and how much it costs you to sell, bearing in mind that when thinking about 'abroad' you have to include the costs of getting to and from the place, as well as all the entry and exit fees, local costs and taxes.

Also bear in mind that there are ever more developers, property clubs, seminars and so on trying to get you to part with your money to invest abroad. My own advice would be: never buy into anywhere you don't know, where you don't speak the language and where your only interest is that whipped up at an expensive property investment seminar, fly-to-buy trip, property exhibition or unsolicited post or e-mail.

The golden rule is: if you are interested in investing abroad, make sure you have done all your research before going out to view a yet to be built development or are seduced by sales talk. Never forget that property salespeople are most probably much better at selling than you are at resisting. Also never forget that the costs stack up far more than you can ever believe – before you have completed on the sale.

Finance and mortgages

By far the greatest majority of people who buy abroad finance the purchase either by downsizing on their main UK home, or by remortgaging, to free up the minimum 20–25 per cent of the purchase price needed before being granted a mortgage. There are now very many mortgage options for buying abroad, but across Europe they all work broadly on the same principle, which is that they are available for up to 75 per cent of the purchase price.

To set up the mortgage, you will have to pay an administration fee to the lender, plus a valuer's fee (non-refundable), legal fees, land registry charges and the notary's fees. The notary, a legal personage without an exact equivalent in the UK, usually acts for both buyer and seller, and has to examine and assess all relevant paperwork for the sale to proceed. You are also responsible for the lender's legal fees, so need quite a lot of spare cash to complete the sale.

As with obtaining a mortgage in the UK, lenders have to know your exact financial position, and will assess your ability to pay the mortgage. If you are hoping to cover the mortgage by renting out the property, they will have to be satisfied that enough of a rental market exists.

Buying property abroad on a mortgage gives some checks on the purchase, as lenders will not advance money for a complete ruin. At least, so one hopes!

In many countries, there is high VAT levied on new properties, so you would need to know whether this applies. It has now been introduced in Cyprus, for instance.

International property expert Wayne Mottley advises: 'In some countries you have to set up a company in order to buy property. In certain Eastern European countries, for instance, it is not possible to buy land, or an off-plan villa, without first setting up a company.

'In order to do this, you have to engage a local lawyer who knows the set-up. Apart from the fact that the local lawyer is likely to be more conversant with the laws of his own country than one in your home country, it can be very expensive to set up a company to buy a foreign property from the UK.'

If you have the money, is it better to buy a foreign property with cash or take out a mortgage? Again, Wayne Mottley advises: 'Obviously there are pros and cons to both options, but if you take out a mortgage, you can buy two (or more!) properties instead of one, and there may also be significant taxation advantages to having a mortgage. Personally, I would lean towards a mortgage even where you have the cash as this enables leverage and in some countries, there are taxation and inheritance tax advantages. For instance, in Spain, there is 40 per cent inheritance tax on property bequeathed to both spouses and children. There is no way out of this, but if the property has a mortgage on it, the amount of tax can be considerably lessened.'

Another major issue surrounding mortgages is whether it is better to take out a mortgage in the local currency or in the UK. 'Mostly I would advise buyers to raise a mortgage in the same country as they are buying,' adds Wayne. 'The main reason for this is that if you intend to rent out your property, it is best to have your assets and liabilities in the same currency to avoid currency fluctuations between countries. Obviously you want the value of your foreign property to increase so you want to have as little currency fluctuation as possible. Such fluctuations can make it difficult to establish the value of your property.

'Before finally deciding, though, you have to look at comparative interest rates and also hidden costs. There are often more mortgage options in the UK than in other countries, and interest rates may be lower. The paperwork might be more difficult to understand in other countries, as often the legal language is very different and more archaic than the spoken and conversational language, as in English legal documents. Again, you need the services of a reputable local lawyer.

'The other thing you can do is to buy forward currency, where the rate can be guaranteed for 24 months. By using specialist forward currency companies – H I Effects in the UK is one of the biggest – you get a much better rate than at a local high street bank.'

As to whether a particular property will prove to be a good investment, one of the best ways of deciding is to use yourself as an example. 'If you are intending to rent out the property, would you want to go there yourself on a regular basis? Would you yourself want to pay 400 euros a week to stay there? If the answer is no – however cheap the property seems – you should walk away from it,' Wayne Mottley advises. 'Established markets are – well, established, and emerging markets are riskier. It is also essential to look at the overall economics of the particular country that interests you, and to be aware of the overall plans over the next five to 10 years. Obviously nobody knows anything for sure, but the established markets can often offer a better guaranteed return.'

It is still the case that more people want to go to France and Portugal for holidays than Romania, for instance.

Tax matters

There are no reliable figures to show how many overseas investors rent out their overseas homes without declaring the income, but a new EU Directive requires banks throughout the community, plus the Channel Islands, Isle of Man and other tax havens such as the Cayman Islands and Gibraltar, to disclose the identity of account holders to their home tax authority.

If you have been receiving income from a foreign property, but have not declared it to HM Revenue and Customs, there will most likely be an investigation which could go back many years, and result in large fines and possibly other penalties.

These rules do not apply to companies or trusts, only to individual account holders. If you have funds in an overseas bank, they will not reveal your identity without your consent, so if you receive a letter asking to reveal this information, you can be pretty sure that a tax investigation is under way.

Either this, or the bank will automatically deduct a withholding tax of 15 per cent from your account.

At the time of writing, banks in Hong Kong and the Bahamas are not included in this Directive, but it could only be a matter of time before it actually becomes impossible to evade tax on foreign investments.

The best advice, as ever, is not to take the risk but to make sure all income received from overseas properties is declared.

As ever, take advice from a good accountant conversant with foreign tax matters before going ahead with an investment.

Profitability

The wise investor also undertakes extensive research when it comes to the possibility of capital growth. For this, you would have to know the average resale prices of similar properties in the area. If very many new developments are going up, you are unlikely to make a profit on resale for a very long time, as who would buy a two-year old apartment or villa at a premium price, when they can get a brand-new one at a discount?

On the other hand, it would be hard to lose out on a beachfront apartment, ultimately, simply because there are limited areas of seashore, as opposed to inland. But if buying right on the beachfront, you would need to make absolutely certain that there is no possibility of a huge building going up in front of yours, obscuring your view and decimating the value of the place.

Private, gated developments are also unlikely to lose value, although it may take a long time for them to realize their full potential. As in the UK, it is usually the case that you have to hold the property for at least 10 years to make a decent profit on resale. A friend with a property in Boca Raton, Florida, held onto it for 11 years before it became profitable. In that time, the value of the house went down before it went up again.

There is huge development going on in many popular resorts and destinations, whether new or established, such as Croatia, Bulgaria, Cyprus, Spain, Dubai, Portugal, France, Florida, South Africa, Shanghai and Australia, and very many of these developments are specifically aimed at the foreign investor. They tend to be heavily marketed at investor shows, where cheap inspection trips are on offer.

Beware of these. Before enthusiastically signing up for an apparently cheap fly 'n' buy trip, you need to know about the developer's track record and whether it is a good idea to reserve off-plan in the belief that you can make a significant profit on resale. In Florida, many investors are 'flipping', which means they sell their off-plan property on completion, without ever having lived in the place. Many investors also hope to do this in Spain, but first you would have to be sure that the property will make you a handsome profit in that timescale.

Although Spain has been a mature market for many years and has experienced phenomenal growth, there have been reports of such massive overbuilding that investors cannot hope to make a profit on their properties for many years, if ever. And during 2008, the previously ever-upward values on holiday and retirement properties all seemed to be going in reverse. For instance, a luxury villa valued at 900,000 euros in 2006 sold in 2008 for 415,000 euros. In 2006, Britons were responsible for 60 per cent of foreign demand in Spain; by 2008 this had gone down to 20 per cent, indicating that the Brits' long love affair with Spain might be over at last.

In fact, what happened is that owing to reports about illegal land grabs, property prices going into free fall, and corrupt officials, the British became scared. And it is true that many people did lose out. These were mainly inexperienced investors trying to flip. But because of falling property values, they found themselves left with an unsaleable, unlettable property on which they have a mortgage they can't pay. This is the situation with Heather and Simon, who bought in Turkey and Bulgaria: completely inexperienced investors who should never have been let loose on foreign soil, except for a short holiday. They simply had no idea what they were doing, and the sums they put down as deposits were too large for them to lose.

Turkey is tricky, but Spain represents a golden opportunity for the type of investor profiled at the beginning of the book; the experienced or canny property buyer with money, the person who carefully carries out all the research necessary into roads, airports, popular holiday destinations and rental yields before buying. When sellers are desperate, somebody who comes along with money will be able to make a killing.

This is because, if an offer is subject to being able to raise finance, in a buyer's market you will very likely have lost the sale before the finance is in place. The golden rule is, always have the finance ready when you are buying in a depressed sales market.

It is more than likely that the situation in Spain will climb back up. It remains a highly popular country for holidays, and although the property market there may be, in estate-agent speak, 'correcting' itself, this situation will not last for ever.

We spoke about repossessions and distressed property assets earlier in the book. Since 2008, there has been a major distressed asset industry going on in Spain, where the property market all but collapsed. But experts warn that in fact, there are few genuine bargains to be had and that the real bargains are being snapped up by the bank staff, who then try to offload the dogs onto unsuspecting investors.

The severe downturn in Spanish property prices has been caused by four major factors, at least so far as UK buyers are concerned: massive oversupply in new apartments and falling demand; the credit crunch causing money owed by developers to be demanded back very quickly, and this has led to developers being forced to sell at almost any price they can get; the fall in the value of the pound against the euro causing large numbers to default on their mortgages; and confidence in the property market dented by corruption in Spanish Town Halls, as seen on a number of property programmes on television.

All this has meant that property values in Spain have taken a severe tumble and it may take years for them to climb back, if ever. Some good news is that the Spanish government is in the process of knocking down villas and apartments built without planning permission and tightening up the regulations on planning.

But buying repossessed property in Spain, known as 'repo' property, is fraught with problems. The bank or mortgage lender will start repossession proceedings when the owner has not paid the mortgage for three consecutive months, as in the UK. Until these have been concluded and the bank now owns the property, it cannot be bought by another person. The whole process takes between 18 and 24 months.

While court proceedings are under way, a potential buyer can only buy the debt on the property, not the title. By the time the title is available, many of these properties will have been on the market for up to two years, during which time no interested buyer has come forward, because the property is in a poor location, badly built, difficult to rent out or with some other investment no-no.

Many repossessed properties in Spain are offered for sale directly by Spanish banks and buying from a bank has its problems. There is a lot of paperwork, which may be difficult for a non-Spanish speaking person to understand. Also, the bank will often offer the property at an inflated price as it wants to grab its own commission on the sale. Further, mortgage approval for the property may be on the bank's own terms rather than a competitive product.

It is also possible to buy a cheap property directly from the developer, but not all of these may have the proper paperwork in place. The property must possess a First Occupation Licence to attract a mortgage and be already connected to mains utilities. Many distressed properties are on huge sites where many properties may remain empty. This is why you should never buy a property directly from a website or even from going on an inspection trip, but make your own way there and do your own research.

Bargains may be had on small finished developments that are being sold directly by the developer and which have the First

Occupation Licence already in place. This means that most of the units have already been sold and the developer is desperate to sell the remaining few. But the remaining unsold properties may not be in the best parts of the development, which is why it is vital to go and inspect in person, and not with a sales team hovering over you.

Clearly there will always be a property market in Spain as it is popular not only with Brits but with the Russians, French, Germans and Dutch, and it is undoubtedly the case that there are bargains to be had. But the main two things you need to know are (a) does the property have resale value and could you sell it at considerably more than the purchase price?; and (b) would the property rent out to holidaymakers for long enough and at a high enough rent to make the purchase worthwhile in the meantime?

A few years ago, a friend bought a luxurious £6 million villa in Spain. The idea was that she would keep it for a few years, then sell at a big profit and that would provide a handy inheritance for her grandchildren. But then the property market collapsed, the pound fell against the euro, my friend could not keep up the mortgage payments and the lovely villa was repossessed and sold off at less than half its purchase price.

As with the UK, property prices in other countries are subject to fluctuation, and the presence or absence of cheap airlines, international airports, exchange rates and economy upturns and downturns can all make a dramatic difference in a very short time. A cheap airline going bust could wipe out all your investment, for instance. There are always many unknowns, and it is impossible to have a crystal ball to foresee them all.

Because 'abroad' is a big place, and to describe everywhere in detail would take a big book in itself, here are a few examples of popular markets outside the UK. For a fuller picture, see the author's *Complete Guide To Buying Property Abroad*, published by Kogan Page.

Existing markets

Spain and France continue to be the most popular 'abroad' countries for UK nationals, with Florida now coming up close behind.

In 2003, £57 billion was taken out of UK property, and most of this money went into buying properties abroad, with Spain and France the top favourites for investment.

Demand for France also remains strong, in spite of much competition coming now from newer entrants to the overseas market. Paris and Nice are well-established hotspots, attracting much foreign investment, and apartments in these two cities are popular with the rental market.

Normandy is becoming increasingly popular with Brits as property prices are much cheaper than UK properties, the area is easy to get to, at least from Southern England, and the historic Normandy landings sites mean that it is a much-visited tourist and holiday location. Much real estate in Normandy is sold with a lot of land so is ideal for those who want to grow their own vegetables, want to keep horses or have peace and privacy.

Also, many British people are establishing businesses in Normandy. The website www.FindyourFeetinNormandy.com gives financial and accounting advice for setting up a business, and discovering whether there is a ready market and potential customers for the skills you are able to provide. Business registration procedures in France relaxed in 2009 and it is now easier than before for foreigners to set up and run a commercial concern there, such as a gite, property management, restaurants, business consultancy, IT, estate agency or graphic design, for instance.

The Invest in France agency provides support for those wanting to set up commercial businesses in France and Normandy is good strategically as it opens out to the rest of France and the whole of Europe.

One reason why France and Spain continue to be popular, apart from their being known quantities in many ways, is that the buying process is now well established. In emerging markets such as Croatia and Bulgaria, it can be difficult to establish title, and because these markets are relatively new, nobody knows what might happen when these former communist countries get properly on their feet with a market economy.

In countries which have the euro, you can now get a euro mortgage whether or not you have a euro income.

Portugal

Portugal is a mature market, with – some believe – still a long way to go before it reaches saturation point. The overwhelming attraction of Portugal lies in the sporting facilities, particularly golf. Investors are advised to look for developments which have championship quality golf courses, not just ordinary ones. There are many huge new developments going up in Portugal, where the entry level is higher than Spain, and the whole place seems to be more upmarket.

The most popular buys are new, lavish apartments with private swimming pools in gated developments right next to a wonderful golf course. Guaranteed rental schemes are a particular feature of new developments as a way of hooking investors, and as ever, investors have to be sure there is a genuine rental market once the guarantee period ends.

Leaseback deals are also heavily marketed. Here, you buy a room, or suite, in a hotel, on a lease, and it is rented out for you, with some of the profits coming back to you. With most of these schemes, you are allowed to use the room yourself for a certain number of weeks. It can cost into six figures to buy one of these deals so again, you would have to do a lot of number-crunching and ignore the glossy brochure to see if it makes sense from an investment point of view.

Lengths of lease vary, and can be from 5 to 99 years, depending on the deal.

Emerging markets

Eastern Europe

Much of Eastern Europe is considered an 'emerging market' because, although there have been some spectacular property price increases since the fall of communism, most experts believe there is still more to come. However, this does not mean that unprecedented riches will automatically be showered on anybody who invests in Eastern Europe. Because many countries have not fully established themselves since communism, nobody really knows what will happen in the future, and whether all this foreign investment will continue to be welcomed, especially when the idea is not to benefit the country concerned, but the individual investor.

For every potential investor, there is a lot of homework to be done. Chris Howard, managing director of 4:you Property Partners, plc, believes that assessing the pace of change is an important factor. But it can be difficult in some Eastern European countries to access good information about price trends and economic growth. We are used to being able to access such figures in the UK, United States and established European markets, but in some of the newer entrants to market economies, as opposed to communism, such figures may not be available or, if available, unreliable.

The most contentious issues surround legal title and ownership and whether foreign nationals are actually allowed to own property, or whether you have to form a company in the chosen country. There is also the fact that in many of these new market economies, the profession of estate agent is not established at all, and you have to rely on websites which may not be particularly reliable.

Property developer Alan Goss has decided to invest in the Czech Republic – but only after undertaking massive research. In 2005, he bought a 1920s apartment in Brno, the second city after Prague, which he has rented out to Czech law students. Alan's partner is Czech, which obviously helps with language problems, but before ever investing, he drew up a fact sheet giving details of population, neighbouring countries, age demographics, population growth, GDP, currency, literacy levels, type of government, national holidays, temperature variation, official language and international airports.

In other words, he carried out the most thorough research that it was possible to do, before deciding to take the plunge. His first purchase cost £46,000 and he is now negotiating for more properties, with a view to investing in the native rental market.

Emerging Eastern European markets which are welcoming foreign property investors include Croatia, Poland, Estonia,

Hungary, Latvia, Slovenia, Lithuania and Bulgaria. Do not, whatever you do, lump all these countries together and imagine they are all identical, just because they are all former communist countries. They not only have their separate identities, pluses and minuses, but their emerging economies are very individual, as well.

Most property experts believe the Eastern European countries have a long way to go before they reach their peak, investment-wise, but you could have a long wait.

Dubai

Massive new developments are going up, some the last word in luxury. But many property experts believe that the Muslim Sharia laws, which mean that women cannot inherit property, for instance, will have to be changed or modified to fit in with Western ideas, before investments there become profitable.

At the time of writing, all countries in the United Arab Emirates operate under Sharia law, and it is essential to understand the terms of any property contract and the ways in which it may differ from a UK or European contract. Many European women are now investing in fast-growing Dubai, which welcomes foreign investment but, as the laws of inheritance and ownership may differ from those applying to a man, make sure you ask about this before putting down any money in this heavily hyped country.

South Africa, Australia, China and New Zealand

These rapidly emerging markets are worth looking into, as foreign investment is being actively encouraged. Again, these places are heavily marketed at property fairs, with inspection trips usually offered as part of the deal.

Cyprus (on the cusp of emerging and mature)

Cyprus, which joined the EU in 2004, is highly popular with UK nationals and it is easy to see why. Because of British occupation, Cyprus has a definite 'British' feel and many people speak English as well. Their laws are based on British laws, so are not too diffi-cult to understand.

Since 2004, property developers and investors have been tar-geting Cyprus in the confident expectation of a huge property bonanza. In contrast with, say, Florida, it is not possible to build and build because Cyprus is an island with only a very limited amount of land available for development. The small size of Cyprus is one of the main factors beckoning investors. Because it is hot and dry, there are also fears about water shortages, and this as well is limiting development.

Cyprus adopted the euro on 1 January 2008.

Local banks can offer mortgages of up to 75 per cent of the pur-chase price over 15 years, with interest rates typically 2.5 per cent above the UK rate. The Cypriot government must normally approve foreign purchases, but investors tell me this is only a formality.

Purchase tax is 3–8 per cent, depending on the price of the property, and stamp duty is also payable on a sliding scale.

If you stay in your Cyprus holiday home for more than 182 non-consecutive days in one year, you may have to pay Cypriot income tax. Most non-Cypriot residents pay 5 per cent, although it can go up to 30 per cent. You may also be liable to pay tax on any rental income.

Since joining the EU, property prices in the South have enjoyed 15–20 per cent annual growth. Lettings for residential and short-term holiday lets have increased as ever more property manage-ment companies set up on the island.

EU membership has also meant more work and investment opportunities, more budget airlines and vastly more develop-ments, from simple studios to magnificent detached villas with their own swimming pools and wonderful sea views. You could also buy a 100-year-old stone house with character, although by far the great majority of UK purchasers buy off-plan. The most popular tourist area is around Paphos, very heavily developed now, and entire village developments are going up in the area, most of which are expected to be sold to UK nationals. Golf is a big draw, as with many sunny spots in Europe.

With apartments, all tenure in Southern Cyprus is freehold. There is no such thing as leasehold, and this is another plus as when you buy a leasehold property abroad – as in the UK – there is usually a head freeholder who wants to make money out of you, the leaseholder, and you may not have much control over service charge increases and swingeing levies. Whenever buying leasehold property in another country, pay close attention to the terms of the lease and ask for explanations of any clauses not fully understood. An apparently cheap apartment can become very expensive when you have to pay your share of exterior decoration, for instance, or landscaping the grounds.

When it comes to the Northern (Turkish) part of Cyprus, the situation becomes complicated, as when the Greek Cypriots fled the Northern part after partition in 1974, whole villages were abandoned. In some cases, it may not be known who actually owns the derelict properties, or the land on which they sit.

So far, Northern Cyprus is less populated than the South, it tends to be poorer, and there is much unemployment. On the plus side, property is also cheaper than in the South, and there are many beautiful areas, including some of the island's best beaches. If interested in buying into Northern Cyprus, which, along with the Southern Greek part, is being heavily featured at property investor shows, the most important aspect of the purchase is ensuring that there is a clean legal title, and that nobody will come and claim it after you believe you have bought.

Last word on buying abroad

If you are buying purely for investment, you have to do a lot more number-crunching than if buying that dream place in the sun for your own pleasure.

The best advice is to go to the place where you are interested in investing, get to know it, get a 'feel' of the place, do all your homework regarding demographics, infrastructure, political set-up, healthiness or otherwise of the economy, before ever making a down payment. All too many people get carried away at property shows, and sign up for a wonderful-looking off-plan apartment they have only seen on the internet. That, of course, is the idea!

The best advice remains the traditional advice: before ever buying into a new or unknown country, go on a two-week holiday that you pay for entirely yourself. Fly 'n' buy and inspection trips are not holidays but marketing exercises operated by very clever salespeople on high commissions. Beware of any capital growth predictions provided by the company selling the properties.

Although nobody can know what will happen to any property or any country in two or three years' time – nobody saw the credit crunch coming, for instance, not even the cleverest financial brains in the world – the most sensible thing is to gather as much independent information on the country as you can before visiting it, and certainly before visiting any new developments or lavishly-appointed marketing suites.

And also never forget that once the property is yours, wherever it may be, it becomes your responsibility. You are responsible for repairs and upkeep, for paying service and maintenance charges and local rates and taxes. You cannot just buy a property abroad and forget about it, as with a stock or share.

All financial experts give the same important advice when buying abroad, which is: always be aware of the hidden costs. In some countries it actually costs more to buy a property than in the UK; in others interest rates may be higher and in yet others, there may be taxation issues when you come to sell.

Hidden costs can, for instance, include unexpected service and maintenance charges on apartments. If the swimming pool needs cleaning and clearing, you will be liable for your share of this cost; likewise if the management company decide the communal gardens need landscaping, or the communal areas need redecorating. You will also have to pay your share of landscaping, maintenance and general upkeep when buying into a gated apartment in another country.

If intending to rent out the apartment or villa, you have to be sure these extra costs can be met out of the rent.

Increasingly, people are buying foreign properties as investments rather than to improve their own lifestyle and if you are one of these, you have to be sure that the purchase will constitute a genuine investment rather than an expensive folly.

9 SIPPs and REITs

It is generally accepted that as a nation, we do not save enough to give ourselves a comfortable retirement. But it is difficult enough to save any money out of taxed income, unless you are extremely rich. My grandparents, along with most other people of their generation, saved hard out of earnings to be able to supplement their old-age pension in retirement. But today, by contrast, most people live on credit and borrowings rather than being able to put money away for a rainy day. Many of the over-50s, even, are deeply in debt even though they are approaching retirement and coming to the end of their working years.

In fact, for many, the whole idea of saving has become completely theoretical. Most people believe they do not have enough money to get by day to day, let alone save.

Added to that, even those who have saved or put money into a pension fund have often seen these savings eroded through inflation or bad management of the pension fund. It is with retirement, or a nice nest-egg, in mind that people have been investing in buy-to-let, holiday homes or properties overseas since easier mortgages became available from 1998. The idea was that by the time retirement was reached, either the mortgages would be paid off and the rents would actually count for something, or, alternatively, the investment properties could be sold for a substantial capital gain which would give a welcome boost to retirement funds.

One of the original reasons so many people started investing in buy-to-let was dissatisfaction with existing pension schemes. Unless you had a generous employer's pension, which these days most people do not, it was difficult to see how you would ever be able to save enough money for a decent retirement. Added to that, in the old days, when people started working at 16 and retired at 65, they would have 40 years of employment in which to save for retirement. Nowadays, not only do many people not start work until the age of 21 at least, they almost always graduate from university with debts which take many years to pay off. Also, very few jobs these days are secure, many people may get divorced at some stage and, increasingly, employer's pensions are becoming a thing of the past, except for people working in the public sector who, by and large, still have comfortable salary-linked pensions to rely on in retirement.

For the self-employed, or those working in fragile businesses or industries liable to collapse with huge debts at any moment, the future is far from secure.

Many heavily advertised pension schemes have not performed well, or have been downright fraudulent, with the result that very many people have lost their faith in the pension industry to provide them with a proper pension. Pension funds are almost always invested in stocks and shares, which may perform well or ill and nobody knows what may happen in the future.

So – enter the huge rush to invest in property in recent years, as an alternative investment. As we have seen, it has been possible to put commercial property into a self-invested personal pension (SIPP) since 1989, but the majority of ordinary, individual investors have tended to steer clear of this sector.

The government announced its intention to allow people to put residential property into a SIPP from 6 April 2006, and then dramatically backtracked on this in December 2005.

So what does this last-minute reversal actually mean in practice?

It means that you can no longer wrap up property such as a second home or buy-to-let in your pension scheme, although you will still be able to put commercial property into a SIPP, as before.

Aparthotels

One other type of property investment you can still put into a SIPP is investments in Aparthotels. These are a new (ish) idea whereby you buy a room for, say, 99 years and the room is rented out for that time on your behalf. Aparthotels are well established in the US and have been in existence in the UK since about 2004. They are also now a feature of many popular holiday destinations in France and Portugal, for instance.

What happens is that you, the investor, buy the room or apartment in the hotel, but you do not have control over the rental and you cannot ever use the room yourself. Nor can you stay in the same hotel in another room at a beneficial rate.

There are no concessions anywhere when you buy a share in a hotel to put into a SIPP and as such, the investment works in much the same way as buying a stock or a share in that it is a purely financial transaction. It is completely different from, say, timeshare, where you are sold a week or two in an apartment or hotel for a certain length of time. Instead, you are investing in the property in much the same way that you might invest in any other commodity.

Investment expert Keith Boniface explains: 'For people who want to buy residential property to put into a SIPP, this is now the nearest they can get. The rule is, though, that you can have no beneficial use of the hotel room yourself, but you receive a proportion of the profits in just the same way as a share dividend.

'One of the main companies dealing with Aparthotels to put into a SIPP is Galliard Homes. There was a big question mark as to whether this type of investment would survive the budget, but it has, and this method of investing in property looks set to grow fast.'

In very simple terms, a SIPP is a 'wrapper' into which you can put pension assets. In the past, these have included equities, bonds, cash deposits and commercial property assets such as hotels, guest houses, nursing homes, ground rents and pubs and restaurants. This facility still applies.

In normal circumstances, any profit made on your property is subject to one or other – or maybe all three – forms of taxation. Rental income is subject to income tax and all properties apart from your own home (at the time of writing at least) are subject to capital gains tax when you sell. In addition, all property, and all assets come to that, are liable for inheritance tax when you die, with the sole exception being assets which pass directly to your spouse or civil partner, so long as this is made clear in your will.

If you put your assets into a SIPP, by contrast, the assets become tax-exempt, although the eventual income or pension you receive is subject to income tax, as ever. It's just that while everything remains inside the SIPP, it is sheltered, in modern parlance, from the taxman.

All well and good. But by putting property – or any other asset – into a SIPP, you cannot ever take out the entire lump sum. You cannot, for instance, put an investment property into a SIPP, where you shelter it from income tax and capital gains tax, and then sell it, thereby pocketing a nice wodge of tax-free money. Why not? Because it is no longer yours. You have sold it, in effect, to the SIPP which now owns it.

A property-based SIPP acts in exactly the same way as any other pension fund, in that only a small proportion of the money invested may be taken out as a lump sum. The rest has to be kept in the fund, and you the pensioner take out an income which amounts to interest on the capital.

It is all highly complicated and, in some instances, it may not be a good idea to put money into a SIPP. Some people in any case would not be eligible for a SIPP, bearing in mind that the letters refer to self-invested personal pensions. If you receive a company pension, for instance, you may not be eligible as the pension is not then self-invested. Also, you have to have income or other funds to put into a SIPP in the first place.

Here, the labyrinthine rules and regulations are explained by SIPP experts.

Property investment expert Geoffrey Summers clarifies some of the important issues regarding SIPPs: 'If you put property into a pension fund, it is owned by the pension fund, rather than by you personally. The advantages are that if the property is sold, there is no capital gains tax payable by the pension fund, although the sale has to be properly conducted, and estate agents and stamp duty paid as usual.

'There may, however, be capital gains liability the other way round, such as when you dispose of your property to a SIPP.'

Supposing you have five shops, the SIPP can purchase all five, in a proper sales transaction. Obviously, the SIPP already has to have enough money in it to buy the properties, just as with an individual, and this can come from an existing pension fund or from contributions that you have made. It is clear that you cannot put property into a SIPP if there is already nothing in your pension fund. You don't just bung it in; there has to be a proper transaction once the SIPP is already set up.

The point about pension funds is that they operate independently of you, the beneficiary of the fund. This is because the fund is considered a separate entity from you, unlike when you have liquid assets in the bank.

If you have a bank account containing £100,000, this will typically yield interest of £4,000 a year on which you pay tax. You can also go at the capital as much as you like, eventually eroding it down to nothing.

If, however, you have £100,000 in your pension fund, you can draw down the interest or income after a certain age, but you cannot get your hands on the bulk of the capital. The incentive for keeping your money in the pension fund is that the money becomes free of tax. But the capital is unavailable to you for ever. You cannot get it out, whatever you try to do, once you have taken out the initial tax-free sum allowed, usually 25 per cent of the entire fund.

Exactly the same thing happens when you put property into a SIPP as with any other pension scheme. Another SIPP expert, James Hughes, of the City Trading Post, sheds some more light on the subject: 'A pension is basically a trust fund where you are the beneficiary. This is the case with all pensions, whether the funds are invested in equities or property. If you have £500,000 sitting in the bank, you can do what you like with it, but if it is in the pension fund you can never take it out even though you remain the only beneficiary.'

So, one might ask, why did the government change its mind on residential property and SIPPs at the last minute?

Some experts believe the Chancellor suddenly realized the system could be open to abuse, with already wealthy people wrapping up all their properties into pension funds, and benefiting from generous tax breaks. Maybe then Chancellor Gordon Brown bowed to pressure from some sections of the media.

Commenting on the U-turn, *The Guardian* – which had campaigned long and hard against allowing residential property into a SIPP – said that SIPPs would give £3 billion a year in tax breaks to already well-off property investors, and push up prices for first-time buyers who were trying to get a foot on the property ladder.

When you set up a SIPP, you are setting up a trust which is a legal entity in its own right. This entity can hold assets, be taxed, be sued. It owns the assets on behalf of the beneficiary and, as the beneficiary, you can draw income from the funds. A trust consists of assets owned by that trust.

Such trusts can also be advantageous when it comes to inheritance tax. Again, James Hughes explains: 'If properties or money are unwrapped, you are blasted by IHT and there is very little you can do about it. But if the assets are in a SIPP, they can pass to your descendants, who in turn become the beneficiaries of the pension fund. If you have a million pounds' worth of assets in a SIPP, your descendants can inherit it for their own retirement. This means that your children can have a nice juicy income on their own retirement, thanks to your SIPP taken out many years earlier. All this still applies, except that residential property no longer forms part of the scheme.'

SIPPs will allow investment in commercial property by borrowing 50 per cent of the fund value. Once a property is invested in a SIPP, rental income will have to be reinvested in the fund and used to pay off any outstanding mortgage. Of course, as with any other pension fund, if you put rented properties in a SIPP, you will not be able to take advantage of the rental income until you reach retirement age – or the age decided on when you start to invest in this way. In any case, you would have to be aged over 50 to take out any funds for your own use as income.

You can only buy commercial properties for inclusion in a SIPP if you can afford the 50 per cent deposit. This means that if you have an existing SIPP containing £250,000, you can invest in a hotel or B&B home valued up to £375,000. Then the income will be yours free of tax. Any rise in the value of the property will also be tax-free. If the mortgage on the property is paid off by the time you retire, the rental income on investment properties can provide your pension. This is of course subject to income tax, but you could, if you wished, sell off the properties when you retire and take 25 per cent of the fund as a tax-free sum. If, on retirement, you have a SIPP of maximum value £1.5 million, this means you could take out £375,000 for your trip to Las Vegas or that round-the-world cruise – and still have £1.125 million in the bank. Not a bad retirement sum!

The things to watch out for, as with any investment in property, are a sudden downturn in property prices or rents, or upsurge in interest rates. It may also be the case that the pension fund administrators will want to let and manage your properties themselves, charging a 15 per cent management fee.

Once you have confirmation that you have enough money to start a SIPP, you will then have to fill in a form giving details of all old or existing schemes which you obtain from your pension provider, or a company handling SIPPs, and they will manage the transfer – for a fee, of course. Then, once the SIPP is up and running, you can either manage it yourself, or hand over the management to a financial adviser. The more you hand over the management, the more you pay.

The usual pension fund situation is that the fund is active and can be added to until you reach the age of 75, when it stops, and you have to buy an annuity. Also, usually when you die, your pension dies with you, however much it may have accumulated. But SIPP investors can keep the fund going beyond this age and also include their children and grandchildren in the pension, so they will inherit, although in time – when the Treasury gets round to it – this perk may disappear and be taxed along with other inherited income.

The two aspects which make property-based pensions attractive are (a) tax relief on your contributions and (b) tax-free investment growth, as all your rental income and capital gains will be tax-free. Supposing you earn £100,000 in a year, none of which you need to spend. If you put that entire sum into your SIPP you will not have to pay tax on it.

Geoffrey Summers, of SIPPs advisers Hartley-SAS, advises those who are interested in SIPPing into the future, to:

▌ Start a SIPP now by making personal contributions, which must in general be based on income from an occupation or trade and not rental or investment income.

▌ Maximize the value of your pension fund by making contributions at the highest level you can to benefit from tax relief. You can transfer money from an existing pension fund into a SIPP once it is set up, but this is not always in your best interests, so it is necessary to take professional advice (if possible, from more than one adviser).

▌ Consider using your SIPP to start buying commercial property now. Interest rates or property prices may rise in the near future.

But – self-invested pensions are not for everybody. All advisers stress that they are an option, and dependent on your general financial circumstances. Also, you will definitely need to take advice if you are divorced or separated, or considering divorce, as former spouses and civil partners can now raid pension funds as well as other assets.

What you cannot do is get your money out of the pension scheme once it is in. According to the rules pertaining to pension funds, it has to stay there until you are over 50, and only then can you take out 25 per cent (as with any other pension scheme). However, you would still have to take an income from the rest of the pension. So you have no choice but to put the money in some other type of investment, or let it sit there, doing nothing.

REITs (Real Estate Investment Trusts)

REITs (Real Estate Investment Trusts) have been successfully established in the USA, Netherlands and Australia for many years and were launched in the UK in January 2007.

They are intended to act as a replacement for residential investment in SIPPs in that they can be put into a pension fund, but work in a completely different way. With REITs, you buy a share in a specially set-up property company rather than buying property direct. This means that you can buy a stake in a residential or commercial property for as little as £5,000, after which your investment will work in much the same way as any other stock or share, in that you the investor will be paid regular dividends.

Investment expert Richard Cotton, of Cluttons estate agents, explains how REITs work in practice, and why the UK government is now backing them. 'Looking back, SIPPs – where you were going to be able to put residential property into your pension fund and then benefit from huge tax breaks – were always too good to be true. But REITs have been tried and tested in other countries and have been hugely popular with investors. REITs work in much the same way as any other company except that they are exempt from corporation tax and investors will only pay once, on profits on their dividends.'

A major advantage for the Exchequer, Richard Cotton believes, is that REITs will stay on shore and money invested in them will not go out of the country. 'REITs are very much private investor-friendly and you won't need large sums to invest. These are the two most positive aspects to REITs as a serious drawback to conventional, or direct, investment in property is that you need a large capital sum to start with, and there are also very high entry and exit costs in the property market. Here, the company buys the properties and also looks after and manages them.'

The key issue to REITs, and the aspect which makes them unique as investment vehicles, is that the companies who operate them will have to invest in rent-producing properties, whether these are residential or commercial. They must all be income-producing to qualify as a REIT. The companies operating REITs will be highly regulated and this will also act as a safety net for the investor.

Of course, dividends paid to investors will depend on how the rental market, in both the residential and commercial sectors, performs in future. This is of course an aspect nobody can know for sure but historically, property does go up all the time, although there can be blips. But the private rented sector is growing all the time as ever more people see the financial advantages of renting, rather than owning property.

Liam Bailey, investment expert at Knight Frank, adds: 'REITs must be set up by specialist companies and 98 per cent of the profits must come from rental income. The REIT company can retain 10 per cent of the profits for improvements, but that's all and everything else must be paid to the shareholders.'

Most property professionals believe that REITs will put buy-to-let on a much more professional basis. Until REITs were allowed, there was very little corporate interest in the private rented sector and most landlords were more or less amateurs. Liam Bailey believes that as REITs become ever more established, the days of the amateur landlord will be numbered, and rented apartments will be properly and professionally managed. At the moment, it is all very much a hit and miss affair.

Kevin Fleury, of Conti Financial Services, is Canadian, and has seen REITs operate at first hand. He believes they will prove to be a far better bet than SIPPs would ever have been. 'The problem with SIPPs was that they would have had to be run by a fund manager and this would have meant huge incremental fees, as I see it, and these would have almost totally wiped out the tax advantage. Speaking purely personally, I am glad that SIPPs have gone and that REITs have arisen out of the rubble of the SIPP fiasco.'

If you are interested in investing in a REIT, you should go to a reputable independent financial adviser who knows all about this type of investment. Most IFAs now have details of how REITs operate and can advise accordingly. Always go for companies with a proven track record and make sure you obtain complete clarification of how the tax breaks operate and how they will benefit you.

Jonathan Morley, investment adviser at AWD Chase de Vere, the largest IFA in Europe, adds: 'The big advantage of REITs is that, unlike direct investment in property, they are a flexible, liquid investment where you can sell your share at any time. They have been massively popular in the USA and Australia and as they have been tried and tested in other countries, should also work well in the UK.

Companies that operate REITS have to invest in income-producing properties, whether these are residential or commercial.

In fact, they must already be income-producing to qualify as a REIT. Dividends paid to investors will depend on how the rental market, in both the commercial and residential sectors, performs and this of course can never be guaranteed.'

However, as Jonathan Morley says, 'Although there is always some risk with any investment, REITs should provide a nice income from the start. Interested investors should always go for property companies with a proven track record, as there will inevitably be people jumping on the REITs bandwagon.

'REITs are a kind of stock exchange for property and as such, a brand-new investment vehicle.'

Last word

As with any type of investment, there is no certain or guaranteed way of making money out of property. On the other hand, it has to be said that when you look at newspaper Rich Lists, at least half of the richest people in the world will have made their money out of real estate, one way or another.

And even those whose primary fortune does not come from property will almost certainly have invested a significant amount of their wealth in property. This tells you that there is a lot of money to be made from property. There always has been and there always will be.

Sir Paul McCartney, for instance, with seven or eight valuable homes scattered around the world, continues to buy up properties in his main location, Peasmarsh, in East Sussex, although his main income still probably derives from his music royalties. Locals predict that before long, Sir Paul will own the entire village in much the same way as squires and the landed gentry of old.

So how can you maximize your chances of joining the property investment bonanza?

First of all, you not only have to have a definite 'feel' for property, but also be prepared to take on the responsibility of caring for bricks and mortar. One friend who invests in the stock market told me he would not want to have to be responsible for four or five ceilings falling down, ten tenants not paying rent and being in another country when the roof on one of his properties fell in.

Nobody wants these things to happen, but the difference between the successful and the unsuccessful property investor is that the successful ones know they can handle such events. If the whole thing simply terrifies you, then you may be advised to leave property investment alone.

You also have to be able to give it time. It takes more time and effort to invest successfully in property than in stocks and shares, and you have to be prepared to put in this effort. Any effort you expend in investing in the UK has to be doubled and tripled for successful investment overseas. And the more unknown or 'emerging' the market, the more effort you have to put in. Never rely on hype or marketing coming from those wanting to sell you a very expensive product. Do your own research, and then see whether your results match those of the developer.

I would say also that in order to make money from property, you really have to enjoy every aspect of the process. You have to actively enjoy viewing places, doing the number-crunching and also look forward to decorating, furnishing and marketing your properties. You have to get a buzz from it all – even when it goes wrong. You have to look forward to putting things right, rather than wringing your hands in despair.

Although I am a complete dumbo when it comes to numbers and figures, funnily enough this doesn't apply when I am working out figures when considering whether to buy, sell or rent property. Suddenly, my number-blindness leaves me, and everything becomes crystal clear.

The more research you put in, the more you are prepared to be hands-on, the less likely you are to make a very expensive mistake.

In my life, I have made very many mistakes over all kinds of things but looking back, I find I have made very few mistakes with property. This is because I have only bought after undertaking extensive research. And then, even after I have bought, I continue doing my research, to see if I have done the right thing, or could do better.

For instance, I bought a holiday flat on the south coast apparently on impulse. But talking to a friend about it years later, I realized I had actually put a great deal of research into the purchase. Before buying, I had investigated neighbouring towns and resorts, thought hard about the pros and cons of each and before buying, drew up a blueprint of my ideal purchase.

And then, after buying, I continued to investigate, to make sure I had done the right thing. And I still investigate, by viewing every new development, making forays into neighbouring areas to see if there is something better for me to buy, and making sure I keep thoroughly up to date with all small shifts in the market.

The result is that there are very few developments, very few properties, in West or East Sussex that I don't get to know about. And I keep expanding my area of expertise. I now know about investing in Devon, for instance, and I have also investigated Hampshire.

And during 2009, I thoroughly investigated Oxford and kept an eye on it for many months. I made several visits, which enabled me to pinpoint the right location for me and at the same time, I researched the surrounding areas and haunted estate agents' windows and websites.

There is no substitute for going to places yourself, getting a feel of the place and, most of all, discovering which properties go fast, which ones hang around, and why. A property that looks charming on a website can look very different in reality, and you also need to know what is happening in the location.

I would always go in person to any property I was interested in buying, anywhere in the world, and then stay in the place, talk to locals, investigate the shops and businesses and generally get a definite feel for the place. I would also have to decide whether it felt 'me'. Properties and locations are much like people in that some are on your wavelength and some aren't, not always for a reason you can pinpoint.

I have been considering investing in Auckland, New Zealand, where many properties are aimed directly at the British buyer, and of course they all look wonderful on the websites. But when you actually view them and walk round the area, very often they don't seem so marvellous and have hidden drawbacks that never show up on a website or agent's particulars.

When investing in property (or anything else come to that) it is always very tempting to hand everything over to a company that purports to do all the work for you, and which hypes up the investment potential of the products it is trying to sell.

But bearing in mind how the 'discounted' off-plan property market collapsed, and how so many hopeful investors who had been persuaded to buy-up a number of properties were simply unable to cover their running costs, let alone make a profit on resale, I am always very wary of taking much notice of any company promising a low purchase price and high returns.

Many investors also came a cropper when they invested in dilapidated Victorian terraced houses in the North-East of England, again heavily hyped by companies that promised to renovate and rent out on behalf of clients. Mostly, the advertised rents were never realized, and most of the companies went bust, leaving the hapless investors stranded. The properties seemed extremely cheap, at least to London buyers, but mostly never realized their advertised potential.

Nothing stays static in the property market for long.

It also helps to have good taste, and to keep your taste honed and up to date by viewing the show homes of new developments, keeping an eye on all the magazines and looking at the current makeover shows on television. This enables you to be aware of how things might be changing, and know what's going on. One interior design friend says she works on a five-year timescale. When she designs a place, she can feel confident that it will look attractive and up to date for at least five years, after which it may well start to look dated. But she cannot plan an interior that will never date – that is impossible, she says.

The décor of properties abroad also dates. It is tempting to imagine that an Italian interior, or Spanish interior, is timeless, unlike a UK interior. But this is not true; nowadays, their ideas change as rapidly as anybody else's – and a Spanish villa with a tired, seventies look could be difficult to sell or rent.

You should also read the business pages of newspapers to keep up to date with interest rates, exchange rates, mortgage deals, bank account deals and investment opportunities. Some people are more interested in interior design, others more naturally turn to business and financial pages. But both aspects count equally, when investing in property.

Above all, investing in property should be an enjoyable activity. The more you enjoy it, the less likely you are to make terrible mistakes, as with anything else. The more you enjoy cookery, the more likely you are to cook wonderful meals; the more interested you are in fashion, the better you will look.

Property is exactly the same. You have to get a definite buzz out of the whole thing, and you can't mock it up. I like looking at even very nasty properties. They may not all please me, but I still find them interesting.

I wouldn't buy a nasty property, though! Or – at least, I wouldn't buy a property I found nasty. Whenever considering an investment property, it is always best to go for properties you like, rather than those you imagine might increase in value. As with all investments, gut instinct works best – at least, after you have done all the research and crunched all the numbers. Even when buying purely for investment, I always try to imagine myself living there, and if this is impossible, I will reject the property on those grounds.

But to be successful, you have to be confident about what you like and what you don't like – and why. There has to be some kind of chemistry between you and the property, as with people.

When the chemistry works, success will follow.

Appendix: Resources

Chapter 1: Determining the market

Auctions

Andrews and Robertson
Tel: 020 7703 2662

Allsop
Tel: 020 7494 3686

Clive Emson
Tel: 01622 630033

Savills
Tel: 020 7824 9091

Ward & Partners
Tel: 01662 859999

Essential Information Group
Tel: 0800 298 4747
www.eigroup.co.uk

www.propertyauctionnews.co.uk

www.auctionpropertyforsale.co.uk

www.RICS.org/auction-guide
(Free guide to auctions.)

Specialist auction finance

DMI Finance
PO Box 3000
Calne
SN11 OYZ
Tel: 01240 822999
E-mail: info@dmifinance.com
www.dmifinance.com

Book

Farrell, Dominic (2006) The *Jet-to-let Bible*, Lawpack, London

Repossessions

www.repossessions.org.uk/index.html
www.nationalhomebuyers.co.uk/repossessions

Seminars and advice on buying distressed assets and repossessions (aimed at investors):
www.distressed-assets.co.uk

Chapter 2: Using your own home

Information on property prices

www.Net-houseprices.com
www.Mypropertyvalue.co.uk
www.Landregistry.com (England and Wales only)
www.Ros.gov.uk (Scotland)
www.Hometrack.co.uk
www.Rightmove.co.uk
www.Propertybroker.com
www.UpMyStreet.com
www.Neighbourhood.statistics.gov.uk

www.Propertypriceadvice.co.uk
(Note: apart from propertypriceadvice, only the official government sites are free.)

Home stagers (quick upgrades to add value)
Tel: 0800 542 8952
www.homestagers.co.uk

Leasehold advice

The Leasehold Advisory Group
www.leaseholdadvice.co.uk

Brighton, Hove and District Leaseholders' Association
Cornerstone Community Centre
Church Road
Hove
BN3 3FL
Information line: 01273 705432
www.leaseadvice.org
(This is a voluntary organization which holds drop-in clinics and can also give telephone advice on leasehold problems.)

The Leasehold Advisory Service
31 Worship Street
London
EC2 2DZ
Tel: 020 7374 5380
E-mail: info@lease-advice.org
www.lease-advice.org
(Government organization which gives advice on leasehold valuation tribunals and other leasehold matters.)

Association of Residential Managing Agents (ARMA)
178 Battersea Park Road
London
SW11 4ND

Tel: 020 7978 2607
E-mail: info@arma.org.uk
www.arma.org.uk
(Can give advice on extending leases.)

Federation of Private Residents' Associations (FPRA)
59 Mile End Road
Colchester
CO4 5BU
Tel: 0871 200 3324/01206 855 888
E-mail: info@fpra.org.ukl
www.fpra.org.uk

Rosetta Consulting Ltd
31 St Petersburgh Place
London
W2 4LA
Tel: 020 7853 2282
E-mail: info@rosettaconsulting.com
www.rosettaconsulting.com
(One-stop shop for advice and information on collective enfran-
chisement and lease extension.)

Books

Callo, Kat (2005) *Making Sense of Leasehold Property*, Lawpack,
London
Callo, Kat (2006) *The Survivor's Guide to Buying a Freehold*, Lawpack,
London

Self-build

SelfBuild and Design Magazine
Tel: 01283 742970
www.plotbrowser.com

Build It Magazine
Trinity Mirror Business
Tel: 020 7772 8300

Advice on self-build

www.Primelocation.com

www.self-build.co.uk

www.self-build.ie
(Exhibitions and magazines on self-build.)

www.mapletimberframe.com

www.ebuild.co.uk

Customs and Excise advice on self-build VAT matters:
Tel: 0845 0109000

Homebuilding and Renovating Show
Tel: 0870 010 9031
www.homebuildingshow.co.uk

www.self-build.co.uk

www.buildstore.co.uk
(This site gives advice on all aspects of self-build from land to materials and raising finance.)

Eco homes

Preschan Homes Ltd
www.Preschan.com

www.whatgreenhome.com
(Provides advice and information on sustainable development worldwide.)

www.ecofriendlyhomes.co.uk
www.yourecofriendlyhomes.com
www.ecofriendlyideas.net

For film and TV locations

The Space Men
8–10 Lower James Street
London
W1F 9EL
Tel: 020 7534 5780
E-mail: info@thespacemen.com
www.thespacemen.com

www.locationpartnership.com
www.locationworks.com/library
www.mylocations.com
(You can register your property online; the companies take 15–20 per cent commission from the film or TV company.)

Advice on inheritance tax

www.thisismoney.co.uk/inheritancetax
www.direct.gov.uk (how and when you have to pay IHT)
www.AdviceOnline.co.uk (IHT and CGT explained)
www.avoidinheritancetax.com (information on how to avoid or minimize this tax)
www.octopusinvestments.co.uk (commercial advice on IHT planning)
www.hmrc.gov.uk/cto/iht.htm (HM Revenue and Customs Guide to IHT)
www.taxcafe.co.uk (tax saving information – not free)
www.IHTCentre.co.uk
St James's Place, The Plain, Goudhurst, Kent TN17 1AE. Tel: 01580 211211
www.thisismoney.co.uk/inheritance-tax-calculator

Books

Scott, Maria (2006) *How to Avoid the Inheritance Tax Trap*, Robinson, London
Lowe, Jonquil (2008) *The 'Which?' Guide to Giving and Inheriting*, (10th edn). Which? Books, London

Islamic mortgages

Ahli United Bank
Property Finance
Tel: 0800 783 3323

HSBC – Home Finance
Tel: 0800 587 7786

Islamic Bank of Britain
Tel: 0845 606 0786

Lloyds TSB
Tel: 0845 600 7786

www.Which4U.co.uk./islamic mortgages
www.islamicmortgages.co.uk
www.islamicmortgageadvice.co.uk

Book

Hodgkinson, Liz (2007) *The Complete Guide to Renovating and Improving your Property*, Kogan Page, London

Chapter 3: Buy-to-let

Mortgages

Landlord Mortgages
www.lml.co.uk

Coleman and Co
E-mail: wpc@wcoleman.co.uk

www.mortgageadvicebureau.com
www.Find-the-Right-Mortgage.co.uk
www.moneysupermarket.com/mortgages
www.thisismoney.co.uk/homes
Intelligent Finance: www.if.com

The Financial Services Authority
www.fsa.gov.uk
(Information on mortgages and finance.)

Right-to-buy specialists (council homes)
www.OwnMyCouncilHome.co.uk
www.buy-to-let.co.uk
www.buy-to-let.com
(This is a site run by David Humphreys, a long-established and reliable expert on buy to let.)

Landlord action

Landlord Action Ltd
Concorde House
Granville Place
London
NW7 3SA
Tel: 0870 765 2005
www.landlordaction.co.uk
(Advice on evicting troublesome tenants quickly.)

National Federation of Residential Landlords
Tel: 01273 600847
Helpline: 01273 600747
www.nfrl.co.uk

National Landlords Association
78 Tachbrook Street
London
SW1V 2NA
Tel: 020 7828 2445
www.landlords.org.uk

ARLA (Association of Residential Letting Agents)
Tel: 0845 345572
www.arla.co.uk
(Useful information for landlords.)

Comprehensive investment site for landlords:
www.riky.co.uk

Black Swan Capital
Godliman House
21 Godliman Street
London
EC4V 5BD
Tel: 0844 888 0575
E-mail: enquiries@blackswancapital.uk.com

Investment properties in the UK and overseas:
Investment Property Portfolio Services
Tel: 020 8213 5222
www.ipps-property.com

Independent Property Consultants
The Business Village
3–9 Broomhill Road
London
SW18 4QJ
Tel: 08707 454601
E-mail: info@buy-to-let.com
www.buy-to-let.com

Specialist conveyancing solicitors

Quoteline: 0845 456 8675
www.bbcbasic.com

Selling your buy-to-let property with tenants in situ

Homelet Ipex
Becor House
Green Lane
Lincoln
LN6 7DL
Tel: 0870 853 2269
E-mail: ipex@homelet.com
www.homeletipex.com

Student properties

Bournston Student Homes
Tel: 0115 952 4960
www.bournston.co.uk

www.charterproperties.net
www.PropertyHotspots.net
www.Assetz.co.uk
www.moneyfacts.co.uk
www.top-lets.co.uk
(an example of how to run student lets with an eye-catching
website.)

Off-plan investment

Urbanlogic
Fourth Floor
Fourways House
57 Hilton Street
Manchester

M1 2EJ
Tel: 0161 236 5505
E-mail: guyd@urban-logic.co.uk

Useful websites:
www.incitopropertyinvestment.com
www.viceroyinvest.co.uk
www.off-plan.co.uk
www.BuyProperty4Less.com
www.urbaninvestor.net
www.new-homes-direct.com
www.serliana.com (free guide)

Book

Hodgkinson, Liz (2008) *The Complete Guide to Letting Property* (7th edn), Kogan Page, London

Chapter 4: Developing property

First time buyers

www.firstrungnow.com

New Homes Direct
Off-plan and new homes from developers
Tel: 0870 432 0790
E-mail: developer-sales@new-homes-direct.com

A Quick Sale
(Buys and sells property at below market price.)
2 Waverley Street
York
YO31 7QZ
Tel: 0800 328 8239
www.a-quick-sale.co.uk

Buying land

Land Investment Association
Tel: 0845 1249857
E-mail: enquiries@landinvestmentassociation.com

Hayden James Land Acquisitions
Tel: 0870 8080 118
www.haydenjames.co.uk

European Land Sales
Freepost NAT7984
98 Stadium Street
London
SW10 OBR
Tel: 020 7242 4242
www.europeanlandsales.com

Useful websites:
www.profitinland.co.uk
www.daltonsbusiness.com

Caution!

www.propertyscam.org.uk/hitdocs/fivemyths.htm

FSA Consumer Helpline (information on land-banking)
Tel: 0845 606 1234

Strategic land investment

Part Exchange Properties for Developers
Tel: 0870 420 4131
www.movewithus.co.uk

Listed Heritage Magazine and Listed Property Owners Club
Lower Dane
Hartlip

Kent
ME9 7TB
Tel: 01795 844939
E-mail: info@lpoc.co.uk
www.lpoc.co.uk

Listed Property Exhibition:
The Listed Property Show
Business Design Centre
52 Upper Street
Islington
London
N1 0QH
(Details from Listed Property Owners Club, above.)

Ground rent and freehold investments

Andrews and Robertson
www.a-r.co.uk

Chapter 5: Holiday lets

Park and Holiday Homes monthly news-stand magazine
www.magazine-group.co.uk

Marsdens Cottage Holidays (Devon only)
2 The Square
Braunton
North Devon
EX33 2JB
Tel: 01271 813777
E-mail: holidays@marsdens.co.uk

Mulberry Holiday Cottages Ltd
The Granary
Bridge Street

Wye
Ashford
Kent
TN25 5ED
Tel: 01233 813087
www.mulberrycottages.com

VisitBritain guide to self-catering accommodation:
Tel: 020 8846 9000
www.visitbritain.com

Park Homes
Tel: 0800 138 0053
www.park-resorts.com/cmc

British Holiday and Home Park Association
PO Box 28249
Edinburgh
EH9 2YZ
www.ukparks.com

For ideas on how to set up a holiday cottage website, go to:
www.worthingbeachapartments.co.uk
www.willow-cottage.net
www.earlscroftfarm.co.uk

Chapter 6: Commercial property

Mortgages for Business
Tel: 0845 345 6788
www.mortgagesforbusiness.co.uk
(Mortgages for commercial and property development.)

www.mortgages4commercial.co.uk
www.cpfconsultancy.co.uk
www.generalfinancecentre.co.uk
www.freshcommercial.co.uk

Assetz Ltd
251 London Road
Stockport
Cheshire
SK7 4PL
Tel: 0161 456 4000
www.assetz.co.uk
E-mail: enquiry@assetz.co.uk

For advice on commercial property:
www.commercialpropertyadvice.com
www.propertymall.com

Tax information

www.taxcafe.co.uk
www.taxconsultants.guide.com

Document on commercial property from RICS

www.ipf.org.uk
www.7dials.com

www.propertyinvestment.co.uk

Book

The Guide to Commercial Property Investment 2008, published by
Property Investor News. Tel: 0208 906 7772

Chapter 7: Setting up a B&B

Bed and Breakfast News
Tel: 01565 65283
E-mail: mail@bandbnews.co.uk
www.bandbnews.co.uk

(Monthly subscription magazine; also members-only website. Contains ads for buying and selling B&Bs.)

VisitBritain
Tel: 0208 563 3000
(Publishes *The Pink Booklet*: legislation advice on B&Bs.)

Finance

Cumberland Building Society
Tel: 01228 403135

Walbrook Commercial Finance Ltd
Tel: 0800 7312967

Supplies

Out of Eden
Tel: 01768 372 939
www.outofeden.co.uk

B&B insurance

JW Group
7 Market Street
Galashiels
TD1 3AD
Tel: 01896 758 371

Chapter 8: Buying property abroad

Book

Hodgkinson, Liz (2008) *The Complete Guide to Buying Property Abroad* (7th edn), Kogan Page, London

General information on buying property abroad
Exhibitions

Homes Overseas Exhibitions (information line: 020 7939 9852)
www.international-homes.com

The Property Investor Show
Information: www.propertyinvestor.co.uk

Seminars

John Howell and Co
The Old Glass Works
22 Endell Street
London
XC2H 9AD
Tel: 020 7420 0400
www.europelaw.com

Property Economics and Investment Training
Tel: 0151 482 5525
E-mail: info@bewarethesharks.com
www.bewarethesharks.com

Jet-To-Let Magazine
Tel: 0800 177 336
www.jet-to-let-magazine.com

The official website of the Federation of Overseas Property
Developers has fact sheets you can download for each country:
www.fopdac.com

Information on mortgages and investments in France, Spain,
Southern Cyprus:
Assetz Ltd
251 London Road
Stockport

Cheshire
SK7 4PL
Tel: 0161 456 4000
www.assetz.co.uk/investors
E-mail: investors@assetz.co.uk

Advice and information about buying repossessed properties in Spain:
www.bank-repossessions-spain.co.uk/index.htm
www.spanishrepossessions.eu

Country Properties Overseas Department
41 High Street
Baldock
Herts
SG7 6BG
Tel: 01462 895122
E-mail: overseas@country-properties.co.uk

Overseas Property Investments
Princess House
Princess Way
Swansea
SAT 3LW
Tel: 0800 180 4544
E-mail: enquiries@opiuk.com
www.opiuk.com

Australian investments:
Auswest Property Group
www.auswestpropertygroup.com

Dubai investments:
Key2Dubai
www.key2dubai.co.uk

World Property Centre
www.worldpropertycentre.com

Cyprus investments
www.cybarco.com

Portugal investments:
Algarve Retreats
Tel: 0870 742 8100
www.algarve-retreats.co.uk

Finance for overseas properties

Conti Financial Services Ltd
204 Church Road
Hove
BN3 2DJ
Tel: 01273 772811
E-mail: Kevin@mortgagesoverseas.com
www.mortgagesoverseas.com

Capital Financial Partners Worldwide
Tel: 0800 883 0838
E-mail: waynem@cfpworldwide.com
www.cfpworldwide.com

Chapter 9: SIPPs and REITs

Hartley Pensions Administration Ltd
PO Box 1198
Bristol
BS99 2QZ
www.hartleysas.co.uk

Assetz
Tel: 0161 456 4000
www.assetz.co.uk

TEBC Ltd
Victoria House
Desborough Street
High Wycombe
Bucks
HP11 2NF
Tel: 07900 881 883
E-mail: info@tebc.co.uk
www.sipps2006.co.uk
(Information and advice on investing in Aparthotels.)

REITs

MoneyWeek Magazine
info@moneyweek.com

www.rics.org
www.investmentadvice.co.uk/reits-uk.htm
www.citywire.co.uk
www.hammonds.com

Index

Index of advertisers